Communications
in Computer and Information Science   1004

Commenced Publication in 2007
Founding and Former Series Editors:
Phoebe Chen, Alfredo Cuzzocrea, Xiaoyong Du, Orhun Kara, Ting Liu,
Krishna M. Sivalingam, Dominik Ślęzak, Takashi Washio, and Xiaokang Yang

More information about this series at http://www.springer.com/series/7899

María José Abásolo · Telmo Silva ·
Nestor D. González (Eds.)

Applications and Usability of Interactive TV

7th Iberoamerican Conference, jAUTI 2018
Bernal, Argentina, October 16–18, 2018
Revised Selected Papers

Editors
María José Abásolo (iD)
CICPBA - III-LIDI
National University of La Plata
La Plata, Argentina

Telmo Silva (iD)
Department of Communication and Art
University of Aveiro
Aveiro, Portugal

Nestor D. González (iD)
Department of Social Sciences
National University of Quilmes
Buenos Aires, Argentina

ISSN 1865-0929   ISSN 1865-0937 (electronic)
Communications in Computer and Information Science
ISBN 978-3-030-23861-2   ISBN 978-3-030-23862-9 (eBook)
https://doi.org/10.1007/978-3-030-23862-9

This Springer imprint is published by the registered company Springer Nature Switzerland AG
The registered company address is: Gewerbestrasse 11, 6330 Cham, Switzerland

Preface

The 7th Iberoamerican Conference on Applications and Usability of Interactive TV (jAUTI 2018) was held during October 16–18, 2018 in Quilmes (Argentina), and was organized by the Transversal Program of Digital TV of the National University of Quilmes.

jAUTI 2018 was the seventh edition of a scientific event promoted by the RedAUTI Thematic Network on Applications and Usability of Interactive Digital Television. RedAUTI currently consists of more than 200 researchers from 32 universities and industry from Spain, Portugal, and 11 Latin American countries (Argentina, Brasil, Colombia, Costa Rica, Cuba, Chile, Ecuador, Guatemala, Perú, Uruguay, Venezuela).

These proceedings contain a collection of extended selected papers originally presented at jAUTI 2018, and later peer reviewed, that cover the development and deployment of technologies related to interactive digital TV, second screen applications, interfaces for TV, audiovisual content production and user experience studies of TV-related services and applications.

May 2019

María José Abásolo
Telmo Silva
Nestor D. González

Organization

Program Chairs

Daniel González   National University of Quilmes, Argentina
María José Abásolo   III-LIDI, National University of La Plata, Argentina
Telmo Silva   DigiMedia, University of Aveiro, Portugal

Program Committee

Jorge Abreu   DigiMedia, University of Aveiro, Portugal
Pedro Almeida   DigiMedia, University of Aveiro, Portugal
Fernando Boronat   Polytechnic University of Valencia, Spain
Bernardo Cardoso   University of Aveiro, Portugal
Teresa Chambel   LASIGE, University of Lisbon, Portugal
Fernanda Chocron Miranda   Federal University of Rio Grande do Sul, Brazil
Rostand Costa   LAVID, Federal University of Paraiba, Brazil
Armando De Giusti   III-LIDI, National University of La Plata, Argentina
Daniel Gambaro   University of São Paulo, Brazil
Israel Gonzalez-Carrasco   Carlos III University of Madrid, Spain
Raphael Irerê   Projection University Center, Brazil
Anelise Jantsch   Federal University of Rio Grande do Sul, Brazil
Raoni Kulesza   LAVID, Federal University of Paraiba, Brazil
Oscar Mealha   DigiMedia, University of Aveiro, Portugal
Tiago Maritan Ugulino de Araújo   LAVID, Federal University of Paraiba, Brazil
Ana Martins   DigiMedia, University of Aveiro, Portugal
Carlos Matheus-Chacín   Carlos III University of Madrid, Spain
Rita Oliveira   DigiMedia, University of Aveiro, Portugal
Patrícia Oliveira   DigiMedia, University of Aveiro, Portugal
Antoni Oliver   Universiy of the Balearic Islands, Spain
Ana Margarida Pisco Almeida   DigiMedia, University of Aveiro, Portugal
Emili Prado   Autonomous University of Barcelona, Spain
Alcina Maria Prata   Higher School of Business Studies (ESCE), Portugal
Tânia Ribeiro   DigiMedia, University of Aveiro, Portugal
Miguel Angel Rodrigo Alonso   University of Córdoba, Spain
Josemar Rodrigues de Souza   University of Bahia State, Brazil
Rita Santos   DigiMedia, University of Aveiro, Portugal
Cecilia Sanz   III-LIDI, National University of La Plata, Spain
Juan Carlos Torres   Private Technical University of Loja, Ecuador

Enrickson Varsori	DigiMedia, University of Aveiro, Portugal
Ana Sofia Velhinho de Sousa	DigiMedia, University of Aveiro, Portugal
Valdecir Becker	LAVID, Federal University of Paraiba, Brazil

Contents

Testing and User Experience of IDTV Services

Contexts of Application of the IDTV

A Systematic Literature Review of iDTV in Learning Contexts

Vagner Beserra[1](✉) , Alan César Belo Angeluci[2] ,
Rafael Guimarães Pedroso[1] , and Monica Navarrete[1]

[1] Universidad de Tarapacá, 18 de Septiembre 2222, Arica, Chile
vagner.beserra@gmail.com, rafaelgpedroso@gmail.com,
mnavarre@uta.cl
[2] Universidade Municipal de São Caetano do Sul.,
Av Goiás 3400, São Caetano do Sul, Brazil
aangeluci@uscs.edu.br

Abstract. In early 2000s, several countries have experienced the technological transition from Analog Television to Interactive Digital Television (iDTV). This fact has impacted in diverse areas of knowledge, among them, education. However, to date, there has not been a systematic study of the works using this technology in learning environments. This paper presents a systematic literature review in order to contribute and to better understand the state-of-art using DTV in learning contexts. To do so, literature data search and collection was performed in ACM, BioMed Central, ERIC, IEEE, Ingenta Connect, ScienceDirect and WOS databases; boolean expressions were used as search terms for papers published between 2014 and 2017, and full texts not mentioning the word "learning" were not considered. It was found 521 papers, being selected 18 through double peer review for systematic analysis to identify the most relevant characteristics and outcomes. Results showed positive outcomes during the teaching-learning process, as in participation and motivation of the students. Most of the analyzed studies were originated in Latin American countries and are related to the historical period of discussion and implementation of DTV technology.

Keywords: Systematic review · Interactive digital television · Learning

1 Introduction

Interactive Digital Television (iDTV) has been usually used as a synonym of a new technology for television that leaves behind the traditional unidirectional flow model and promotes new forms of consuming audiovisual contents in a more interactive way (Reyes et al. 2015). The contemporary environment of digital convergence put in evidence multiple uses of television not only focused in entertainment and journalism, but also for contexts in which health, education and public services can take advantage of interactivity and high quality of sound and image.

Educational opportunities using multiple platforms are growing exponentially. The technological implementation has created conditions for exploring distance education. This offers for nontraditional learners possibilities to have access to learning options,

© Springer Nature Switzerland AG 2019
M. J. Abásolo et al. (Eds.): jAUTI 2018, CCIS 1004, pp. 3–13, 2019.
https://doi.org/10.1007/978-3-030-23862-9_1

dodging time and place restrictions and making learning process more flexible. Learning management systems have evolved significantly as synchronous, asynchronous, and hybridized delivery options provide new forms of teaching-learning and professional development, surpassing the traditional face-to-face classrooms.

Regarding educational scenarios, the convergence between television and rich video contents with computer technologies has led to require a closer relationship of cooperation and conjunction of concepts between teaching practice, didactics and software engineering. Many challenges are presented tough. Television has its own language and tradition in consumer electronics market. Although many interactive strategies have been presented and experienced in narratives and technologies for television, the user experience is fundamentally more passive than active. When trying to make closer education and entertainment landscapes, it is worthy considering different methods for making the learner more active and engaged.

This paper focuses specifically in the conveniences of iDTV in learning scenarios. Typically, the use of iDTV for teaching-learning contexts emerged from t-learning frameworks, in a way users can have access to educational content in different manners and forms from TV for acquiring knowledgement (Reyes et al. 2015). Depending on the historical moment of a country and its researcher's appropriation of the term, iDTV can be also found as Interactive Television (ITV) with slight different concepts in learning scenarios. These nuances will be further explored in the next lines.

2   Method

2.1   Research Question

Although along the history plenty of papers show the potential of using iDTV for enhancing learning scenarios (Pemberton 2002; Aarreniemi-Jokipelto 2006; Angeluci 2013; Angeluci et al. 2015; Bureš 2017), there is a lack of studies that systematize and categorize how iDTV has been explored considering learning contexts. That could put some light on trends and perspectives for future studies since the subject has been frequently appearing in the literature in the last 15 years and seems to have reached a certain degree of conceptual maturity. Consequently, the aim of this paper is to address: "what evidences in the literature shows characteristics of studies related to the use of iDTV in learning scenarios?". In order to do so, the review is focused in categorizing the papers so these evidences can emerge.

Database Searched for Data Collection

Databases searched in this paper where chosen by their relevance in education, technologies and social science fields: ACM (Association for Computing Machinery), BioMed Central, ERIC (Education Resources Information Center), IEEE (Institute of Electrical and Electronics Engineers), Ingenta Connect, ScienceDirect and WOS (Web of Science).

Search Terms and Selection Criteria of Papers for Inclusion in the Review
Search terms included were extracted from a preliminary and exploratory bibliographic research and generated the following boolean expression:

("DIGITAL TV" OR "INTERACTIVE TELEVISION" OR "DIGITAL TELEVISION" OR "DIGITAL TERRESTRIAL TELEVISION") AND ("LEARNING" OR "EDUCATION")

Full texts not mentioning the word "learning" were not included in the review. Also, it was only considered papers published between 2014 and 2017 in form of articles in journals and magazines – papers from event proceedings or books were excluded. Duplicate papers in different databases were disregarded in the counting of databases with higher occurrence of articles and considered in the smaller ones. Finally, a double peer review of papers' titles and abstracts meeting the select criteria previously mentioned was done, and papers not directly related to the use of iDTV in learning settings were excluded.

2.2 Data Analysis

The papers meeting full inclusion criteria were coded in order to carry out data analysis. A categorization proforma was created based on the preliminary and exploratory bibliographic research, aiming to extract systematic information from all selected papers in nine specific categories that helps to salient dimensions of evidences searched in learning scenarios. Part of the categories are more methodology-driven and the other related to the implementation of iDTV: (1) paper's purpose; (2) educational content; (3) country of the host institution; (4) research methodology used; (5) sample size, gender and public age range; (6) learning activities characteristics; (7) mode and technology of interaction; (8) digital television system; and (9) learning results types: quantitative, qualitative or mixed.

3 Results

3.1 Papers Identified by Search Terms

Table 1 shows the number of papers in each of the databases that were identified using search terms. As the table shows, the search terms identified a large number of papers (521) demonstrating high interest in iDTV in learning context during the time period assigned. During the process of double peer review of titles and abstracts 18 papers were selected and half of them were found in WOS database, becoming the most popular database for the queries investigated.

Table 1. Number of papers identified by selection criteria.

Database	# identified in search	# mentioning "learning"	# between 2014 and 2017 in form of journal articles	# selected after double peer review of titles and abstracts
ACM	1.691	144	7	3
BioMed Central	25	12	4	0
ERIC	697	127	5	3
IEEE	20.777	977	301	1
Ingenta Connect	1.591	184	43	0
ScienceDirect	3.848	650	143	2
WOS	2.098	79	18	9
Total	30.727	2.173	521	18

3.2 Paper's Purpose

Regarding paper's purpose, 12 referred to the iDTV and related technologies used or applied to learning tool, thus meeting the main objective of this work. They analyze, study, describe or validate variables related to the use of iDTV in learning context.

There were four papers related to technology applied to iDTV, i.e. the main objective of these works was to develop new techniques or technologies for iDTV and to do so, they used learning contexts as tools. It should be noted that these four works were nor eliminated of this paper, since they have valuable information about using iDTV as a possible learning tool, although that was not the aim of these studies. In addition, two theoretical works were found describing methodological proposals for development of educative contents for iDTV.

Of the papers selected, none of them can be classified as a survey or literature review (Table 2).

Table 2. Paper's distribution by purpose and country

Region	Country	Paper's purpose	Authors
Latin America	Brazil	Technology applied to iDTV	Monteiro et al. (2016)
	Brazil	iDTV as Learning Tool	Santos et al. (2016)
	Brazil	Technology applied to iDTV	Furtado et al. (2014)
	Brazil	iDTV as Learning Tool	Neto et al. (2015)
	Colombia	Theoretical	Reyes Gamboa et al. (2016)
	Colombia	Theoretical	Reyes et al. (2015)
	Mexico	Technology applied to iDTV	Vásquez-Ramírez et al. (2014)

(*continued*)

Table 2. (*continued*)

Region	Country	Paper's purpose	Authors
North-America	USA	iDTV as Learning Tool	Turner and Turner (2017)
	USA	iDTV as Learning Tool	Proctor and Bumgardner (2016)
	USA	iDTV as Learning Tool	Revelle et al. (2014)
	USA	iDTV as Learning Tool	Lightner and Lightner-Laws (2016)
	USA	iDTV as Learning Tool	Reddy (2014)
	USA	iDTV as Learning Tool	Olmsted (2014)
Europe	Spain	iDTV as Learning Tool	Costa et al. (2017)
	Spain	iDTV as Learning Tool	Baldassarri et al. (2015)
	Czech Republic	iDTV as Learning Tool	Bureš et al. (2017)
	Latvia	iDTV as Learning Tool	Kapenieks et al. (2015)
	Serbia	Technology applied to iDTV	Krstic and Bjelica (2016)

Among the works that considered ITV as a learning tool, there are those that refer to the use of TV in remote classes with the transmission of live lectures, being these works the ones developed in the USA (Table 2).

It was possible to observe from the chronology of the publications that the most recent papers are related to learning tools with applied technologies from previous works, suggesting an initial concern with the development and evolution of the technologies and, later, the application of them as learning tools. Moreover, in the case of Brazil, this period coincides with the implementation and first years of the terrestrial DTV system operation, which may explain the interest in researches about technology development and, later, its use in education. In Colombia, where the digitization process was later, only theoretical works were found, carried out by Reyes et al. (2015) and Reyes Gamboa et al. (2016). It should be noted that in one of the papers, Monteiro et al. (2016) presents the proposal of a structure that can be applied to ITV, but in their experimental work, other technologies were used.

3.3 Learning Contents of Application

Several learning contents were subject of the applications or the courses which the research was carried out. Among the contents are: Math (two papers), Biology, Sociology, Literacy, Communication, IT, Artificial Intelligence, Cognitive Application, Health Care, Dental Hygiene, Manager Training, Teacher Training and MBA.

3.4   Country of the Host Institution

Of the 18 papers analyzed; seven were from Latin America: four from Brazil, two from Colombia and one from Mexico. Six were performed in the USA and five in Europe: two from Spain, one from Czech Republic, one from Latvia and one from Serbia.

American studies were about questions and comparisons between the different delivery methods courses offered by the American educational institutions: traditional classroom course, online course and ITV course; meanwhile Latin American's and European's works were about different themes, such as technology, methodology and even theory.

3.5   Methodology of Research Used

Of the non-theoretical studies analyzed, eight of them were case studies and the other eight were experimental studies, of which, one also presented characteristics of a quasi-experimental study (Table 3). In comparison with Sect. 3.2, it was possible to observe that, of the selected papers, among those that presented a case study, there was two papers referring to technology applied to ITV and six referring to learning tools. The proportion was maintained for the experimental studies, being two works on technology and six works on use as a learning tool.

Table 3. Paper's distribution by method and purpose

Paper's purpose	Method	Authors
iDTV as Learning Tool	Case Study	Santos et al. (2016)
iDTV as Learning Tool	Case Study	Neto et al. (2015)
iDTV as Learning Tool	Case Study	Proctor and Bumgardner (2016)
iDTV as Learning Tool	Case Study	Revelle et al. (2014)
iDTV as Learning Tool	Case Study	Reddy (2014)
iDTV as Learning Tool	Case Study	Baldassarri et al. (2015)
Technology applied to iDTV	Case Study	Furtado et al. (2014)
Technology applied to iDTV	Case Study	Vásquez-Ramírez et al. (2014)
iDTV as Learning Tool	Experimental	Bureš et al. (2017)
iDTV as Learning Tool	Experimental	Lightner and Lightner-Laws (2016)
iDTV as Learning Tool	Experimental	Olmsted (2014)
iDTV as Learning Tool	Experimental	Kapenieks et al. (2015)
iDTV as Learning Tool	Experimental	Costa et al. (2017)
Technology applied to iDTV	Experimental	Monteiro et al. (2016)
Technology applied to iDTV	Experimental	Krstic and Bjelica (2016)
iDTV as Learning Tool	Quasi-experimental	Turner and Turner (2017)

3.6   Sample Size, Gender and Public Age Range

The sample sizes in the case studies and experimental studies varied between 22 and 382 individuals, and three case studies and one experimental study did not indicate sample size. Only six studies indicated gender distribution and, in three of them, the distribution was approximately 50% for each gender. Other three report predominantly women, as can be seen in works of Baldassari et al. (2015), Olmsted (2014) and Bureš et al. (2017). None of the studies present an analysis of the difference of the results by gender, which can be explained by the fact that only three papers presented a sample with a distribution around 50%, with a small sample size still.

Regarding to public age range, one work was addressed to children's public (8–14 years old) and another one to basic education (8–14 and 15–18 years old). Six studies had university public (19–30 years old) and two works related to adult public (19–30 and 31–59 years old). Two papers were focused on the elderly audience (over 60 years of age). Finally, seven papers do not indicate public age or this characteristic does not apply, as in the two theoretical papers.

3.7 Learning Activities Characteristic

Papers have mostly activities with exclusively individual learning mode – being a total of eight papers following this profile. Five papers presented the learning conference mode, since they referred to studies on remote class. These studies were carried out in the USA as previously mentioned. Monteiro et al. (2016) and Revelle et al. (2014) presented proposals with games characteristics. In the first, this was a small functionality of the platform, allowing creating of challenges between users. The second study of Revelle et al. (2014) involved a proposal with collaborative and competitive learning characteristics, the proposal was an augmented reality game, in which users needed to collect virtual objects (balls) scattered in the environment and throw them onto the television. Finally, for three studies, including the theoretical ones, the individual, collaborative or competitive classification does not apply.

Regarding the learning type, as expected in this survey, the works that presented ITV as a learning tool are predominantly those that involve distance learning. Twelve studies did deal with a distance-learning proposal and two papers presented mixed proposals that applied distance learning combined with instances of presential methods.

It is worth mentioning that, even in comparative studies between distance and face-to-face courses, when ITV was used exclusively in the distance course, learning type was classified as distance. The cases in which the distance ITV method also incorporated presential instances are considered mixed. Lightner and Lightner-Laws (2016) and Monteiro et al. (2016) presented this mixed type learning.

3.8 Mode and Technology of Interaction

Most of the works presented interaction mode through individual devices. Seven of the analyzed manuscripts used remote control to interact with iDTV. Bureš et al. (2017) indicated in his work, besides the use of remote, that the interaction was potentialized with a pointer device. Also, Baldassari et al. (2015) used, in addition to the remote, an IP camera that had an important role in the interaction with the system, capturing the user's emotions from facial recognition.

In the five remote class researches, the mode of interaction with iDTV, as it might be suppose, was through personal computer or video conference system. It should be noted that in these works their authors consider video conferencing and remote class systems as iDTV.

In three proposals, the interaction was made by smartphone, and for Krstic and Bjelica (2016), the user's choices in his device were used to recommend new content, in addition to Monteiro et al. (2016) and Revelle et al. (2014) which, as mentioned earlier, applied game elements in their projects, also using mobile devices for inter-action. This latter made use of a stylized case that gave to the device a playful design to turn it into an object of the game.

In three works, the interaction mode did not apply or was not specified; for example, Vásquez-Ramírez et al. (2014) presented a proposal addressed to android TV, that is a platform with multiple possibilities of interaction. However the work does not materialize a study with an application generated in the platform and, therefore, there is no interaction reported.

3.9   Digital Television System

Of the proposals that used or were developed for terrestrial TV, three were made for the Brazilian-Japanese standard (ISDB-t) and two for the European standard (DVB).

The five USA works related to remote class had their own conference system. Two proposals were directed to the market of Smart TVs. Vásquez-Ramírez et al. (2014) had their project directed to the Android TV platform and Rivas Costa et al. (2017) pre-sented an independent prototype platform and executed it in a HTPC simulated envi-ronment. Revelle et al. (2014) used an OnDemand video system (VOD).

For five papers, the system on which the project was executed was not specified or this characteristic does not apply. Among them, Bureš et al. (2017), in which the prototype was run in a set-top box, but operating system was not indicated.

3.10   Learning Results Types: Quantitative, Qualitative or Mixed

Regarding the results, the criterion for analysis was the presentation of results in terms of education, either in learning (knowledge and skills acquired) or behavioral (moti-vation and engagement). Of 11 analyzed papers, six presented principally qualitative results, two papers presented mainly quantitative results and three presented mixed results.

All these studies indicated that there was learning using ITV, and seven of them concluded that learning with ITV was better than other methods. Two studies found that learning with ITV, compared to other methods, was equal. For two proposals, this characteristic does not apply because there was no comparison with another scenario.

Of the papers that presented results related to education, ten also indicated advances in engagement and motivation. Olmsted (2014) demonstrated gains in learning in his study, but do not mention behavioral analysis.

Seven papers did not present results, or this characteristic does not apply to the proposal presented by them. Furtado et al. (2014) presented an integrated production method for ITV applications, and therefore did not seek learning results, but results in ease of use. Vásquez-Ramírez et al. (2014) performed a heuristic usability analysis of an application produced for ITV on the proposed platform. Presenting adequate learning objects was the result sought by Neto et al. (2015), which showed a recommendation system. Krstic and Bjelica (2016) proposed a personalized guide system, so the results were related to the adequacy of the contents suggested by the system. Kapenieks et al. (2015) assessed results in terms of reduction of dropout rate in the course studied. Finally, two papers did not present results in education because they are theoretical.

4 Conclusion

Although it is worthy pointing that the reduced sample can induce to bias, this limitation do not short the relevance of the findings based on the strong structured data collection. The data showed some important evidences in this research field and addressed the research question previously pointed.

Most of the papers identified are research results from Latin American countries. There are differences in approaches regarding the concept of iDTV; in the USA, the concept of iDTV is closer to distance education, and ITV is a more used term than iDTV in north-american works. The greatest occurrence of papers on the subject in a given period is related to the country's historical moment in the discussion about the implementation of DTV technology, as in the case of Brazil.

Regardless of the type of methodology used, most studies have investigated the use of iDTV as a learning tool rather than purely technological issues, with a very varied spectrum of interest in terms of public profiles and educational contents. It is also important to note that most interaction activities occurred in remote education contexts using computers, smartphones and other devices as interaction resources. In general, most studies showed advances in learning process, also in engaging and motivation of the public involved.

As future works, expanding the time period, including papers from 2008 to 2013 and 2018, giving a wider perspective, as the period analyzed (2014 to 2017) is understood as not the boom period for research in DTV in Latin America and also for USA and Europe - although it was important for a proper understanding of the current state-of-art of iDTV in learning scenarios in a contemporary set.

Acknowledgements. This work has been funded by the Comisión Nacional de Investigación Científica y Tecnológica (CONICYT) under the Call "Apoyo a la formación de redes internacionales para investigadores(as) en etapa inicial", Grant Agreement nr. REDI170043.

References

Aarreniemi-Jokipelto, P.: Modelling and content production of distance learning concept for interactive digital television. Helsinki University of Technology (2006)
Angeluci, A.C.B.: Recomendações de IHC para uso de aplicativos interativos em televisão e segunda tela a partir de infraestrutura de TVD (Doctoral dissertation, Universidade de São Paulo) (2013). https://doi.org/10.11606/t.3.2013.tde-10032014-153029

Angeluci, A.C.B., Calixto, G.M., Morandini, M.L., de Deus Lopes, R., Zuffo, M.K.: Interactive TV interoperability and coexistence: the GLOBAL ITV project. In: Abásolo, M., Kulesza, R. (eds.) Applications and Usability of Interactive TV. CCIS, vol. 389, pp. 3–16. Springer, Cham (2015). https://doi.org/10.1007/978-3-319-22656-9_1

Bureš, V., Mikulecká, J., Ponce, D.: Digital Television as a Usable Platform for Enhancement of Learning Possibilities for the Elderly. SAGE Open, **7**(2) (2017). https://doi.org/10.1177/2158244017708817

Pemberton, L.: The potential of interactive television for delivering individualised language learning. In: Workshop on Future TV: Adaptive Instruction in Your Living Room (2002)

Reyes, A.X., Soto, D.E., Jimenez, J.A.: MADCE-TVD-model agile development educational content for digital television. IEEE Latin Am. Trans. **13**(10), 3432–3438 (2015). https://doi.org/10.1109/TLA.2015.7387251

Coded papers

Baldassarri, S., Hupont, I., Abadía, D., Cerezo, E.: Affective-aware tutoring platform for interactive digital television. Multimedia Tools Appl. **74**(9), 3183–3206 (2015). https://doi.org/10.1007/s11042-013-1779-z

Costa, C.R., Anido-Rifón, L.E., Fernández-Iglesias, M.J.: An open architecture to support social and health services in a smart TV environment. IEEE J. Biomed. Health Inform. **21**(2), 549–560 (2017). https://doi.org/10.1109/JBHI.2016.2525725

Furtado, E.S., Cardoso, R.P.L., Neto, H.B.: An integrated view of communicational, educational and technological categories applied to the content production for IDTV and mobile devices. Int. J. Inform. Commun. Technol. Educat. (IJICTE) **10**(4), 41–52 (2014). https://doi.org/10.4018/ijicte.2014100104

Kapenieks, A., et al.: User behavior in multi-screen eLearning. Procedia Comput. Sci. **65**, 761–767 (2015). https://doi.org/10.1016/j.procs.2015.09.021

Krstic, M., Bjelica, M.: Personalized program guide based on one-class classifier. IEEE Trans. Consum. Electron. **62**(2), 175–181 (2016). https://doi.org/10.1109/TCE.2016.7514717

Lightner, C.A., Lightner-Laws, C.A.: A blended model: Simultaneously teaching a quantitative course traditionally, online, and remotely. Interact. Learn. Environ. **24**(1), 224–238 (2016). https://doi.org/10.1080/10494820.2013.841262

Neto, F.M.M., de Carvalho Muniz, R., Burlamaqui, A.M.F., de Souza, R.C.: An agent-based approach for delivering educational contents through interactive digital TV in the context of T-learning. Int. J. Distance Educ. Technol. (IJDET) **13**(2), 73–92 (2015). https://doi.org/10.4018/IJDET.2015040105

Olmsted, J.L.: Direct assessment as a measure of institutional effectiveness in a dental hygiene distance education program. J. Dent. Educ. **78**(10), 1460–1467 (2014)

Proctor, J., Bumgardner, T.: Transitioning from Traditional Courses to Technologically Supported Classrooms, pp. 1–8. IDEA Paper# 62. IDEA Center, Inc. (2016)

Reddy, C.: Educating laboratory science learners at a distance using interactive television. Am. J. Distance Educ. **28**(1), 62–69 (2014). https://doi.org/10.1080/08923647.2014.868746

Revelle, G., et al.: Electric agents: combining collaborative mobile augmented reality and web-based video to reinvent interactive television. Comput. Entertainment (CIE) **12**(3), 1 (2014). https://doi.org/10.1145/2702109.2633413

Reyes Gamboa, A.X., Jimenez Builes, J., Soto Duran, D.E.: An Agile model for the development of T-learning content. Cuad. Activa **8**, 41–47 (2016)

Santos, R.A., de Goes Brennand, E.G., Soares, I.M.: Interactive applications as multiple enhancing intelligences. ETD Educação Temática Digital **18**(2), 465–484 (2016). https://doi.org/10.20396/etd.v18i2.8635194

Monteiro, B.S., Gomes, A.S., Neto, F.M.M.: Youubi: open software for ubiquitous learning. Comput. Hum. Behav. **55**, 1145–1164 (2016). https://doi.org/10.1016/j.chb.2014.09.064

Turner, C., Turner, K.D.: The effects of educational delivery methods on knowledge retention. J. Educ. Bus. **92**(5), 201–209 (2017). https://doi.org/10.1080/08832323.2017.1331989

Vásquez-Ramírez, R., Alor-Hernández, G., Sánchez-Ramírez, C., Guzmán-Luna, J., Zatarain-Cabada, R., Barrón-Estrada, M.L.: AthenaTV: an authoring tool of educational applications for TV using android-based interface design patterns. New Rev. Hypermedia Multimedia **20**(3), 251–280 (2014). https://doi.org/10.1080/13614568.2014.925004

Design and Implementation of a Home Automation System with an Interactive Application for Digital Television Based on the Ginga Middleware

Belén Enríquez[1](✉) 🆔, Diego Villamarín[1,2](✉) 🆔, and Freddy Acosta[1](✉) 🆔

[1] Universidad de las Fuerzas Armadas ESPE, Sangolquí, Ecuador
{baenriquez2,dfvillamarin,fracosta}@espe.edu.ec
[2] Universidad Politécnica de Madrid, Madrid, Spain
dvz@gatv.ssr.upm.es

Abstract. In this work we present "DomoiTV", a home automation system and its communication protocol with a graphic interface for the Brazilian digital terrestrial television standard ISDB-Tb.

This project is divided into three main phases, the design and implementation of the home automation system, the development of the graphic interface for DTT and the communication protocol between these two areas.

For the automation phase, six areas are covered: intrusion alarms, technical alarms, lighting control, blinds and shades control, access to cameras, and pre-programmed scenarios. To meet the requirements of these six areas, a controller with different sensors and actuators are installed providing a safe, comfortable and controlled environment.

The user interface, designed as an interactive TV application based on the Ginga middleware, is the way to represent the automation devices installed, therefore the user can visualize the status of each sensor and take action on its actuators. In addition, a mobile user application was implemented to provide interoperability and usability in multiple devices.

The communication protocol is developed in order to manage data sent from the application through TCP communication; and by means of a translator the information is redirected to a Real-Time cloud database, where the controller has access to complete the communication between both parties.

Testing of operation and Start-up of the automation system is carried out, in addition to the application usability tests on several devices. The final system resulted in an integrated, robust and reliable system in terms of operation; and friendly and intuitive to the user.

Keywords: DomoiTV · Ginga · DTT · ISDB-Tb · Home automation

1 Introduction

In the technological development area, the advance of electronics and communications has contributed enormously to the growth of new technologies in different fields, directly affecting the way we live. Currently, there are several research papers in the

M. J. Abásolo et al. (Eds.): jAUTI 2018, CCIS 1004, pp. 14–27, 2019.
https://doi.org/10.1007/978-3-030-23862-9_2

home automation area as well as in the Digital Terrestrial Television (DTT) area and its interactivity. However, there is a lack in terms of the state of the art in the association of these two fields.

Currently, buildings around the world lack monitoring and control systems, and although the facilities provide basic services, home automation systems provides greater efficiency and comfort, which translates into a better quality of life and energy savings. The new technology applied to sensors, actuators, controllers, and wired and wireless communications, allows the exponential development of intelligent environments. By integrating these devices and technologies we can obtain information about the inhabitants and the space around them, perform a variable treatment over the information and apply a control over the entire system, improving this way the user experience with a controlled environment [1].

On the other hand, by digitalizing the television signal, different features have been integrated into television sets, bringing great benefits. Beginning with the increase of the programming transmitted by the same channel, varying the quality of audio and video for each transmission[1]. At the same time, internet connection and data management are enabled with the Ginga middleware[2], giving way to new interactive television services such as radio channels, surveys, program guides, voting applications, among many others [2].

The little interaction of electrical and electronic systems with digital television devices and applications has motivated this project to encourage the use and incorporation of these technologies in favor of the population, since the benefits of these embedded systems include the improvement of the users' quality of life, grants greater autonomy within their environment, the possibility of use the automation home system in multiple devices, in addition to assisting vulnerable groups such as the elderly, or people with limited or reduced capabilities [3].

In the bibliography of the Home automation by digital television, there are a patent home automation apparatus using a digital television receiver for use in a building by Jeon and Kim Patente [10]. The apparatus contains a signal processor, a memory unit, a microprocessing unit, a display unit, a sensor input unit, an interface unit, and a controller. But an obvious weakness of Jeon and Kim Patente is the requirement of additional hardware. Also, in [11] De Lucena et al. Paper there are a proposal of a new infrastructure that allows the exchange of data from the interactive digital television systems (iDTV) to home automation devices, such as sensors, mobile devices, among others. This model is supported by Java's open services gateway initiative (OSGi), as a framework for networked devices, and the Brazilian reference middleware, Ginga. The principal advantage of our proposal is the development of a domotics signals interpreter programed in LUA.

---

[1] Digital television allows the broadcasting of High Definition (HD) and Standard Definition (SD) programming through the same transmission channel.

[2] Ginga middleware is a heterogeneous software layer that provides interactivity for the Brazilian ISDB-Tb standard and for IPTV according to the International Union of Telecommunications.

2   Design and Implementation of the Home Automation System

2.1   Facility

The home automation system was implemented in a scale model of a real house as can be seen in Fig. 1. The model has the features of a house, has gardens, parking, rooms, social area, kitchen and bathrooms, so it's ideal for the presentation of an electronic system that shows the benefits of automation in a cohesive manner.

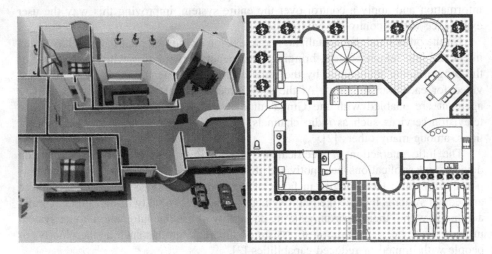

Fig. 1. Scale model of the facility.

2.2   The System Description and the Functions to Be Performed

The implemented home automation system has a centralized control architecture (see Fig. 2). The controller device manages the entire system according to the programming and the information obtained from the peripheral devices (sensors, actuators and user interface). The sensors monitor the environment and capture data for transmission to the system while the actuators execute the commands triggered by the controller. The communication path between the controller with the peripheral devices is wired[3], while the communication with the multiplatform user interface through the cloud database is wireless[4].

---

[3] For the control signals the twisted pair cable is used as a guided transmission medium, while for the power lines, Topflex cable is used for electrical installations.

[4] The standard 802.11 (Wi-Fi) is used as a non-guided transmission medium.

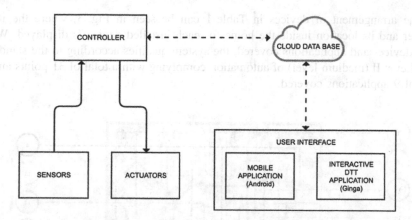

Fig. 2. Architecture of the domotic system.

The AENOR EA0026 standard on the certification for installation of automation systems, technical management of energy and security for facilities [4], highlights the different applications and devices taken into consideration to classify an installation according to its level of automation[5], of which the ones shown in Table 1 have been chosen according to the needs of this project.

Table 1. Applications and devices arranged in the installation.

Applications	Item number	Devices	Quantity	Points
Intrusion alarm	1	Presence detector	3	9
	2	Electronic key	2	
	3	Indoor siren	1	
	4	Magnetic contacts	3	
	5	Motor for doors	1	
	6	Doorbell	1	
	7	Cameras	1	
Technical alarm	8	Butane gas detectors	1	2
	9	Fire detector	1	
Video intercom	10	Video intercom	1	1
Blind control	11	Motors for blinds	3	1
Lightning control	12	Lighting circuits	6	7
Multimedia Network	13	Wifi Router	1	1
User Interface	14	Mobile Device and TV	1	5
Presence Simulation	15	Controller	1	3
Hour schedules				2

[5] The AENOR EA0026 standard qualifies the facilities according to their automation level (high, medium or low), according to the installed devices and the covered applications, giving a score according to their evaluation table.

The arrangement of devices in Table 1 can be seen in Fig. 3, where the item number and its location inside the home for each installed device is displayed. With these devices and applications covered, the system qualifies according to the standard for a Level II (medium level) of automation complying with a total of 31 points and a total of 9 applications covered.

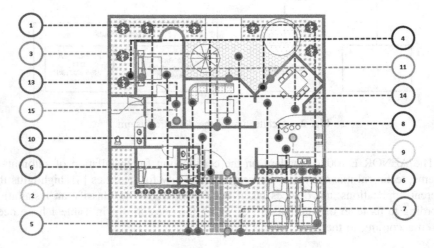

Fig. 3. Arrangement of devices in the facility.

2.3 Cloud Data Base

The implemented system has an orientation towards the Internet of Things (IoT), that is, a system of interrelated objects and devices with the ability to transfer data over a network [5]. In the area of home automation this translates into a connection of sensors and actuators to the internet network, in order to monitor and control in Real-Time what happens inside a facility [6]. As a basis for obtaining Real-Time information through an internet connection, a cloud database is needed primarily. The implemented system has a database on the Firebase server, which is a free cloud service that provides different resources such as user authentication, Real-Time database, file storage, among others, which are used by the automation system.

2.4 Controller Programming

The system driver program is embedded in a Raspberry Pi3 card, this program is done in Python language in its 3.0 version. Five sections are programmed (access, alarms, lighting, blinds and scenarios), these five sections cover the different domotic devices and the controller makes decisions based on the data received, the programming is sequential with interruptions.

Figure 4 shows an example of the lighting area. In the first instance the initial state of the lights can be observed in the scale model and it is reflected in the cloud database (arrows in blue) where "0" represents the lights off and "1" the lights on, on the other hand when an order arrives, the state of the variable changes in the cloud database and the control signal is sent to the corresponding relay to activate the lighting of the room (arrows in orange).

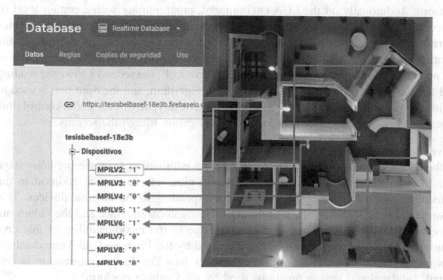

Fig. 4. Sending and receiving data from the cloud to the controller and vice versa. (Color figure online)

3 Design and Development of the Interactive Application and the Communication Protocol

3.1 Development of the Ginga Application

The main objective of "DomoiTV" is to provide the user the personalized perception of the devices installed in the facility though the application for the digital television based on the Ginga middleware. The application covers different programming environments, allowing communication between the user interface with the cloud database and the home automation devices installed.

Figure 5 shows the path that the information goes through, beginning with the declarative language of Ginga NCL that represents the structural part of the program, to the Real-Time database and vice versa [7].

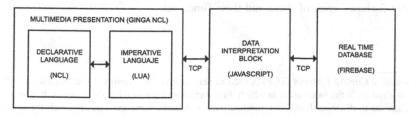

Fig. 5. Interconnection of data between interactive application and database.

In the stage corresponding to the multimedia presentation environment (Ginga NCL), programming is done in the NCL and LUA language. In the NCL section, all the elements that allow the user to know about the home automation system (buttons, indicators, videos, images, text, etc.) are specified, and actions are assigned to each one of them. Additionally, in the LUA environment, programming with a certain level of processing is needed. In this language, information about the user and the variables corresponding to the devices are collected, and with three types of algorithms this information is transferred to the next stage. The first algorithm allows the connection of the application to the Internet through the TCP protocol[6], the second allows the reading and writing of the variables state, using the first algorithm, and the third one is used to define alphanumeric characters by using the numeric keypad of the remote control, this procedure is mainly used for user login and navigation trough the screens.

Development of the communication protocol
In the data interpretation block we collect all the information from the previous stage and we validate and transfer the user authentication information, in addition to the transmission of the status of the variables corresponding to the domotic devices. This information is provided by the user through the graphical interface and the values are provided by the algorithm in LUA, however due to the incompatibility of this programming language with the algorithm managed by the Firebase Real-Time database this interpretation block is needed. In this block (see Fig. 6) the information is collected, validated and sent to finally be used by the Firebase platform.

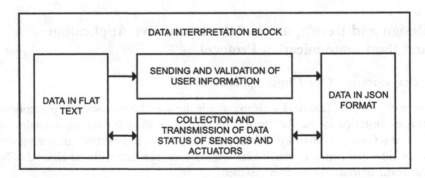

Fig. 6. Data interpretation block.

Under this protocol, a total of 12 main screens are implemented.
Table 2 shows each of them and their function.

---

[6] Transmission Control Protocol (TCP) is used to send a data flow, ensuring that the data is delivered to its destination in the same order in which they were transmitted and without errors. It also provides a mechanism to distinguish different applications within the same machine, through the concept of ports.

Table 2. Screens of the interactive application for the DTT.

N°	Screen	Description
1	Start	Welcome to the application, gives the option to login or help
2	Login	Allows the user to login with their previously registered data through the mobile application
3	Principal Menu	Shows the sections of access, alarms, cameras, scenes, lighting and blinds, for the visualization and control of the system
4	Access	Shows the user the status of the following devices: the bell, the interior, exterior and garage doors, allowing it opening
5	Alarms	Muestra al usuario los indicadores del estado de los sensores de seguridad: sirena, detector de gas y de incendios, detectores de movimiento y contactos magnéticos
6	Cameras	Shows the user the real time video of the security camera and the video intercom
7	Scenarios	Presents different options of pre-programmed scenarios: "good morning", "good night", "sunset", "leaving home" and "travel", which can be used at the user's convenience
8	Lighting	It allows modifying the status of the lights of the following rooms: master bedroom, living room, dining room, kitchen, corridor and gardens. Also the RGB lights can be modified
9	Blinds	It allows modifying the status of the blinds in the following areas of the home: master bedroom, living room, dining room
10	User	It allows the user to get help and close the session
11	Information	It contains a brief explanation of the use of the remote control within the application
12	Help	Provides the user with information about the contact for system maintenance

Figure 7 shows an example of sending and receiving values on the lightning area, where you can first see how the application reads the current state of the variables (arrows in blue), where "0" represents the lights off and "1" the lights on, and also when the user performs an action it is reflected in the database (arrow in orange).

3.2 Development of the Mobile Application

The mobile application of "DomoiTV" is an extension of the interactive application for DTT, so the user can have access to the system remotely. The application is developed by App Inventor [8], a Software-Free programming environment, used for the application development for the Android operating system. The application has the same screens implemented for the DTT application shown in Table 2, so that the design harmonizes in the different platforms. In addition, in the mobile application there is an extra screen of registration, a screen of deactivation of alarms, an improved user screen and finally has different pop-up screens (See Table 3).

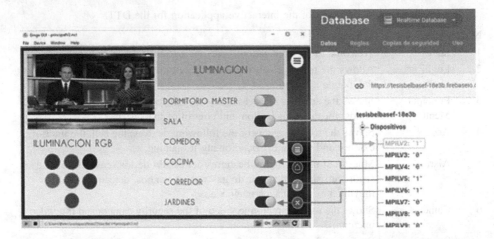

Fig. 7. Simulation of sending and receiving data from the application to the database. (Color figure online)

Table 3. Additional screens implemented in the mobile application.

N°	Screen	Description
1	Registration	Allows the user to enter the data and register as a user of the application
2	Deactivation	Allows to stop the emergency alarm, after verification by the user of the various sensors, whether technical (gas, fire), or intrusion (movement and magnetic)
3	User	Allows the user to personalize his profile, consult information and close the session
4	Emerging	The pop-up screens (bell, gas and fire sensor, siren) are displayed when system sensors are active and need to be checked

4   Results

The evaluation is performed in a real scenario with a television signal transmission, where audio, video and data[7] are multiplexed, modulated and sent by air over the same channel. Next, in the reception area, the signal is demodulated and decoded so the audio, the video and the data can be shown on the TV. On the other hand the automation system takes the information from the peripheral devices and the graphic interface, and stores it in the database.

In the case of the DTT application, the information is sent through a data interpretation block, which allows the information to be stored and subsequently used by the area of the TV signal transmission, thus ending the cycle traveled by the information.

---

[7] The data corresponds to the interactive application and the status of the variables handled by the automation system.

As a final result we obtain an integrated, robust, fail-safe system with a user-centered approach. Figure 8 shows the final scheme where you can see the automation area integrated with the DTT area through the data translator.

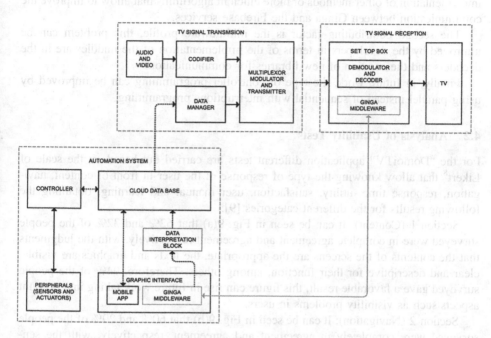

Fig. 8. Integrated scheme of the automation system "DomoiTV".

4.1 Analysis of Performance Tests

Different tests were carried out to verify the stability and functionality of the "DomoiTV" system. Unit and integration tests in terms of software, and tests of operation, continuity and reaction time in terms of hardware. Giving as a result that the behavior of the system is the expected for each of the points analyzed. In both hardware and software, "DomoiTV" is a robust and fail-safe system. Regarding the performance tests, the average results of the system response time are shown Table 4.

Table 4. Response time of the "DomoiTV" system.

	Mobile application	Ginga application
Average response time [s]	2,36	6,95

It can be seen that the response time of the system to an order coming from the DTT interface is 2.94 times longer than the response of the mobile application, this is due to different factors, the first and most important is that the distance traveled by the data from the application to the database and vice versa is much longer than the distance traveled by the data in the mobile application, that is, the data travels from the NCL environment of Ginga, through the algorithms of LUA and the interpretation block until finally reaching the Real-Time database. This problem can be solved through the implementation of other methods or more efficient algorithms that allow to improve the communication between Ginga and the Firebase services.

The second contributing factor is the middleware profile, this problem can be improved by the developers in terms of the implementation of the middleware in the decoders and the creation of new libraries for communication.

Finally, in future work, the type of controller programming can be improved by using parallel instead of sequential with interruptions programming.

4.2   Analysis of Usability Tests

For the "DomoiTV" application different tests are carried out based on the scale of Likert[8] that allow knowing the type of response of the user in front of content, navigation, response time, utility, satisfaction, user manual and learning, obtaining the following results for the different categories [9].

Section 1 (Content): It can be seen in Fig. 9(a) that 62% and 32% of the people surveyed were in complete agreement and agreement respectively, with the judgments that the contents of the screens are the appropriate, the texts and graphics are visible, clear and descriptive for their function, among others. Therefore, 94% of the people surveyed gave a favorable result, this figure can rise in future work taking into account aspects such as visibility problems in users.

Section 2 (Navigation): It can be seen in Fig. 9(b) that 60% and 29% of the people surveyed were completely in agreement and agreement, respectively, with the sentences referring to the application being intuitive, navigation within of the screens is easy, they can easily find what is required, among others. Although this section gives 89% favorable results, this number can rise exponentially with the user education about the interactivity in digital television and the way of using the colors in the remote control.

Section 3 (Response time): It can be seen in Fig. 10(a) that the favorable responses on the response time of the system are 53% (13% completely adequate and 40% adequate). As analyzed in the results of the operation tests, the response time of the mobile application is 2.36 s and the application for the DTT is 6.95 s, this delay in the system is reflected in the level of satisfaction of the users, and in the figure a certain level of dissatisfaction can be observed, 7% of the users think that the reaction time is not adequate and 40% remains impartial.

Section 4 (Utility and satisfaction): In this section it can be seen in Fig. 10(b) that 97% of the users surveyed show a favorable outcome against judgments about whether the application is useful, about the services it offers and if they would use it again or not. 7% of the respondents are impartial in front of these judgments and this may be

---

[8] The Likert scale is a psychometric scale to evaluate the opinions and attitudes of a person in front of a topic. When responding to an item on the Likert scale, the user responds specifically based on their level of agreement or disagreement.

due to the fact that users prefer traditional systems, however this figure can be favorable with the presentation of the benefits offered by advanced systems and education in the same.

In Fig. 11(a) the results show that 33% of the users considered necessary to use a user manual while 47% considered that it was not necessary, these divided opinions are due to the difference in the ages that exist among the users, as can be seen in Fig. 11(b), people with lower ages consider that it is not necessary the user manual and as the ages advance it becomes more necessary the use of it, this is because the digital native people have a greater facility to adapt to new and complex systems over the digital immigrant people[9] [12, 13].

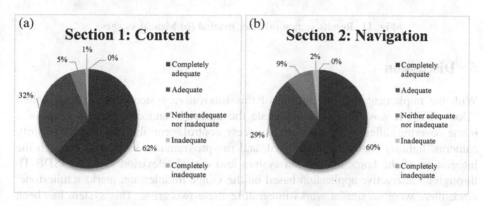

Fig. 9 Results section (a) Contents (b) Navigation.

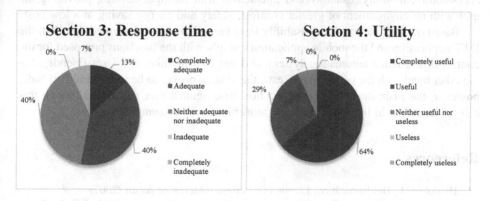

Fig. 10 Results section (a) Response time (b) Utility and satisfaction.

---

[9] The concept of digital natives and digital immigrants is used to describe the generational change in which people are defined by the technological culture with which they are familiar. Given that digital natives are people who were born in the digital era and grew up using technology, while digital immigrants are people who have adapted to this medium.

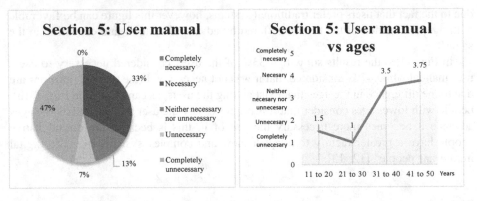

Fig. 11 Results section (a) User manual (b) Manual vs ages.

5 Discussion

With the implementation and testing of this innovative system that we have called "DomoiTV", it was possible to automate the electrical and electronic systems of a home covering different aspects such as access control, central alarm system, security cameras, lighting control, blind control, and pre-programmed scenarios. Through the integration of the home automation system and digital television standard ISDB-Tb through an interactive application based on the Ginga middleware, marks a milestone, since there were no similar works integrating these two areas. This system has been designed based on the IoT so, as a complement to the interactive interface of the DTT, a mobile application was created for the Android platform, which allows improving accessibility, mobility, usability and interaction with multiple devices, providing the user with an environment of greater comfort, safety and energy saving at a low cost.

Based on the functional and usability tests carried out, it was verified that both the DTT application and the mobile application comply with the functions proposed for the control of the home automation system, and are also intuitive and User-Friendly. On the other hand with the performance tests, the system proves to be robust and Fail-Safe, however, the main drawback is the reaction time against user requests, although this can be improved in the future with the aforementioned recommendations.

References

1. Huidobro, J., Huidobro, B.N.: La domótica como solución de futuro (2007)
2. Calixto, G.M., Keimel, C.: Analysis of Coexistence of Ginga and HbbTV in DVB and ISDB-Tb (2014)
3. Morais, W.O.: Architecting Smart Home Environments for Healthcare: A Database-Centric Approach (2015)
4. AENOR: Reglamento particular de la marca AENOR para intalación de sistemas domóticos en viviendas. España (2006)
5. Ducatel, K., Bogdanowicz, M., Scapolo, F., Leijten, J.: Scenarios for ambient intelligence in 2010 (2010)

6. Boubeta-Puig, J., Ortiz, G. and Medina-Bulo, I.: Integración del Internet de las Cosas y las Arquitecturas Orientadas a Servicios: un Caso de Estudio en el Ámbito de la Domótica (2013)
7. Soares, L.F.: Ginga NCL: the declarative environment of the Brazilian digital TV system. J. Braz. Comput. Soc. **12**, 37–46 (2007)
8. Sánchez, E.: AppInventor: Programación para móviles al alcance de todos. Madrid, España (2014)
9. Sánchez, A.: Psicología Social Aplicada. Pearson Educación S.A., Madrid (2002)
10. Jeon, B., Kim, S.: Home automation apparatus using a digital television receiver, US Patent 5,822,012, 1998 - Google Patents (1998)
11. De Lucena, V.F., Chaves Filho, J.E.: A home automation proposal built on the Ginga digital TV middleware and the OSGi framework. IEEE Trans. Consum. Electron. **55**(3), 1254–1262 (2009)
12. García, F., Portillo, J., Romo, J., Benito, M.: Nativos digitales y modelos de aprendizaje. Universidad de País Vasco (2005). http://ceur-ws.org/Vol-318/Garcia.pdf
13. Errandosoro, F., Elissondo, L.: Nativos Digitales: Características que influirían en la aplicación de TIC en el proceso educativo - Situación en la FCE – UNICEN. http://recursos.portaleducoas.org/sites/default/files/12911.pdf

The Concept of Interaction Triggers in Audiovisual Design Model and Its Application to Develop an Interactive Museum

Valdecir Becker$^{(\boxtimes)}$ ⓘ, Rafael Toscano ⓘ, Amanda Azevedo ⓘ,
and Daniel Gambaro ⓘ

Audiovisual Design Research Group, Informatics Center,
Federal University of Paraíba, João Pessoa, PB, Brazil
audiovisualdesign@lavid.ufpb.br

Abstract. This article describes how the methodology of Audiovisual Design was used in the production process of audiovisual content for an Interactive Museum, named Student Citizen. It focuses on how Interaction Triggers were developed considering the diversity of the Museum's audience, especially high school students. To validate the methodology, personas and user scenarios were developed focusing on interaction and role changes. Each role described in the Audiovisual Design model has associated affordances to engage (Triggers of Action) or to relax (Triggers of Inertia). How individuals change roles and behave at each level represent a central element in production of contents for complex audiovisual systems.

Keywords: Audiovisual Design · Interactive Museum · Triggers · Fruition

1 Introduction

The Interactive Museum of Court of Audits of Paraíba State (in Portuguese, TCE-PB) is a project that merges applications, games, augmented reality environments, interactivity and audiovisual contents with the objective of making people aware and involving society in actions towards combating corruption and expanding social control. The resources are designed to lead the visitors to engage in activities focused on fighting corruption daily. The Court of Audits is responsible for monitoring public expenditures and overseeing public works.

The theoretical and methodological model Audiovisual Design (AD) proposed by Becker et al. (2017a) was the conceptual and methodological basis of interaction systems and audiovisual productions for the Museum. The model describes four roles individuals can assume while consuming audiovisual content: Audience, Synthesizer, Modifier and Producer. Each role has its enhanced levels, described as Players, when individuals engage and use all available resources. One important concept of the Audiovisual Design Model are the Interaction Triggers, namely Triggers of Action (ToA) and Triggers of Inertia (ToI). These are elements responsible for calls to action and calls to inertia and should be considered and included in each designing phase of a production. ToA may consist of visual and sound elements or even intrinsic

M. J. Abásolo et al. (Eds.): jAUTI 2018, CCIS 1004, pp. 28–39, 2019.
https://doi.org/10.1007/978-3-030-23862-9_3

motivations (e.g. personal and cultural) provided by the content. ToI usually are present during moments that require high levels of attentiveness. Sometimes the viewer may be unconscious of ToI, although they are central elements in storytelling and long narratives.

This article describes the production process of the audiovisual content and development of interaction strategies to engage people. We will focus on how triggers were developed considering the diversity of the Museum's audience. The project includes around 100 min of institutional videos and content produced by high school students. The project also includes, apart from the Museum, other two visualization systems, one online and other suitable for big audiences, such as lectures and classes in auditoriums.

Each role described in the Audiovisual Design model has associated affordances to engage (ToA) or to relax (ToI). The theme of the museum is 'Fight Against Corruption'. This way, when individuals move from the role of Audience to higher levels of engagement encouraged by ToA, they shall also develop greater awareness of control of public matters. The highest level of engagement is to produce content to be included in the Museum's collection. ToI encourage enjoyment of the institutional videos and content produced by students. Consequently, the whole experience of producing and visiting the Museum should engage all roles described in the Audiovisual Design model.

The outcomes also depicted in this paper formulate the planning process of those interaction triggers applying a use scenario. A persona named Student interacts with audiovisual systems (audio and video content and software) using native media affordances (physical, graphic and symbolic) developed according to each Design Line provided in the DA model, based on actions, or sequences of actions, expected in each role.

This paper is structured as follows: the section two describes the Audiovisual Design model, its roles, affordances and triggers. Section three presents the system architecture, components and resources; section four describes the proposed interactions, based on a persona named Student and a use scenario. The fifth section discusses the museum's triggers and analyses interaction strategies. Finally, section six offers some conclusions and future work suggestions.

2 The Audiovisual Design Model

The Audiovisual Design (AD) initially proposed by Becker et al. (2017a) and developed in studies of Becker et al. (2017b), Toscano et al. (2017), Gambaro et al. (2018) and Becker et al. (2018b) is a theoretical-methodological model for analysis and content development for traditional media and complex audiovisual systems[1]. The AD arises from theoretical propositions of integrating concepts and processes of media studies, (Souza 2003; Jenkins et al. 2015), and Human Computer Interaction, (Barbosa and Silva 2010; Preece et al. 2015). In order to contribute to these studies, AD develops

---

[1] Audiovisual systems are understood here as the set of audio, video and software elements, with their respective interfaces of enjoyment (Toscano et al. 2017).

an interdisciplinary arrangement that considers elements such as content, interfaces and multiple levels of engagement as essential to audiovisual fruition.

The model is based on the description of four roles individuals can assume when consuming audiovisual contents: Audience, Synthesizer, Modifier and Producer. The Audience's role represents the "passive" behavior of the individual during enjoyment of audiovisual contents. The Synthesizer has the skills to compile, classify, comment, recommend and share content, thus building a digital "identity", a profile staged in a social network. The Modifier dominates software to manipulate and recreate content, broadening the notion of engagement to appropriation. Finally, the Producers, which may correspond to a person or a group of people who create original content autonomously, independently or collaborate with large media corporations, are responsible for the design and creation of content.

In addition, each role has its enhanced level, described as Players, which corresponds to an enhancement of the individual's actions when engaging and making the most of available resources. The Player superposes all other roles because it refers to individuals who completely use the tools available on each level. They are treated as Audience-Player, Synthesizer-Player, Modifier-Player, and Producer-Player.

The model also describes Designing Lines, which correspond to product modeling and expected actions of the roles in four aspects: Identity, Motivation, Experience and Content, as conditions to guide both audiovisual production and interaction. The design, using the Lines, can be summarized in: (a) Design with focus on the individuals, through the Line of Identity, idealized by the Producer, or Modifier, for Audience; (b) Design with focus on motivation, through the Line of Motivation, idealized by the Producer, or Modifier, for Synthesizer; (c) Design with focus on the experience, through the Line of Experience, idealized by the Producer for Modifier and Player; (d) Design through the Content Line, which is central at all times, for all roles. It is in content inferences of quality and utility are centered and the intersections between the roles occurs.

Another analysis of the Designing Lines starts from interaction, or from the fruition point of view, and considers the change of roles from an increase in engagement and interaction. The Audience identifies itself with the content and shares it, motivates itself to modify it, and then develops the experience of producing it. Since AD is a set-based model, this change of roles is not necessarily linear, and there may even be action on two or more roles simultaneously. For example, when watching a television program (Audience), the individual, with his cellphone shares comments about the show in a social network (Synthesizer) and records excerpts for a Youtube channel (Modifier or Producer). Figure 1 shows the Audiovisual Design architecture.

Considering interaction happens through interfaces, a concept relevant to Audiovisual Design is Affordance, characteristics of interfaces that are quickly identified and intended for specific uses. From this definition, the authors use the concept of Media Affordances (Becker et al. 2017b), which represent indicative elements present in traditional media and audiovisual systems, which point to meanings and means of enjoyment. Changing roles depends on a correct perception of those affordances, associated with the environment of fruition.

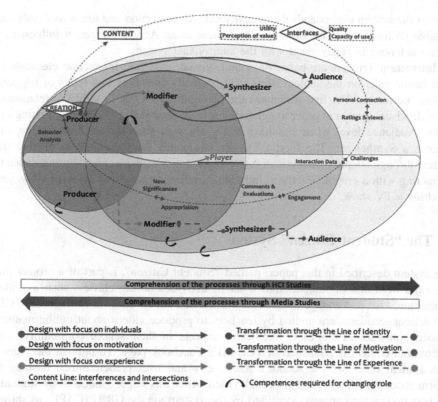

Fig. 1. Audiovisual Design architecture (Source: Audiovisual Design Research Group).

The affordance concept was discussed initially by Gibson (1977) and applied to the media sphere by Becker et al. (2017b), who summarized them in: (a) Physical, affordances that can be actively manipulated, with potential uses easily perceived, composed by technologies used to enjoy content; (b) Graphic, affordances present in interactive graphical interfaces implemented by software and responsible for the mediation between individuals and content; (c) Symbolic, affordances present in narrative or embedded in audiovisual content, where physical affordances are more subtle and cognitive and sensory relations depend not only on technology and interfaces, but also on understanding narrative elements.

The correct identification of possibilities and means of interaction impacts from simple reception, through propagation (Jenkins et al. 2015), and reaches actions that are not foreseen by the Producer, but which contribute to the experience of the individual (who feeds his "identity" into social media profiles) or collectively to a content-related group, such as fan communities, discussion, and technology enhancement.

The action materialized from the perception of value, or utility, of the individual on system's affordances acts as a Trigger, or a element planned by the Producer during the interaction to reach a certain objective (consumption, propagation, participation, attention). A perceived affordance, understood as a call to a certain action, results in a trigger. For example, when entering a share button within the content, the individual in front of the system understands that a new mode of interaction and use is available and possible (Affordance). This button, in turn, acts as an Action Trigger, it influences a certain behavior in engagement with the audiovisual system.

Interaction Triggers are based on sound, visual, interface, interaction elements or even action calls on the content itself. AD basically considers two types of triggers: Action and Inertia. The first stimulates the perception of value or utility in relation to the audiovisual system in order to generate more engagement, for example, getting out of the Audience level when watching a TV show to share impressions online and become a Synthesizer. The Inertia Trigger stimulates the individual to receive the content through attention, analysis or interpretation. For example, after sharing data and interacting with a graphic interface, individuals return to a passive mode of view, just watching a TV show.

3   The "Student Citizen" System

The system described in this paper, named "Student Citizen", is part of a project that integrates high school students into a set of activities during classes, such as video production, visit and engage in Court of Audits of Paraíba State (in Portuguese, TCE-PB) actions. Students are invited by teachers to produce videos about public matters, focusing on success stories or inefficient aspects in their school community. The audiovisual content is published in TCE-PB's Facebook page. To publish the videos, each student describes the school's name, city and uses predetermined hashtag to inform about the content present in each video. After this stage, conducted by students, teachers review the contents, identified by the system via the GRAPH API[2], as shown in Fig. 2.

This data collection (video, user name and school) serves two systems: Advanced and Collaborative Visualization System via Paraíba State Map and the Support System for Lectures, also called as a Custom Video Generator.

Fig. 2. Management panel

---

[2] API provided by Facebook to use information from external web services.

3.1 Advanced and Collaborative Visualization System

The contents are visualized in a Collaborative Map (Fig. 3), which can be accessed on line or viewed on the Interactive Table in the Museum. On line a video gallery presents the students' productions and information about which schools are producing content. In the Museum a touch-sensitive screen contains only the map. In it the teacher defines videos to be presented and chooses a photo from the school. The system generates a personalized video, opening with images from the school, followed by the students' videos and respective credits. The video can be shared with a QR Code, the last image of the video.

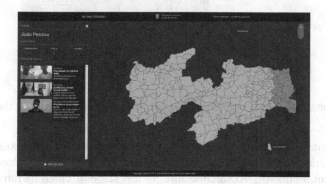

Fig. 3. Collaborative map

3.2 The Custom Video Generator

TCE-PB receives high school students to visit its physical structure and the social actions carried out by it. One strategy to integrate these visitors in themes such as social control and fiscal education, a system of lecture support was developed to integrate institutional audiovisual products into the collaborative production of students, with the purpose of personalizing the experience of each class that visits TCE-PB facilities.

Applying the Audiovisual Design architecture in the development of this system, we have the following proposal: from an institutional video, which defines the Content line and conceptualizes people's importance in supervision and monitoring public matters, videos produced by students are inserted as integral elements of the narrative (Line of Identity and Motivation), according to Fig. 4.

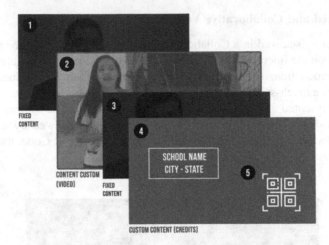

Fig. 4. Abstraction of narrative personalization.

The personalized video, generated based on students' data has the following structure:

Part 1: Contextualization on aspects of mismanagement and corruption, and how popular participation is important in combating and monitoring failures in public management. Following AD architecture, in this stage of video narrative resources (rhythm of editing, soundtrack, forms of expression, among others) have to be coherent with students spectating in such a way as to stimulate the attention and interest about the subject.

Part 2: Examples of social control attitudes based on student videos. Following the architecture of AD, the use of students' videos acts as a Trigger and stimulus to attention and formation of Identity and affinity with the content.

Part 3: Experts explain students' acts represent social control, a fundamental role in whole society. Following the architecture of AD, this stage of the video uses the principles of the Content and Identity Line, since the participation of the students is handled at the content level, as a partner of TCE-PB.

Part 4: Movie credits with names of participants (experts, school and students). This step is also a Trigger, it acts as a stimulus to attention and formation of Identity and affinity with the content.

Part 5: Providing QR code for video sharing. Following the architecture of AD, this step acts as an Action Trigger, forming the Identity to stimulate the student (Audience) to switch the role to Synthesizer, by sharing data in their own social media.

Other Designing Lines can be impacted by the system are Motivation and Experience. Since this personalized material from individuals' data is made available in a file format compatible with social media (Youtube, Facebook or WhatsApp) it is possible to enable scenarios in which students can modify, edit or even remix the content.

To guarantee a scenario of enjoyment and interaction, the following functional requirements for the system were delineated: stablish connection with Facebook via

API Graph; Incorporate hashtag, video, student name and school from a public post on Facebook; Insert imported data into the video project "Student Citizen"; Render all material (fixed institutional videos, customizable and data) to generate a single video file compatible with HTML5 and services like Youtube and Vimeo.

4   The Proposed Interactions

To detail the strategies of interaction and engagement, a system usage scenario based on a persona Student named Wellyngton is described below. Use scenarios are verbal narratives objectively situated, with contextual details, aiming to characterize the context of interaction and define relationships of individuals with technology. They are useful in design to visualize uses of the system in development. Personas are archetypes that represent a set of users for whom the design is done (Lowdermilk 2013; Preece et al. 2015). The focus of the scenario lies in students because it is through them the general objective of the project, related to citizen and fiscal awareness, is supposed to be reached. To create this persona and understand user requirements, a user research was conducted with 1205 high school students, using face-to-face interviews and online questionnaires.

4.1   Persona Student

Wellyngton studies in second year of high school, has lessons weekly about History, owns a prepaid internet access smartphone he uses while the daily data limit lasts. In addition, he connects to the internet using wi-fi at school, where he spends the day. Wellyngton has accounts in several social networks, but mainly uses Instagram, Youtube and Facebook. He thinks all politicians are corrupt, but is intrigued because the History teacher, Cida, spoke during a class it is everyone's responsibility to monitor and control public spending, including those at school.

4.2   Use Scenario

In School: During the History class teacher Cida presents the Portal Student Citizen[3] (ToA 1), which has a Map of State of Paraíba with municipalities and schools. Wellyngton is very interested in videos produced by students from other schools about public management, enforcement and denunciations about unfinished public works. When teacher finishes showing videos, she asks if their class also wants to produce and include videos in the Portal. Cida then shows a movie about how to record and share videos on Facebook (ToA 2), which will then be included into Student Citizen Portal.

Wellyngton creates a group with his friends and records two videos, one about an unfinished bridge on the way home and the other about an abandoned ground next to the school where people throw garbage. They share the videos on Facebook, with hashtags describing the content and the school name (ToA 3).

---

[3] In Portuguese, Aluno Cidadão. The portal can be accessed at this link: http://controlesocial.tce.pb. gov.br/.

In the next class, teacher opens the Student Citizen Portal, clicks on the Alagoa Grande municipality, in the name of the school Josué Gomes da Silveira and all videos produced by the class are listed (ToI 1). The class attends and discusses the origin of the problems, responsibilities and how to solve them. To compare, the teacher shows videos of students from Padre Hildo Bandeira State School, from the neighborhood, who also recorded a video on the unfinished bridge of Wellyngton's group.

4.3   Scenario of Use Visiting the Interactive Museum

The school receives an invitation to visit the TCE-PB facilities, through the School and Citizenship Project. Wellyngton is elated to know TCE, which he has only heard about on television. At TCE students are received with snacks and juices and invited to enter the auditorium (ToI 2). A lecture begins on recycling garbage, with a TCE professional speaker. During the lecture, video clips are shown, among them those produced by school students, such as Wellyngton's, relevant to the subject (ToA 4) and incorporated into the presentation by the speaker.

At the end of the lecture a QR Code appears on the board (ToA 5). The speaker explains that by photographing it students have access to the whole video, can copy it or share it on social networks. Wellyngton immediately photographs the QR Code and shares it in his social media profile, commenting that his video has appeared in a TCE event.

The speaker then invites Wellyngton's class to visit the TCE Interactive Museum, where Cida begins by showing the games, virtual reality, the coworking space, and a theater to watch movies. Then the class goes close to a touch-sensitive monitor, which contains the same Student Citizen Portal Map (ToA 6). The teacher again selects the municipality and the school names. But this time there does not appear the list of all the videos produced by the class: the best videos act as "symbolic affordance" (ToA 6) and are assembled in one workpiece. Cida elucidates the videos she chose about public works and explains the responsibility on roads and bridges can be as much of the city hall as of the state and federal governments. She selects "play videos" (ToI 3), which now start with a photo and name of the school. When the video ends, teacher's name and the students who recorded the videos also appear on a black background, such as on TV. A QR Code offers the option to share the video (ToA 7). Wellyngton leaves TCE-PB facilities talking to his colleagues about themes of next videos they will record.

5   Trigger Definition and Analysis

Methodologically, according to the Audiovisual Design framework, once established the objective to be reached with the content, the Designing Lines are defined, according to a utility perception of each role. Considering purpose and utility, media affordances are developed, resulting in triggers to promote notions of system quality, thus guaranteeing good experiences of individuals. Each Designing Line provides tools to achieve the individual's goals.

Every change of role begins with the perception of a media affordance and is performed using triggers, which may correspond to action or to inertia. In the case of

Student Citizen project, there are changes of roles proposed by the system, and the persona Student will alternate among Audience, Synthesizer and Producer. Modifier actions are focused on teachers and speakers. Table 1 describes the Triggers of Action (ToA) and Inertia (ToI) designed to change roles using the four Designing Lines: Identity (LI), Motivation (LM), Experience (LE) and Content (LC). The triggers were developed based on the use scenario and how individuals should change roles while using and interacting with the Student Citizen system, including getting contact with social control matters.

Considering the purpose of this project, specifically raising awareness about social control and involving society in actions to combat corruption, individuals together play a key role. It is considered that high school students have a central role in medium and long term in this process. The main Designing Line that guides audiovisual enjoyment is Identity. Allied to the Content Line, this Line represents the contact of the individual with the premise of awareness. The stimulus to share is materialized through Motivation Line, focused on the role played by Synthesizers.

From the theoretical point of view, the Audience, when creating the identity with the theme, is encouraged through Triggers of Action to change to the role of Producer. In this role, production and sharing take place (remembering by describing the AD in form of sets, the Producer has the abilities of all antecedent roles). By enjoying videos in the classroom (Trigger of Inertia), the student, who acted as a Producer, returns to the role of Audience. It is important to consider the change from the role of Audience to Producer goes beyond engagement through identification. The stimulus to active participation is part of life experience, which, as a citizen, leads to produce contents relevant to this context. Likewise, we cannot ignore that Identity Line will also be fundamental for students who do not produce, for, identified as citizens, to be motivated to at least watch the videos.

At this point, the teacher is a mediator between objectives of the system (defined by TCE-PB) and Audience, serving as a trigger, both of action in the first moment and of inertia in the second. Already when the teacher moderates videos that compose the Portal and creates the playlist of personalized videos in the Museum, he himself acts as a Modifier. In the case of moderation, Modification happens at a macro level, since the teacher changes the whole system by selecting which videos compose the Map; in the Museum this Modification happens at a micro level, generating a video with data of the students.

A similar relationship can be established when the Audience watches the contents in the Auditorium and in the Museum. In both cases, a modified content is offered to the Audience with a trigger to share at the end (Synthesizer), represented by the QR Code. By photographing it and sharing the video, student moves from Audience to Synthesizer.

The media affordances prevail in defining triggers of this system are symbolic. Calls for action or for inertia are part of the teacher-student relationship within the classroom and in the Museum, as well as speaker and audience, in the auditorium. In addition, there are elements of awareness, central objective of the project, that lead to the action of the Audience. This process of awareness takes place at psychological and motivational levels, where perception of a possible agenda for the video can also become a Trigger of Action (as is the case of the unfinished bridge of the use scenario). The QR Codes, used in two moments, correspond to visual media affordances, centered on the video graphical interface.

Table 1. Triggers for Student Citizen.

ToA/ToI	D.L.	Description	Goal	Role change
ToA 1	LI and LE	Access to Student Citizen portal, whose content is based on collaboration	Awakening the Audience's attention to record	Audience for Producer
ToA 2	LI and LE	Teacher encourages students to produce videos	Motivate the Audience to produce	Audience for Producer
ToA 3	LM	Students use hashtags when sharing videos	Develop identity and generate new engagements	Producer for Synthesizer
ToI 1	LI	Students watch and discuss videos in classroom	Reinforce identity	Producer for Audience
ToA 4	LE	Teacher modifies the students' videos, concatenating several productions, professional and amateur, to compose the presentation	Enable presentation assembly options to the Speaker (Modifier)	Audience for Modifier
ToI 2	LI	Students attend lectures	Reinforce identity	Producer for Audience
ToA 5	LM	Students share content from the lecture	Create identity on social networks	Audience for Synthesizer
ToA 6	LE	Teacher concatenates various productions by entering information about the school and the students	Enable content to be assembled for school representation in the system	Audience for Modifier
ToI 3	Li	Students watch the video	Reinforce identity	Producer for Audience
ToA 7	LM	Producer Design to create identity in social networks	Create identity in social networks	Audience for Synthesizer

6 Conclusions and Future Work

This article describes how the methodological process of Audiovisual Design was used in the production process of customized audiovisual contents for an Interactive Museum. The development of Interaction Triggers is described, based on the museum's objectives and the visitor profile. Each role described in the Audiovisual Design model has associated affordances for Triggers of Action (ToA) or of Inertia (ToI). Role change is a central part in the production of content for complex audiovisual systems.

A methodological approach was designed starting from the objective to be attained through the content, considering different possibilities of fruition. From the objective relevant Design Lines were defined, aiming to awaken the notion of system utility (audiovisual content, interfaces and interaction). From this logical construction, relevant medium affordances have been defined, which lead to Triggers. All these steps should result in system quality, central element of usability for individuals' satisfaction.

The research on the construction of generative audiovisual systems is still undergoing. The next parts are user tests to validate usability and engagement. As future activities, this research has two actions. The first one, theoretical and conceptual in nature, is related to an extended description of the relationship between tools needed in each Designing Line with development of media affordances and triggers. The second action consists of evaluations of software development quality and usability tests with students, teachers and employees of TCE system users. In this way, we intend to validate the development described in this article, specially aspects related to the Motivation Line, with development of engagement.

References

Barbosa, S., Silva, B.: Interação humano-computador. Elsevier, Brasil (2010)

Becker, V., Gambaro, D., Ramos, T.S.: Audiovisual design and the convergence between HCI and audience studies. In: Kurosu, M. (ed.) HCI 2017. LNCS, vol. 10271, pp. 3–22. Springer, Cham (2017a). https://doi.org/10.1007/978-3-319-58071-5_1

Becker, V., Gambaro, D., Ramos, T.S., Toscano, R.M.: Audiovisual design: introducing 'media affordances' as a relevant concept for the development of a new communication model. In: Abásolo, M., Abreu, J., Almeida, P., Silva, T. (eds.) jAUTI 2017. CCIS, vol. 813, pp. 17–31. Springer, Cham (2017b). https://doi.org/10.1007/978-3-319-90170-1_2

Becker, V., Gambaro, D., Ramos, T.S., Bezerra, E.P.: Design Audiovisual: a interseção dos estudos de audiência com a Interação Humano-Computador. Conexão-Comunicação e Cultura 17(33) (2018b)

Gambaro, D., Becker, V., Ramos, T.S., Toscano, R.: The development of individuals' competencies as a meaningful process of the audiovisual design methodology. In: Kurosu, M. (ed.) HCI 201. LNCS, vol. 10901, pp. 68–81. Springer, Cham (2018). https://doi.org/10.1007/978-3-319-91238-7_6

Gibson, J.: The theory of affordances. Perceiving, acting, and knowing: toward an ecological psychology, pp. 67–82 (1977)

Jenkins, H., Ford, S., Green, J.: Cultura da conexão: criando valor e significado por meio da mídia propagável. Aleph (2015)

Lowdermilk, T.: User-Centered Design: A Developer's Guide to Building User-Friendly Applications. O'Reilly Media Inc, Sebastopol (2013)

Preece, J., Rogers, Y., Sharp, H.: Interaction Design: Beyond Human-Computer Interaction. Wiley, Hoboken (2015)

Sousa, J.P.: Elementos de teoria e pesquisa da comunicação e da mídia. Edições Universidade Fernando Pessoa, Porto (2003)

Toscano, R., Becker, V., Ferreira, L., Samara, C., Burgos, L.: Arquitetura de design colaborativo para imersão temporal e espacial em vídeos de altíssimas resoluções e HFR. In: O futuro da videocolaboração: perspectivas. Publisher: Simpósio Brasileiro de Sistemas Multimídia e Web: Workshop do CT-Vídeo – Comitê Técnico de Prospecção Tecnológica em Videocolaboração, 1st edn., pp. 13–53. Gramado, Rio Grande do Sul (2017)

Design and Implementation Techniques of IDTV Content and Services

TV Drama, Representation and Engagement

An Analysis Through the Lenses of the Audiovisual Design

Daniel Gambaro[1] , Thais Saraiva Ramos[2] ,
and Valdecir Becker[3](✉)

[1] Postgraduate Program in Audiovisual Media and Processes,
School of Communications and Arts (PPGMPA),
University of São Paulo, São Paulo, Brazil
[2] Communication School, Anhembi Morumbi University, São Paulo, Brazil
[3] Postgraduate Program in Computer Science, Communication and Arts
(PPGCCA), Informatics Centre, Federal University of Paraíba,
João Pessoa, Brazil
audiovisualdesign@lavid.ufpb.br

Abstract. This paper comments on the *status* of TV drama productions in the Iberian-American scenario, with a special focus on Brazil. According to descriptions of transmedia strategies presented on the last Obitel annual reports, most of the workpieces place the spectators within high levels of inertia, being a real challenge to TV producers to promote the action of the audiences. One probable cause is the rooted values of TV, normally strong enough to legitimate the passive fruition of content. In the special case of Brazil, the stories have been formed around matters of a construed national identity, public and personal affairs, and social issues, topics that draws attention from the audience. This always generated strong ties between the stations and viewers, who identify themselves within the narratives and feel represented. Today, the distribution of content through other platforms is changing the scenario, with other forms of representation taking place. This article observes Iberian-American productions through the lenses of the Audiovisual Design, a theoretical-methodological model developed to afford the creation and analysis of complex audiovisual systems, including television content, interfaces based on software and considering the variable behaviour of the audience. The study proposes that TV stations are still tied to old triggers of audience engagement, instead of seeking new forms of interaction to complement, through the experience with the content, the identity ties that characterise the regular TV production.

Keywords: Television · Audiovisual Design · Transmedia · TV drama · Identity

1 Introduction

The media ecosystem presents, today, challenges and potentialities to the television. TV channels are starting to renovate their operational strategies, trying to occupy the different spaces a programme or its derivates may circulate. In Brazil, such matter

© Springer Nature Switzerland AG 2019
M. J. Abásolo et al. (Eds.): jAUTI 2018, CCIS 1004, pp. 43–59, 2019.
https://doi.org/10.1007/978-3-030-23862-9_4

becomes even more important as the analogue transmission is being switched off. Considering the broadcast TV and complementary web platforms altogether, the challenge is to produce more content and comply with new demands from the audience, while keeping the values that are rooted in original TV drama genres.

In Brazil, the 'rooted values' are structured from a balance of a construed national identity, the discussion of social matters, personal and family affairs and a fascination for the television technique, a mix whose best examples are the telenovelas produced by Rede Globo, the most important TV broadcaster in the country [1–3]. Consequently, ties are formed as the spectators recognise in themselves what they see on the screen and vice-versa, a process that have guaranteed that the fans act beyond the simple enjoyment, through conversations between themselves and interactions with the producers. The digital tools, based on interfaces provided by software, gave the viewers a wider range of possibilities to express their links with the drama productions, e.g. exchanges through social media. Today, they can even occupy a position as coproducers when they add modifications to the original TV content. Producers, then, must use such interactive mechanisms to augment the production's reach. At the same time, they shall observe how viewers are behaving, what may generate information to be used to adjust new productions.

Nonetheless, despite the advances in the use of social media tools witnessed during the last years, the reality is far from the prospects. Reports released annually by the Observatório Iberoamericano de Ficção Televisiva (Obitel, Iberian-American Observatory of Television Fiction) showed that the offer of interactive content by TV channels, such as transmedia drama productions, has remained in primary levels [4]. The main triggers for fan action are still based solely on the identification formulae corresponding to old-style TV drama, and do not expand to other methods of engagement. In other words, the planning of the audiovisual workpieces do not consider in full the additions brought by the digital tools. Nearly all of the television creations reinforce the most basic level of audience (an inert viewer) and allow little space for developing a more active individual.

This is an issue targeted by the Audiovisual Design (AD), a set of theories and methods to assess the planning of fictional work with interactive extensions. By using the AD to describe the elements and agents involved in the creation and distribution of audiovisual content, one may create strategies adequate to different positions occupied by the viewers, in terms of activity or inertia relative to what is being watched. For the AD workflow, audiovisual content is analysed at the same level of tools provided by software, such as interaction interfaces. Considering that interactivity and engagement strategies use these tools to encourage individuals to interact, AD workflow suits the analyses conducted by the present research.

This paper addresses the problem and opens a discussion, where we believe the AD methodology can be applied. In the next section, a brief review of academic papers will show the identification processes operated by spectators regarding TV drama content. Section three discusses the Audiovisual Design workflow, with its theoretical and methodological approach. Next, data from the analysis of TV programmes illustrate the importance of interactive tools to expand the identity and engagement relations with content. Finally, the current online offer of the main free-to-air TV channels is presented to enable a comprehension on which actions the broadcasters expect from their audiences. As a conclusion, it is discussed the importance of a production planning that considers the individual engagement through the Lines of Design.

2 Questions of Identity in Drama Productions

A screens culture results from a broad set of technological and social developments, where audiovisual technologies becomes the translators where the world is represented, where the public intertwine with the private [5]. The language of television is based on the ties created with viewers, consecrating the medium as a mediator of the reality through the factual coverage of the news and through the reconstruction of the life as perceived in the drama productions [2]. Three decades ago, Jesus Martín-Barbero [6] indicated that television had a remarkable capacity to understand the social demands and to hold opportunities and experiences that might be worthy to society.

Telenovelas, as the flagships of drama programmes in almost every Latin-America country, emphasise the collective daily habits. In the past, this genre reached the leadership in audience ratings by following a 'sentimental' style, incorporating characteristics of society and presenting the social changes in a slow, progressive way, through long story arcs that took weeks—sometimes, months—to develop [3]. In Brazil, this narrative form became one of the most resilient constant of TV production, according to Eugênio Bucci, to whom the television developed under 'unwritten laws', such as the 'telenovelas had to present a synthesis of Brazil' and 'TV simultaneously reproduces and integrates the social divide and the class prejudice" [1; pp. 31–32]. The author proposes that the sophistication of television script allows a major part of the audience to recognise and understand the figurations proposed by the stories, in different levels. In summary, the connection of the individual with the TV production—in special the television fictional works—is legitimised by the self-recognition performed by the viewers (of their realities, even if romanticised) in what they watch on the screen.

Even though sociotechnical innovations become evident and are incorporated to the productions, the classic genres still repeat consecrated patterns and reproduce formulae, specially the telenovelas, which are in the crossing of cultural matrices (such as melodrama) and industrial formats [7]. On the other hand, some transformations can be perceived. Even though the telenovelas has sustained their bases and the codified intentions still similar, the development of the format brought a structural change pointed by Martín-Barbero [8, p. 173] as the passage of a 'creative' telenovela to a 'productive' telenovela, based on precise commercial variables, and influenced by the conditions of distribution and market articulations, diminishing the writers' and directors' autonomy.

Those transformations reflect the evolution of the society, following the technical and economic movements of advanced capitalism. Thus, the constitution of identity, initially based on nationalism and collective belonging, now considers matters of utter individuality. Following the description given by Lopes [3], after a 'sentimental' phase of telenovela there was a 'realist' one, in which a story would achieve success by presenting 'novelties' and embodying the private life, triggering the interest, the commentary, the debate among viewers and among other media, in addition to the consumption of related products such as books, records and clothes. Now, still according to the researcher, we are witnessing a 'naturalist' phase, in which the individual becomes even more complex. At least partially, the emphasis in the collective is switching into the valorisation of the individualism.

It is possible to assert that the television drama is reflecting the weakening of the collective identities, since the representation of individualities have been receiving more importance for some decades now, reinforcing the idea of an emancipated subject [9], whose identity reflects the fragmentation of every aspect of quotidian life [10]. The logic of consumption [11, 12] enables strategies that the contemporary individual resorts to construct a coherent *self* and to achieve a sensation of freedom that seems to be historically conquered. In other words, in the most recent years consumption has become an imperative, and the industries use communication strategies to feed a sensation of *welfare* by means of access to products supposedly individualised, be them physical or a work from the symbolic field, such as a movie or a TV show.

The consequences are—at least for the Brazilian TV fiction—more obstacles to sell the old 'television reality' that the telenovelas have built. It is necessary to shift the techniques and the storytelling forms of drama productions, so to keep creating debates and representations of experiences that define television as a means of communication and expression. Important changes must be considered, such as the development of digital platforms and the new composition of the audience, which is migrating to new spaces of content fruition. The one-way, massified distribution form of the broadcast is being reshaped with 'inclusion' and 'participation', giving space to an apparently greater freedom of choice for viewers. According to Vilches [13], technologies affect formats, quantity and quality of the informative flow, but also invoke subtle and profound aesthetical, social and symbolic shifts. Informatics applied to television is, then, affecting the support, the terminals and the networks through which the information flows, as well as the economic models and the systems of production.

Due to the relevance of television as a communication means, new digital platforms of media convergence do not need to produce new content every second, they may instead do the management of the content already produced by key companies, as well as facilitate the relations between the users and that production[1]. That management requires the platforms to be present in the daily lives of the audience. Thus, the planning of a media content must consider a renovated environment of distribution: there is an innate necessity for strategies that incite a more active performance of the media consumer [14].

Since television do not have any more the monopoly of distribution of audiovisual information, web-based platforms of content distribution act both as repository and sociability spaces [13]. Consequently, the circulation of original TV production via digital interfaces (securing the legitimacy inherited from the initial means) prolongs the life of a work through the 'emotional investment' of the fan. In a sense, that would be a way to conciliate the contradictory identity of the individual using the same matrices that defines his or her identity in society.

---

[1] Of course, the new platforms are not comfortable with this business model. Our remark here only shows that the in-house production is not essential – at least until now – to their existence. When the business model of this type of platform requires more investments – such as the current case of Netflix – the tendency is that the other formula will be more efficiently implemented.

Using the Brazilian case as an example, the instituted television logics corresponds to the residual form of the culture [15], adapted to the new cultural paradigm represented by a complex and fragmented individual recomposed via digital networks. Brazil gained more presence in the world's economy in the last decades, and at the same time opened up its boundaries to international standards, also incorporating cultural values from other parts of the world, which became the new 'universal values' in Brazilian culture [11, 16]. To create a tie with this viewer is not a simple task, since his or her involvement with the television product a is now based on more transitory links. Therefore, not always the TV narrative alone will be able to create the necessary rapport to make somebody a fan of the show. The producers (i.e., the stations) must seek models of engagement that bolster the identification of the individual with the work as a cultural product.

3 The Audiovisual Design

The Audiovisual Design (AD) was initially presented and detailed by Becker, Gambaro and Ramos [17]. In a nutshell, the AD proposes the planning and the analysis of the cycle of production, distribution and consumption of audiovisual workpieces in different means and networks. To accomplish such process, it considers a deep understanding and the categorisation of the diverse elements composing the phases of design and fruition of a complex interactive work. Its methodological itinerary shows that people may relate to a given content in different ways, which generate information that feeds back the production phase.

Individuals are classified in accordance to four roles they may assume in relation to the content: *Audience*, all people that watch and interact with the content in a basic level; *Synthesiser*, individuals in a higher level of activity, whose interaction is based on commentary and online sharing of information, but in a simple way; *Modifier*, that is, people who modify the original content via participation, changes or recreation of elements of the narrative; and *Producer*, people or group, independent or hired by a company, responsible for the creation of original content. While performing any role, an individual may be elevated to a higher class (Player), if he or she undertakes advanced activities corresponding to the role he or she is performing, whether they are expected or not by the Producers. Players remain classified as the same role (Audience-Player; Synthesiser-Player; Modifier-Player; Producer-Player), since the advanced activity not necessarily implies that they are changing roles.

To this present discussion, it is also important to address the *Lines of Design*, i.e., general orientations that serve as guidelines for the producing teams while conceiving the elements of a workpiece. Following the Lines of Design, the designers are expected to create in compliance with the roles of individuals, as well as the competencies of each role necessary to allow the mobility between roles. There are four lines, the first being the Line of Content. It corresponds to the wills of the Producers to communicate something, by means of the programme plus the distribution interfaces. Around this first line there are the other three: Identity, regarding the focus on the identity and representation of the individuals in any aspect of the story, such as the characters, the situations or the narrative universe; Motivation, which proposes the increase in activities performed by the individuals, normally from the ease of using the original product to communicate something about themselves, e.g., through social media; Experience, when complex activities are to be incorporated in the product's circuit, enabling individuals as coproducers or autonomous creators (Fig. 1).

The individuals must acquire or develop competencies, so they are able to move between the different roles [18]. The AD model also dictates that the different media affordances[2] present in each communicational system may work out as triggers of action (ToA), that is, as components that promote the activity of the viewer during and after the enjoyment of a content; or as triggers of inertia (ToI), that, on the other hand, work to reduce the activity during moments that require more attention to the content or its interfaces [19].

It is becoming a common knowledge that the limitations of the television regarding interactivity has promoted the reorganisation of the programming schedule by the fans of the audiovisual work (time-shifting of consumption) and the reoperation of content in different web-based platforms [20]. Fans are being encouraged to an active attitude towards the creation of taste [21]. Thus, the prevalence of ToA developed via the Line of Identity are evident, leading to a spontaneous evolution from the role of Audience to the role of Synthesiser. Fans who work for the product and for the Producers are prioritised [20], because, as Lopes et al. state [21], only when the viewer get emotionally involved with the plot he or she creates the strong bonds that characterises a fan. Then, the fan will correspond to those who explore the most of something offered by the production, knowing well the characters and the directions of the stories.

Nonetheless, we can observe a lack of complex productions demanding additional actions of the individuals (as Audience-Players, Synthesisers-Players or as Modifiers), that is, the complexity normally associated to transmedia storytelling and its different narrative extensions [22]. According to Franco, Gómez and Orozco [4], Iberian-American TV channels still are in an initial phase, in which barely a few complex productions are made. Only a few countries, including Brazil, advanced into a 'second level' of transmedia, presenting more-elaborated expansions that highlights the activities of the Audience and the Synthesiser. The next section details this discussion by showing some numbers.

It is important to remark AD incorporates a set of knowledges from the fields of Media Studies and Human-Computer Interaction (HCI), to provide analyses and developments of complex audiovisual workpieces, supporting a broader apprehension of possibilities created by digital communication tools. To this model, audiovisual content and digital interfaces are central to the fruition process. Considering the whole workflow of audiovisual production and fruition is based on digital technologies nowadays, those interfaces demand a new status of analyses [17, 19]. To address this point, AD provides elements to consider audiovisual productions and software developments at the same level, whose importance varies according the Designing Lines.

---

[2] We are considering *affordances* as the characteristics of the objects and environment that exist regardless of agents, and that can be planned to be perceived, understood and correctly used to allow actions (and interactions) of actors among themselves and with the elements composing the environment [19].

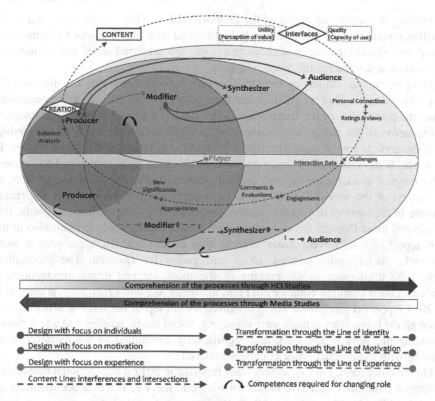

Fig. 1. Audiovisual Design Workflow. Source: Audiovisual Design Research Group

4 Transmedia Production in Obitel Countries

To illustrate this present work, we made a tabulation of data presented by Obitel in the last five years (reports from 2014 to 2018, corresponding to years 2013 to 2017), showing the most common actions taken by broadcasters, as well as the fans response to drama productions [23–27]. This quantification allows to count the occasions that multiplatform actions were considered relevant by Obitel researchers, but it does not show the totality of actions developed in the period. This framework will provide us with a thermometer to understand what the focus of Iberian-American research on the convergent set-ups between TV and other media has been.

Each report focuses on what was predominant or innovative during the analysed year. For example, the 2016 report presented by the Spanish team highlighted the TV series *El ministério del tiempo*, which implemented diverse multiplatform strategies— social media, direct contact with fans, narrative expansions in different forms, including the labour of fans. The way the producers of the series managed the fans' engagement triggered the roles of Audience-Player, Synthesiser and Modifier. The Obitel researchers mentioned an study that identified 'the satisfaction of the fans with the treatment the official teams gave to their artistic creations, some of which were selected to integrate the official products of the drama in the beginning of the second season, recognizing the authorship rights of the creators' [28, p. 314]. On the other hand, the Brazilian report from the same year only highlighted how fans construed communities around the support for couples of characters from their preferred series and telenovelas, a phenomenon known for the word 'shipping'.

The programmes chosen by the Obitel teams to be analysed are, usually, also the most watched ones. This information becomes relevant when it leads to a questioning about: the practicality of the transmedia storytelling in increasing audience ratings, if the expansion of the narrative universe is required to keep high levels of viewership, and if the impacts are the same, regardless the number of programmed interactivities. In this sense, *El Ministério del Tiempo* presentes itself again as an example. The richness of the material available on the web certainly contributed to engage fans and, thus, to the success of the series. This fact is even more relevant if we consider the recent decrease in the number of juvenile audience of linear TV—the segment of public that participated more through the web expansions. Other example was present also in the 2016 report, the telenovela *Anter Muerta que Lichita* had 16 apps, plus a web-telenovela, social media profiles, blogs and games for children. The programme reached the third place in the ranking of the most watched drama productions in Mexico. A third highlight comes from Peru, the series *Al Fondo Hay Sitio*, presented in the 2015 report because, since 2013, it figured on the top of the most watched drama. Although the transmedia actions were timid, e.g. social media profiles and a few videos expanding the story to the web, fans significantly committed to the narrative, contributing with the production of countless material.

On the other hand, the Colombian team reported in 2017 a non-fictional transmedia production with many narrative expansions beyond the TV. It was a documentary on the Colombian health system, called *Paciente*, and included a movie, a web-documentary, official pages in social media, books, conferences etc. The impact of all those actions in the audience ratings and individual engagement was much lower than other productions, that invested much less time and money, but was much more 'commercial'. In the same years, the American team spotted from the analysed workpieces that the programme with more audience was also the one with less presence in other platforms. It was a Disney production, what probably explains why it is not necessary to invest in expansions in order to have a massive success in audience reach.

Once we compared the reports, we noticed changes in how broadcasters invested in events in multiple platforms, as much as in how the researchers observed the set of actions. While in the 2014 and 2015 reports the creation of social media profiles was stressed as a transmedia formula to almost every research team, from 2016 on the observers became more selective. The 2016 report brought a long text from Portugal redefining the knowledge of transmedia as of authors like Jenkins [22] and Fechine [20], but there was no analysis at all. In 2017, the Chileans instead who produced a short text, without evaluations or analysis, emphasising only actions that, under the light of the AD, corresponded to the enlargement of actions directed to the Audience and basic-level Synthesisers. In 2018, most teams stated that the TV stations are not investing in true transmedia storytelling.

During the five years concerning the reports, Obitel investigators from all countries commented on 93 productions, 12 of which were included by Brazilian researchers. The most used tool by TV channels were profiles in social media, that enabled the role of Synthesiser (82 mentions throughout Obitel, 5 from Brazil). In 2015 and 2016, the Brazilian reports emphasised the use of hashtags and social networks to the organic promotion of the drama shows, demonstrating the power of those tools.

The extension models that stress the role of Audience were predominant, as shown in Table 1, with a high number of mentions about the series' websites and extra content. Despite they involve some kind of interaction, the very nature of these types of content usually present more ToI than ToA, thus privileging a limited activity that requires only simple interactive actions between the viewer and the content. Since the viewer sometimes must perform an activity programmed by the Producer in order to visualise a video or a text, than he or she may be empowered as Audience-Player, but even such performance was not prevalent.

Table 1. Summary of complementary media strategies commented by all Obitel reports 2014–2018. Source: Audiovisual Design Research Group (Caption: **Website**: webpage dedicated to the analysed work, whether linked or not to the station's portal. **Extra content**: backstage footage, extra scenes, characters' biographies etc. **Diverse expansions**: documentaries, comics, textual fictions, complex narratives etc. **Video expansions**: webseries, comments on video made by characters (in the form of videoblog) etc., expanding the narrative. **Social Networks - Synthesis:** official profiles on Twitter, Instagram, Facebook, Youtube, used to replicate what has been aired, allowing only commenting and sharing by fans. **Social Network - Expansion:** Profiles related to the characters (own life) or to the environment of the narrative universe (such as fictional companies part of the plots). **Mobile app:** All kinds of app related to the content. **2nd Screen:** Motivation created by the Producers to activities through second screen, using or not a dedicated app. **Games:** Simple activities such as quiz, mobile games etc. **ARG:** Alternate Reality Games, complex activities that requires the user to reunite content from different sources. **Memes & more - Production:** the use of memes, photos, sharable texts created by the Producers. **Memes & more - fans:** Appropriation by fans of characters and original content to create simple derivative produces. **Other fan productions:** Channels with music videos, mash-ups, reedition, highlighted in the analysis because of their relevance.).

	Total analysed	Website	Extra content	Diverse expansions	Video expansions	Social media - synthesis	Social media - expansion	Mobile app	2nd screen	Games	ARG	Memes & more - producers	Memes & more - fans	Other fan productions
2014	12	12	12	2	2	12	2	1	2	0	0	0	3	1
2015	19	17	11	3	5	16	4	2	1	0	0	2	7	3
2016	15	10	10	5	4	13	1	4	1	2	1	0	8	6
2017	25	18	18	6	11	23	0	4	2	6	0	0	5	2
2018	22	8	9	5	4	18	2	2	3	1	0	0	5	3
Sum	93	65	60	21	26	82	9	13	9	9	1	2	28	15

Actions that presuppose more ToA and allow interaction with other people or modification of the original materials were normally undervalued by the broadcasters. In the same line, the use of second screens as a strategy to interaction was referred to only nine times, only once by the Brazilian team. To make the tabulation clearer, we classified the work of fans as 'simple productions', for instance photo edition and memes, and as 'complex production', such as music videos, fanfics, mash-ups etc. Both are related to the labour of the Modifiers, being the second category aligned with the competences of the Modifier-Player. If we consider all Obitel countries, productions by Modifiers were mentioned 28 times, mainly memes and photos, and 15 times the works from Modifiers-Players, in particular fanfics and short videos. These numbers include three citations about memes and three about sophisticated productions made by Brazilian fans (Table 2).

Table 2. Summary of Brazilian complementary media strategies commented by all Obitel reports 2014–2018. Source: Audiovisual Design Research Group.

	Total analysed	Website	Extra content	Diverse expansions	Video expansions	Social media - synthesis	Social media - expansion	Mobile app	2nd screen	Games	ARG	Memes & more - producers	Memes & more - fans	Other fan productions
2014	1	1	1	0	1	1	0	1	0	0	0	0	1	0
2015	2	1	1	0	0	1	0	0	0	0	0	0	1	1
2016	2	0	0	0	0	1	0	0	0	0	0	0	1	1
2017	4	1	1	0	3	1	0	1	1	1	0	0	0	0
2018	3	0	0	2	1	1	0	0	0	0	0	0	0	1
Sum	12	3	3	2	5	5	0	2	1	1	0	0	3	3

It is visible across the observation of the reports that role of Audience was privileged on the multiplatform strategies, reaching only in basic levels the Synthesiser. Although the presence and labour of Modifiers, they are not valued by the broadcasters. If the fans end up creating blogs, webpages, memes, hashtags and even music videos with segments of the series or telenovelas, that happens mostly in a natural way. They move from the inertia of the Audience to the roles of Synthesiser and Modifier, but in a continuity that remains connected to the Line of Identity.

Franco, Gómez e Orozco [4] indicated that most of the countries were still producing transmedia of a 'first level', i.e., they are experimenting and only a few broadcasters may be considered to reach the 'level 2.0', which includes the creation of apps, games, competitions, 360° experiences, web-stories etc. The 2018 report underlined a trend following the past years, when no country presented production of a 'level 3.0', that is, presenting increased user participation and expansion of stories in different platforms [29]. As of the Brazilian case, the slowness to adopt strategies that empower the individual in roles other than the Audience is the consequence of a dogmatism whose origins are at the assembly of the programming schedule. To Becker and Azevedo [30], the broadcasters systematically ignore the irreversible impacts of the technologies and do not overcome the gap between the TV flow and the strategies for the online environment. Still according to the authors, the TV output is outlined as 'recorded, owned, national and unaired', with focus mainly on entertainment. Regarding the expansion of the programming to the web, they indicate a 'low performance of free-to-air broadcasters concerning the elaboration of audiovisual strategies to explore and take content to other digital platforms' [30, p. 3825].

Becker and Azevedo's analysis shed light on two axes to discuss the TV production [30]. One: all informative programmes together take most of the schedule in terms of hours, although the numbers are much close to those of drama and entertainment productions. This configuration is underlined every year by the Brazilian team. While journalistic shows are typically live broadcast, entertainment ones are both live and recorded. Anyway, these are genres of production that make possible a type of interaction where the viewer acts simultaneously with the show. As we saw, the 2nd screen is a new territory little explored by the TV channels, maybe due to a lack of a deep exam on the affordances available through the devices and the content—to be invested by the broadcasters.

The second point is the drama production. The fictional genres—especially telenovelas—would benefit from an integrated strategy, that 'train' the viewers to the online services of the station while keeping them watching the regular output. This will not happen only by empowering the individuals as Synthesisers, but with the engagement that departs from the Line of Identity to the Line of Experience. In other words, it is necessary to plan how the viewers will experience the interfaces, and how they shall find something they can use for their individual representation. Given the high volume of drama productions, it is surprising that there are only a few strategies of online activities. The viability of this proposal is backed up by what Becker and Azevedo [30] and the Obitel teams [26, 27] have found: most of the drama production aired in Brazil is domestic and new, what gives the control to the broadcasters to explore diverse angles of the workpiece.

5 The Online Offer of TV Content

In this section, we will analyse the distribution of content through web portals of dedicated platforms, such as mobile apps, provided by the four main Brazilian TV channels. We expect to provide the reader with a comparative frame of strategies that, as explained in the previous sections, results in low levels of transposition of content from the TV flow to the internet platforms. The analysis was performed during the first quarter of August 2018, and only official websites and apps were included.

BAND: The broadcaster controls the Portal Videos.Band [31], which include content from two channels, TV Bandeirantes (free-to-air) and BandNews (journalistic, pay-tv). The contents are separated in sections, with emphasis in entertainment, sports and journalistic shows—a consequence of low investments in drama. The broadcaster provides a live streaming embedded in each show's webpage. The *Superpoderosas* programme, for instance, was a variety show dedicated to women, transmitted daily until cancelled in November 2018, due to low audience ratings. The webpage however, stills available. It was a show that, supposedly, would connect the TV flow with the internet. Its webpage held a section where a user could share commentaries, texts, photos and videos, which would be incorporated to the show. Although it is not an example of drama production, it shows the capabilities of the station to empower the individual as a Synthesiser or a Modifier. Analysing the content available through the website and the focus on social media, there are initiatives to engage the Synthesiser, despite the concentration in actions of the Audience. Even under the theme 'sports'—mainly 'football'—that naturally may instigate engagement, the webpages restrict it to simply sharing.

Globo: Globo TV provides the streaming services GloboPlay [32] (Fig. 2), with live programming available in some regions, and on-demand content produced internally or by third parts. The first external production acquired by the station and offered through the service was the American series *The Good Doctor*, followed in 2019 by *The Handmade's Tale*, which premiered first in the online platform with all episodes of the first season at the same time. Besides, the station provides complete shows in the same form as when they were aired, programmes with the addition of new scenes and others unaired in the broadcast channel. The service also delivers old and famous programmes, such as comedy shows, telenovelas, children programmes and series, both from the free-to-air station and from the pay-tv channels owned by Globo Media Group. The streaming can be accessed via personal computer, smartphone, tablet, smart TV, Chromecast, Android TV and Apple TV. During the observed period, the live programming was restricted to the metropolitan regions of Rio de Janeiro, São Paulo, Brasília, Minas Gerais, Recife and Manaus.

Fig. 2. GloboPlay app interface [32]   **Fig. 3.** PlayPlus app interface [33]

Record: Record TV released in 2018 the service PlayPlus [33] (Fig. 3), a type of marketplace of streaming with live transmission and catch-up TV. Besides the station's content, third part productions are included in the service, e.g. from ESPN channels, Disney, FishTV and some radio stations. The user may choose between a free subscription or a paid one. The free option includes the live transmission of Record TV and ESPN Extra. Besides this service, the broadcaster keeps the video portal R7 OnDemand [34] mainly with short videos of up to three minutes, usually newscasts' reports and telenovelas' scenes. The portal works as an invitation to the free-to-air TV and to the PlayPlus service. By offering only 'sliced' content and not a complete show, the video portal is a trigger for the Audience to opt for that way of visualisation. Portal and streaming service, considered together, reinforce the focus on Audience, with the other elements converging to the passive visualisation of content, both on TV or on online platforms. On the other hand, all video available through the portal bear the option to share on social media.

SBT: This was the first free-to-air TV station to invest in online content, upon the launch of the portal SBT Videos [35] in the end of the last decade. The portal offers all productions made internally by the broadcaster, accompanied by shortcuts for sharing in social media. The live streaming is available through the website and on mobile apps. There are links to dedicated pages in the broadcaster's website for content acquired from third parts, such as series and movies. TV series such as *Kenan and Kell* and *The Archer* only have descriptions with photos, characters and synopsis of episodes. *Chaves (El Chavo del Ocho)*, on its turn, due to the success of this long-running show, has a section of memes made by the station, based on the characters of the show. So, the content available through the portal is dedicated to the Audience, lacking tools or ToA to the other roles—exception made to the buttons for sharing in social media, targeting the Synthesisers. In general, the portal only presents an option to *like* SBT's page on Facebook and follow the station on Twitter. There is no option to *like* individual programme pages. The Silvio Santos Show, the most traditional auditorium-hosted programme in Brazilian television, has a page on Twitter and the option to start following it from the website.

The analysis of the online output of the four main Brazilian TV stations reveals reticent initiatives to alternate the viewers' roles between Audience and Synthesisers. The four broadcasters implemented ToA on their internet platforms, aiming to engage individuals through their social media. However, in most of the observed cases, those triggers are restricted to sharing the content, without other strategy for engagement, appropriation or creation of identity.

The strategies about streaming platforms indicate stations are implementing projects that go beyond the broadcast model, but still focused on Audience. It represents a different business model, based on subscription, that offers more variety of content than those via broadcast. Yet, the available options of fruition are restricted to watching the live output or creating a playlist with catch-up TV or other available shows. Regarding the TV drama productions, it was not possible even to perceive the use of online platforms as a mechanism to promote more complexity of the storytelling, which would demand other forms of viewership, as foreseen by Mittel [36]. The platforms do not use, or are not yet adapted to, the resources of the online universe in reference to the communication means and the engagement through digital social networks.

Compared to Obitel's reports and their synthesis shown in Table 2, on line strategies from the four biggest Brazilian television stations also focus on Audience and, to a lesser extent, the Synthesizer. Television production is still far away from using resources and digital interfaces to trigger individuals to the roles of Modifier and Producer. Those triggers are commonly used in North American productions as strategies to engage individuals in cinema franchising, as described by Jenkins in his books [14, 22].

6 Conclusion

This paper presented some remarks on how Iberian-American TV stations, in special Brazilian ones, are dealing with cross-platforms and transmedia strategies. The data was acquired from the Obitel's reports from 2014 to 2018, and the study considered the theoretical and methodological approach of the Audiovisual Design. In conclusion, the analysis showed that a great part of the productions keeps the viewers in high levels of inertia. Besides, the examination of the online offer provided by the main free-to-air TV channels in Brazil disclosed that these broadcasters expect their viewers to behave passively. At maximum, it is expected a simple interaction, in order to strengthen the identity and representation bonds that are already common to the TV production.

In summary, the two surveys revealed that most strategies adopted by regular TV stations are devoted to the role of Audience, meaning that the individuals watch and interact in a basic level. Some initiatives directed to the role of Synthesiser were also identified, showing some interaction based on commentary and online sharing of information. No motivations directed to the other roles were identified. It is not clear whether the offering of transmedia storytelling applied to common TV shows positively influence the audience ratings, as exemplified with some examples from Obitel. Rooted structures of TV production are still capable of retaining audience. Nonetheless, there are cases, such as *El Ministério del Tiempo*, whose web expansions were responsible for the success of the show. Another clue to contribute to this discussion: by the Obitel reports we could realise that the fans spontaneously create blogs, webpages, memes, hashtags and even video remixes to be shared on social media. The individual, in this case, leaves the passive status of Audience to the roles of Synthesiser and Modifier. Usually, these processes take place without any planning by the Producers, with exception to some rare encouragement from the TV stations.

On the one hand, the links between viewers and workpiece continue the same as already in place through the Line of Identity, that is, the recognition supported by the narrative. For example, the elements of the Brazilian TV drama that sustain representation and commitment of spectators are historically based on the recognition of the quotidian on the screen. Social problems and personal affairs are mixed in the construction of plots, characters and scenarios where the action develops. This is a recipe to feed a culture of fans that, in different forms, have always appropriated the fictional constructs into their own realities [3]. Hence the broadcasters are inclined to rely only on the Line of Identity, because they have historical proof it works well.

On the other hand, the other Lines of Design—Motivation and Experience—should be more present during the planning of the productions, in order to retain the viewership that fluctuates towards other media. The producing division, to retain control over the circuit of the content, must broaden the scope of actions performed by the individuals through mechanisms other than those linked to the narratives (and more complex than simple buttons for sharing and commenting on social media). Instead of only focusing on the ties created through the narratives, the Producers should test with relations created at the interaction nodes, fomenting the *experience* of the individual with the transmedia set of the production. For example, the invitation to interaction can be supported via online interfaces, and besides allowing the user to show a representation of him or her in the network, it would also offer a more generalised experience with the content (Line of Experience). At the same time, an action programmed to occur outside the TV narrative may trigger the individuals do publicly comment the workpiece (Line of Motivation). In result, these actions would mean to expand the storytelling and incite the spontaneous propagation of the content.

The decision took by the Producer, informed by the other two Lines of Design, would aggregate to the storytelling new strategies to promote sharing, appropriation and modification of the content by fans. Today, as exemplified with the analysis of online content offered by the Brazilian stations, only buttons and links for sharing in social media are available. In other words, because of the ties created with the content, the individuals may want to develop the connection through tools that are not available. The broadcasters must quit the (more and more inefficient) attempt to have control over all their contents, and then reach out to contributions from the viewers.

The integrated analysis of audiovisual content and digital interfaces of interaction is still an incipient task, with little basis in the literature. Usually, media and reception studies and Human Computer Interaction treat their objects of study independently, with no intersections. The processes of creation, modeling and production are different, as is the process of fruition. While media studies are concerned mostly with the impact of content, IHC seeks to facilitate interaction. The AD model, which proposes to analyse the production and fruition of these areas in an integrated way, is recent and is in development. Future studies to largely test AD hypotheses and improve the method of analysis are focused on the Designing Lines of motivation and experience. Concepts such as content appropriation, widely studied in the Communication field, and user satisfaction, common in usability studies, tend to play a central role in the evolution of the AD model. In this way, we intend to continue the integration of these two fields and provide a powerful workflow to create and analyse complex software, or audiovisual, systems.

The audiovisual work, considering content and software, is more than a source of expression, it is also a consumption object, fluid and ephemerous as the whole society. Nevertheless, the expansion of the narrative through the elements aggregated via digital interfaces must consider that a great part of viewers remains in the role of Audience, consuming the story only through the television flow or the streaming services. The advantage of a methodology such as the AD is to foresee that many people will be simultaneously in different positions of interaction, bearing distinct identity bonds, performing diverse roles. It may be helpful in this moment of incipient experiments towards complex narratives by Iberian-American TV channels.

References

1. Bucci, E.: Prefácio. In: O Brasil em tempo de TV. Boitempo, São Paulo (1997)
2. Machado, A.: A televisão levada a sério, 2nd edn. Senac, São Paulo (2001)
3. Lopes, M.I.V.: Telenovela como recurso comunicativo. Revista Matrizes 3(1), 21–47 (2009). https://doi.org/10.11606/issn.1982-8160.v3i1p21-47
4. Franco, D., Gómez, G., Orozco, G.: Síntesis comparativa de los países Obitel en 2016. In: Lopes, M.I.V., Gómez, G.O. (eds.) Uma década de ficção televisiva na Ibero-América: análise de dez anos do Obitel (2007–2016), pp. 25–60. Sulina, Porto Alegre (2017)
5. Machado, A.: Pré-cinemas e pós-cinemas. Papirus, Campinas (1997)
6. Martín-Barbero, J.: La telenovela en Colombia: televisión, melodrama y vida cotidiana. Revista Dialogos de la Comunicación (17) (1987). http://dialogosfelafacs.net/edicion-17/. Accessed 27 Feb 2019

7. Martín-Barbero, J.: Dos Meios às Mediações: comunicação, cultura e hegemonia, 2nd edn. Editora UFRJ, Rio de Janeiro (2003)
8. Martín-Barbero, J.: Narrativas da ficção televisiva. In: Martín-Barbero, J., Rey, G. (eds.) Os exercícios do ver: hegemonia audiovisual e ficção televisiva, pp. 107–174. Senac, São Paulo (2001)
9. Harvey, D.: Condição pós-moderna, 21st edn. Edições Loyola Jesuítas, São Paulo (2011)
10. Hall, S.: A identidade cultural na pós-modernidade, 7th edn. DP&A, Rio de Janeiro (2003)
11. Ortiz, R.: Mundialização e Cultura. Brasiliense, São Paulo (1994)
12. du Gay, P.: Organizing Identity. Sage, London (2007)
13. Vilches, L.: A migração digital. Editora PUC-Rio, Rio de Janeiro; Edições Loyola, São Paulo (2003)
14. Jenkins, H., Ford, S., Green, J.: Spreadable Media: Creating Value and Meaning in a Networked Culture, Kindle Edition. New York University Press, London, New York (2013)
15. Williams, R.: Marxismo y literatura, 2nd edn. Ediciones Península, Barcelona (2000)
16. Ortiz, R.: Universalismo e diversidade. Boitempo, São Paulo (2015)
17. Becker, V., Gambaro, D., Ramos, T.S.: Audiovisual Design and the Convergence Between HCI and Audience Studies. In: Kurosu, M. (ed.) HCI 2017. LNCS, vol. 10271, pp. 3–22. Springer, Cham (2017). https://doi.org/10.1007/978-3-319-58071-5_1
18. Gambaro, D., Becker, V., Ramos, T.S., Toscano, R.: The development of individuals' competencies as a meaningful process of the audiovisual design methodology. In: Kurosu, M. (ed.) HCI 2018. LNCS, vol. 10901, pp. 68–81. Springer, Cham (2018). https://doi.org/10.1007/978-3-319-91238-7_6
19. Becker, V., Gambaro, D., Saraiva Ramos, T., Moura Toscano, R.: Audiovisual design: introducing 'media affordances' as a relevant concept for the development of a new communication model. In: Abásolo, M.J., Abreu, J., Almeida, P., Silva, T. (eds.) jAUTI 2017. CCIS, vol. 813, pp. 17–31. Springer, Cham (2018). https://doi.org/10.1007/978-3-319-90170-1_2
20. Fechine, Y.C.: Transmidiação e cultura participativa: pensando as práticas textuais de agenciamento dos fãs de telenovelas brasileiras. Revista Contracampo 31(1), 5–22 (2014). https://doi.org/10.5327/Z22382577201400310694
21. Lopes, M.I.V., Mungioli, M.C.P., Freire, C., Lemos, L.M.P., Lusvarghi, L., et al.: A autoconstrução do fã: performance e estratégias de fãs de telenovela na internet. In: Lopes, M.I.V. (ed.) Por uma teoria de fãs da ficção televisiva brasileira, pp. 17–64. Sulina, Porto Alegre (2015)
22. Jenkins, H.: Cultura da convergência. Aleph, São Paulo (2008)
23. Lopes, M.I.V., Gómez, G.O. (eds.): Estratégias de produção transmídia na ficção televisiva: anuário Obitel 2014. Sulina, Porto Alegre (2014)
24. Lopes, M.I.V., Gómez, G.O. (eds.): Relações de gênero na ficção televisiva: anuário Obitel 2015. Sulina, Porto Alegre (2015)
25. Lopes, M.I.V., Gómez, G.O. (eds.): (Re)invenção de gêneros e formatos da ficção televisiva: anuário Obitel 2016. Sulina, Porto Alegre (2016)
26. Lopes, M.I.V., Gómez, G.O. (eds.): Uma década de ficção televisiva na Ibero-América: análise de dez anos do Obitel (2007–2016). Sulina, Porto Alegre (2017)
27. Lopes, M.I.V., Gómez, G.O. (eds.): Ficção televisiva Ibero-Americana em plataformas de video on demand. Sulina, Porto Alegre (2018)
28. Lacalle, C., Castro, D., Sánchez, M.: Espanha: Inovação e Tradição. In: Lopes, M.I.V., Gómez, G.O. (eds.) (Re)invenção de gêneros e formatos da ficção televisiva: anuário Obitel 2016, pp. 289–326. Sulina, Porto Alegre (2016)

29. Burnay, C.D., Lopes, P., Sousa, M.N.: Síntese comparativa dos países Obitel em 2017. In: Lopes, M.I.V., Gómez, G.O. (eds.) Ficção televisiva Ibero-Americana em plataformas de video on demand. Sulina, Porto Alegre (2018)

30. Becker, V., Azevedo, A.: As estratégias audiovisuais da TV aberta brasileira no meio digital. In: Lopes, M.I.V., Ribeiro, N., Castro, G.G.S., Burnay, C.D. (eds.) XV Congresso IBERCOM 2017: comunicação, diversidade e tolerância, pp. 3806–3827. ECA-USP, São Paulo; Lisboa, FCH-UCP (2018)

31. Videos.Band. https://videos.band.uol.com.br/. Accessed 28 Feb 2019

32. GloboPlay. https://globoplay.globo.com/. Accessed 28 Feb 2019

33. PlayPlus. https://www.playplus.com/. Accessed 28 Feb 2019

34. R7 Ondemand Portal. https://videos.r7.com/. Accessed 28 Feb 2019

35. SBT Vídeos. https://www.sbt.com.br/sbtvideos/. Accessed 28 Feb 2019

36. Mittell, J.: Complex TV: The Poetics of Contemporary Television Storytelling. Pre-publication Edition. MediaCommons Press (2012–2013). http://mcpress.media-commons.org/complextelevision/

Hybrid DTT & IPTV Set Top Box Implementation with GINGA Middleware Based on Low Cost Platforms

Wilmer Chicaiza[1(✉)] ⓘ, Diego Villamarín[1,2(✉)] ⓘ,
and Gonzalo Olmedo[1(✉)] ⓘ

[1] Universidad de las Fuerzas Armadas ESPE, Sangolquí, Ecuador
{Wrchicaiza, Dfvillamarin, gfolmedo}@espe.edu.ec
[2] Universidad Politécnica de Madrid, Madrid, Spain
dvz@gatv.ssr.upm.es

Abstract. This work shows the implementation of a hybrid STB (Set Top Box) that receives real-time digital signals for ISDB-Tb and IPTV. The implementation integrates middleware GINGA for interactive DTT applications based on low cost platforms. The features of the hardware platform for this implementation are analyzed so that they can integrate USB reception modules for digital TV, support interactive middleware versions and also be compatible with TV playback software by means of internet protocols. After the analysis and evaluation, we found that the most suitable board to achieve this implementation was Raspberry Pi 3. The development of the Android mobile graphic interface is also shown, which emulates a remote control by Bluetooth technology. Finally, the results of the implemented hybrid STB's evaluation are presented; evaluation performed by reception tests of DTT channels with interactivity and free IPTV channels. Also, quantitative readings were made to test the performance and correct operation, as well as qualitative MOS polls to get the quality of user experience when handling the decoder.

Keywords: TDT · GINGA · IPTV · Raspberry Pi · Hybrid television · ISDB-Tb

1 Introduction

In 2010, ISDB-Tb (Integrated Services for Digital Broadcasting - International) was adopted, as a standard for Digital Terrestrial Television (DTT) in Ecuador, which offers a better quality of open television with better services [1]. The infrastructure growth of Internet networks in Ecuador makes it possible to use the Internet Protocol Television (IPTV) service; because telecommunications operators in Ecuador have launched specific studies of the technology in development [2]. The phenomenon of digitalization influenced the Ecuadorian population, a large part of it has changed the analog tuners by digital, and they acquired a television with built-in digital receiver.

In the market there are external tuners that allow receiving digital signals and the user can use monitors without digital television tuner. Currently you can find receiving and decoding units in the market, but only certain equipment includes the

© Springer Nature Switzerland AG 2019
M. J. Abásolo et al. (Eds.): jAUTI 2018, CCIS 1004, pp. 60–70, 2019.
https://doi.org/10.1007/978-3-030-23862-9_5

Ginga middleware, so it is a motivation for us to find a low cost STB (Set Top Box) that integrates the DTT plus the IPTV and also integrates the interactivity option.

The present work is dedicated to the implementation of a receiver and decoder unit or STB with hardware components and software of low cost and open source, including middleware that allows interactivity in ISDB-Tb and player for IPTV. A graphical command control interface for mobiles also is designed using Bluetooth wireless technology with the Android operating system to operate the digital decoder.

A Hybrid approach is needed because it will be permit the integration between the broadcasting TV with the broadband TV content.

The second section explain Hybrid DTT & IPTV Set Top Box architecture, next section describe about the Hybrid STB implementation, hardware and software platforms installation and configurations, the forth section show the evaluation reception tests and result analysis, finally we present the discussion and future works.

2   Hybrid DTT & IPTV Set Top Box Design

Digital Terrestrial Television and IPTV need to encode and compress the information for transmission, as well as decompress and decode them, so both technologies require a digital decoder, this allows show multimedia content (audio, video, data). Here is important to show the relationship between the Digital Terrestrial Television ISDB-Tb standard and the Internet Protocol Television (IPTV) standard to develop this project; both technologies use H.264/MPEG-4 compression for audiovisual content and MPEG-2 as the standard for transporting information [3].

2.1   Hybrid ISDB-Tb and IPTV

A hybrid box is a larger and more complex system than a simple box, in this case an ISDB-Tb and IPTV environment. Figure 1 shows how the environment of a hybrid network can be, also each block of the hybrid network diagram is described [4].

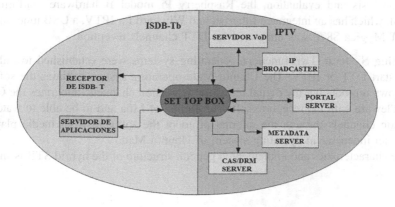

Fig. 1. Hybrid network diagram of blocks

2.2   Hybrid STB Hardware Architecture

The hardware architecture of a Hybrid Set Top Box must have a high performance to support all the video processing and additional GINGA middleware and IPTV technology. Also, it must be able to tune and process the signals from the ISDB-Tb and IPTV system. Figure 2 shows the physical components architecture of STB for DTT and IPTV technologies.

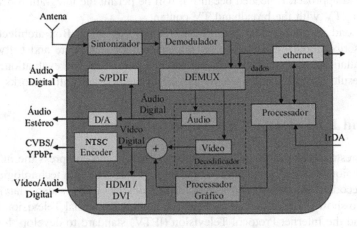

Fig. 2. Hardware architecture of a STB hybrid

3   Hybrid STB System Implementation

3.1   Hybrid STB General Structure

Hardware Platform: First we made an investigation of low cost hardware platforms, focus on find the best characteristics and requirements for implement the project. Then of an analysis and evaluation, the Raspberry Pi model B hardware platform was selected, which has an integrated Ethernet and Wifi card for IPTV, a USB tuner module ISDB-T Mygica S870 was integrated for DTT channels reception.

Operating System: Two functional operating systems were established to independently start DTT or IPTV. The Ubuntu Mate operating system contains the software that allows reproducing the digital terrestrial television channels, integrates the Ginga. ar middleware with the reception software Zamba of Lifia and to be able to watch the television channels through the internet protocol the software Kodi media player is used as an independent operating system of Ubuntu Mate.

The characteristics and implemented general structure of the hybrid STB is show in the Fig. 3.

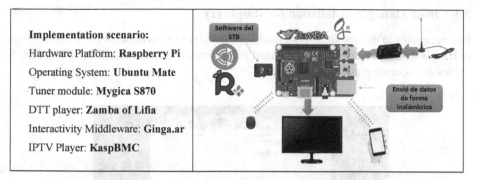

Implementation scenario:

Hardware Platform: **Raspberry Pi**

Operating System: **Ubuntu Mate**

Tuner module: **Mygica S870**

DTT player: **Zamba of Lifia**

Interactivity Middleware: **Ginga.ar**

IPTV Player: **KaspBMC**

Fig. 3. Characteristics and implemented structure of the hybrid STB

3.2 STB Management

An Android application was developed to control the Ubuntu Mate operating system from a mobile phone via Bluetooth. The application was developed in Android Studio. The program sends a character string via Bluetooth using a mobile device, string variables were assigned to use the interactive buttons F1, F2, F3 and F4, in addition to using the escape, enter, right and left mouse clicks, upload and change channel and volume to manage the zapper; the interface can be seen in Fig. 4.

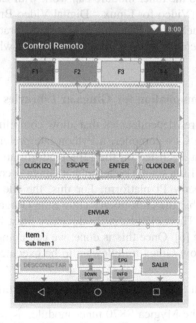

Fig. 4. Android mobile application for remote control interface.

3.3 Boot Manager Installation for Raspberry

It is necessary to use the Berryboot dual boot manager to start one of the Ubuntu Mate or RaspBMC (Kodi) operating systems, it's important to choose a DTT or IPTV, Fig. 5 shows the operating systems installed.

Fig. 5. Boot manager Menu (Berryboot)

3.4 Build and Install Video4Linux Drivers

This step is fundamental to the tuner module can work with Linux, to build the kernel driver module V4L-DVB (Video for Linux - Digital Video Broadcast) is necessary to install headers in the kernel (linux-headers), and install libraries from the Linux terminal: *build-essential, patchutils, libproc-processtable-perl,* which allow working with the drivers.

3.5 Installation and Compilation for Ginga.ar Libraries

Ginga.ar installation requires dependencies that allow compiling the source code. It is necessary have installed a C++ compiler, a Python interpreter and the cmake library. Also external libraries that are listed on the Lifia platform are required [5].

It is necessary modify Lifia source code, so that Ginga is compatible with the ARM architecture of the Raspberry Pi platform. For this, the file *FindGlib.cmake* of the source code is edited, so that the Glib library allows the Ginga source code to be used in the ARM architecture. The *FinGlib.cmake* directory must be added: *lib/arm-linux-gnueabihf/glib-2.0/include* [6]. Once this is done, we can compile and build the Ginga directories, which will allow Ginga middleware to be executed.

3.6 Zamba Multimedia Software Compilation and Installation

Once the installations of the Mygica S870 tuner module, as well as the Lifia Ginga.ar middleware, are completed, the Zamba reception software is installed (Zapper oriented to Set top Boxes) [5].

The dependencies necessary to compile the source code of Zamba, are *Zlib* and *Pulseaudio*, as well as all the libraries that were required to compile Ginga.ar, this is because the reproduction software is linked to the middleware that allows reproducing interactive applications that arrive from a broadcaster station.

3.7 Zamba Zapper Source Code Compilation

Before compiling the Zamba source code in the ARM architecture of Raspberry Pi, is required to modify the *FindGlib.cmake* file part of Kuntur source code of Lifia, using the same principle as in Ginga code. It's necessary to apply two patches to Zamba source code to be compatible with the tuner module. The first patch must be made in the canvas library of the source code, that mean edit the directory *kuntur/lib/dtv-canvas/deps.cmake*. The patch set the VLC library as the default player. The second patch is necessary to make it in the zapper library of the Kuntur source code; we can find it in the directory *kuntur/lib/dtv-zapper/CMakeLists.txt* [5].

Once the patches are established to the source code, a file with cmake extension must be generated to build the reception software, since the cmake configuration file contains the necessary variables to build Zamba [5], then is necessary to copy the directories to the Linux system and be able to open it like any other program.

3.8 System Installation and Configuration for IPTV

The XBMC player is used to solve IPTV, but it works as an independent Ubuntu Mate operating system that contains the Zamba DTT player. The operating system is known as RaspBMC.

The digital video recorder (PVR, Personal Video Recorder), allows to watch IPTV channels. This complement makes possible to upload the content and logos of the television channels by IP, see the electronic program guide or EPG (Electronic Program Guide) and create free channels list.

4 Reception Tests and Results Analysis

The evaluation is done at the performance level, the implemented STB is evaluated with percentage measurements of processor use, start time and processor temperature; these tests are rigorous and important because it refers to quantitative measurements. The second evaluation was done at user level, with qualitative MOS (Mean Opinion Score) measurements, where a group of people will evaluate the final result that is presented.

4.1 Start Time and Temperature

The start time of the Ubuntu Mate operating system is the time that elapses since the decoder is turned on until it starts playing a DTT channel. While the time to view IPTV, is the time it takes to start the RaspBMC system and display a digital channel.

The temperature measurement was made by tuning the channel 4.1 of the DTT signal in Quito-Ecuador with an environment temperature of 20 °C, in the different image qualities that it transmits; the same way free HDTV and SD channels were used to measure the parameters. As shown in the results of Table 1, on average the start time of the DTT system is greater than the IPTV because the XBCM player works independently of the Ubuntu Mate system that contains the DTT playback software, allowing the IPTV system to have better handling fluidity and low overheating presence.

Table 1. STB scenario monitoring

		Measuring 1	Measuring 2	Measuring 3	Average
Initialization time for DTT [seg]		41 [s]	45 [s]	36 [s]	41 [s]
Initialization time for IPTV [seg]		23 [s]	20 [s]	19 [s]	21 [s]
DTT displayed temperature [°C]	HD	52 °C	54 °C	48 °C	51 °C
	SD	40 °C	42 °C	43 °C	42 °C
	One Seg	37 °C	36 °C	37 °C	37 °C
	Interactive applications	49 °C	50 °C	56 °C	52 °C
IPTV displayed temperature [°C]	HD	30 °C	32 °C	31 °C	31 °C
	SD	29 °C	27 °C	25 °C	27 °C

Interactive application download tests were also performed on the Zamba player from Lifia that brings the GINGA middleware embedded, and Zamba was compared running from a PC, the results are shown in Table 2, the download time of the applications that are sent from the air in the laptop is faster, because this PC has better processing capacity compared to the STB implemented in the Raspberry Pi.

Table 2. DTT applications download time that are sent from ESPETV Channel

		Test TS 1	Test TS 2	Test TS 3	Average time
Aplication Interactives Download Time [s]	Set Top Box	19 [s]	22 [s]	24 [s]	21,6 [s]
	Laptop	12 [s]	14 [s]	13 [s]	13 [s]

4.2   CPU Resources Use in DTT

To know the CPU use, the channel 4.1 of the DTT in Quito was tuned with its different image qualities transmits. The Ubuntu Mate task manager was used, it shows a history of CPU utilization of each processor core in percentages (%). The CPU use in Raspberry Pi 3, working with the Ubuntu Mate operating system when viewing Digital Terrestrial TV presents graphs of use history of Fig. 6.

The Fig. 6 graphs represent the CPU use of the 4 Raspberry Pi 3 cores, and allow to know the behavior of each processing core of the platform. The CPU use in HD channels is high, it can be seen the processor cores are in saturation, therefore isn't

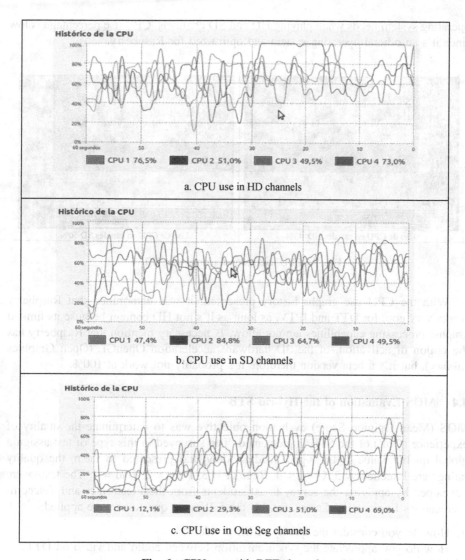

a. CPU use in HD channels

b. CPU use in SD channels

c. CPU use in One Seg channels

Fig. 6. CPU use with DTT channels

recommendable to watch channels in HD because it could damage the status of the Raspberry Pi in a long time, since it saturates the processing and overheating your plate. The use of the CPU in SD and OneSeg channels in DTT, are at acceptable levels so it could remain active without difficulties.

4.3 CPU Resources Use in IPTV

Kodi is designed as a multimedia center; therefore it allows to play almost any video format. Figure 7 shows the history of CPU use when IPTV is displayed, and RaspBMC operating system needs when playing HD and SD channels. CPU use percentage is low since it's an official operating system and optimized for Raspberry.

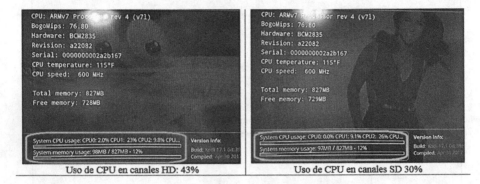

| Uso de CPU en canales HD: 43% | Uso de CPU en canales SD 30% |

Fig. 7. CPU use second scenario in IPTV

With the CPU use graphs history presented, it was determined that Raspberry works very goof for DTT and IPTV, as long as it's not HD content because its limited graphic processing capabilities are not allow. Is necessary mention that Raspberry has the option of activation, of the 3D hardware acceleration OpenGL (Open Graphics Library), but it's a beta version therefore it's probably not work at 100%.

4.4   MOS Evaluation of the Hybrid STB

MOS (Mean Opinion Score) evaluation objective was to determinate the quality of experience (QoE) of the STB implemented. The surveyed in this type of test assign a global quality value to the signal (audio/video/data) presented to them, the quality ratings are Excellent = 5, Good = 4, Regular = 3, Poor = 2, Bad = 1. The tests were developed by applying the survey to 20 students from the Electronics and Telecommunications Engineering Career, for this the following questions were applied:

1. How do you consider the quality of DTT video?
2. How do you appreciate the synchronization between audio and video on DTT?
3. How do you consider the quality of video on IPTV?
4. How do you appreciate the synchronization between audio and video on IPTV?
5. How do you evaluate the presentation of interactive applications?

Figure 8 shows the results, reflect that watching digital terrestrial television in the implemented STB the QoE tends to REGULAR or GOOD, except in the HD quality that is deficient or POOR as justified before, in the same way the QoE when watching TV through the Internet Protocol tends to EXCELLENT or GOOD.

Finally, in the test of execution of interactive applications it's show the locally loaded applications had an excellent appreciation while the applications loaded by the air through the modulator of the ESPETV laboratory, the appreciation was good due to the time it takes to load from the carousel of data because they are transmitted as a data stream by open signal.

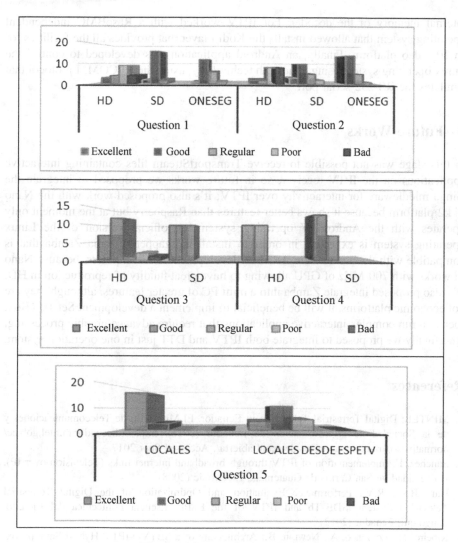

Fig. 8. MOS Results, questions 1-5.

5 Discussion

The main objective of implementing a hybrid DTT and IPTV receiver was reached, the low cost platform chose was the Raspberry Pi 3 because it's the most accessible in the market and there is great support and technical help forums; it was decided to work with the Linux operating system, because it was the most stable and was coupled to the USB DTT tuners that were used, it was able to reproduce in real time interactive applications transmitted by air in a data flow; Zamba the Lifia receiving zapper containing GINGA was configured to be compatible with the architecture of the ARM platform. Also, it was possible to play local interactive applications stored in the internal memory of the decoder. For IPTV worked with a RaspBMC independent operating system that allowed installs the Kodi player that provides all the facilities for an IP video platform. Finally, an Android application was developed to control the Linux operating system using Bluetooth technology, using the RFCOMM protocol that emulates the RS-232 serial port.

6 Future Works

In this stage was not possible to receive TransportStream files containing interactive applications on the IPTV receiver, so in future works we proposed to integrate the Ginga middleware for interactivity over IPTV; it's also proposed work with the Nano Pi k2 platform because it shows better features than Raspberry but at the moment only operates with the AndroidTV operating system, an official version of the Linux operating system is expected, in order to install the zapper of Lifia Zamba that is compatible with the architecture ARM of development minicomputers, because Nano Pi works with 700 MHz of GPU allowing to have great fluidity of reproduction in HD. It's also proposed integrate Zamba into a mini PC of greater features, although they are not economic platforms, it will be beneficial to implement a development Set Top Box, focus on run complex interactive applications that require advance graphic processing. And finally we proposed to integrate both IPTV and DTT just in one operation system.

References

1. MINTEL: Digital Terrestrial Television in Ecuador. El Ministerio de Telecomunicaciones y de la Sociedad de la Información de Ecuador (2016). https://tdtecuador.mintel.gob.ec/normativas-para-concesionarios-de-senal-abierta/. Accessed Sept 2017
2. Sánchez, E. Implementation of IPTV through broadband internet links (Television over IP). Universidad de San Carlos de Guatemala, Electronic (2008)
3. Haro Baéz, R.V.: Performance Evaluation and Optimization of the Digital Terrestrial Television System ISDB-Tb and IPTV of the ESPE. Escuela Politécnica del Ejército, Sangolquí, Ecuador (2012)
4. Ribeiro, H., Lourenco, A., Newton, B.: Architecture of a SBTVD-IPTV Hybrid Set-top box. J. Broadcasting (2008). http://set6.tempsite.ws/revistaeletronica/index.php/revistaderadiodifusao/article/viewFile/157/163. Accessed Oct 2017
5. Lifia. (Junio de 2013). Ginga.ar. de Laboratorio de Investigación y Formación en Informática Avanzada – Lifia. http://tvd.lifia.info.unlp.edu.ar/ginga.ar/. Accessed Oct 2017
6. Espinel Rivera, K.: Evaluation of the performance and features of an interactive content decoder based on the Ginga - NLC on a Raspberry PI. Universidad de las Fuerzas Armadas ESPE, Eléctrica y Electrónica, Sangolquí, Ecuador, January 2016

Dr. Nau, a Web Generator of Interactive Applications for Digital TV

Sandra Casas$^{(\boxtimes)}$, Franco Herrera, Fernanda Oyarzo,
and Franco Trinidad

Lab. de TV Digital (ITA), Universidad Nacional de la Patagonia Austral,
9400 Río Gallegos, Argentina
scasas@unpa.edu.ar

Abstract. This work introduces Dr. Nau, a tool that supports the design of interactive applications for Ginga-NCL and automatically generates them. Dr. Nau was developed with the aim of collaborating with television industry professionals; its goal is to simplify the development process, reduce the cost and time of development, increase the usability of applications, and support their consistent appearance. This work describes the main characteristics of Dr. Nau's use, design, and implementation and also presents a usability evaluation by several groups of users.

Keywords: Interactivity · Digital TV · Ginga-NCL

1 Introduction

Digital TV is a set of technologies for generating, transmitting, and receiving images and sound using digital information. The digital signals send data, video, audio, software applications, and so forth over the transmission channels. In addition to being more efficient than analog signals, the main advantage of digital transmissions is that it is possible to transmit several services through a single channel, which provides efficient use of the transmission spectrum.

An interactive Digital TV (iDTV) application is a multimedia software application that allows viewers to interact with digital TV via remote control [1]. IDTV provides an opportunity to interact with the linked content and make decisions, which gives viewers more control over their television. IDTV applications include surveys, voting, games, natural catastrophe alerts, purchasing, banking transactions, navigation through additional information nodes, and more.

IDTV applications can be classified as offering local, simple, or advanced interactivity [2]. Local interaction offers the possibility of selecting and presenting information, which involves processing the information that comes through the data stream. Typical local applications include local customization, filters, support of preferences, ordering, simple games, and news. Simple interactions, or interactions with upload, involve applications that can send data via a return channel. Typical applications in this category include voting that can alter the result of a TV show and what is known as "Social TV", in which a community interacts through a program. Finally, advanced

M. J. Abásolo et al. (Eds.): jAUTI 2018, CCIS 1004, pp. 71–86, 2019.
https://doi.org/10.1007/978-3-030-23862-9_6

interaction (interactions with upload and download) includes applications that involve sending and receiving via the return channel. Typical applications in this category include downloading applications and data via the return channel, T-Learning, T-Commerce, and T-Banking.

According to [3], in order to optimize the process of developing interactive applications, communications organizations look for mechanisms that (i) simplify the development process, (ii) reduce the cost and time of development, (iii) enhance the usability of applications, and (iv) support the consistent appearance of applications.

Construction of prototypes is recognized as an adequate methodology for the development and evaluation of iDTV design solutions in that they facilitate the validation of producers' requirements as well as early evaluations of usability [2]. However, use of this approach on an industrial scale requires having a software development capability that allows rapid construction of several prototypes/applications for the purpose of analysis and evaluation.

This paper presents Dr. Nau, a web tool that automatically generates NCL code for Digital TV based on usability patterns. The rest of this paper is organized as follows. Section 2 describes related work. Sections 3 and 4 briefly present the context for the present study. Section 5 provides an overview of the Dr. Nau tool. Section 6 discusses the approach that we implemented to automatically generate code. Section 7 presents a usability evaluation of the tool. Finally, Sect. 8 concludes the study.

2 Related Works

An important group of tools is aimed at developers. Among these, code editors and compilers such as NCL Eclipse, NCL Composer [4], and NCL-Inspector [5] require solid knowledge of programming languages for their use. The frameworks of applications such as Frame IDTV [6], Ginga-Game [7], ATHUS [8], and iTV Suite [9] allow a higher level of reuse of code and design, but learning and using these is more complex and requires more technical skills.

Automatic code generators are aimed at users who know the domain well but are not developers. These tools can be compared based on different perspectives, such as the domain for which they are intended, the level of interactivity they support, and the operating environment. One important aspect that must be considered is the extent to which principles and/or usability guidelines are incorporated as abstractions. The following briefly summarizes some automatic code generators.

ITV-Learning [10] is a tool for educational instructors that allow the creation of learning objects, which facilitates development of interactive digital materials by abstracting them from programming knowledge for the creation of iDTV applications.

Crea Digital TV [11] is a tool for creating NCL-Lua applications, aimed at content producers. It implements a graphic timeline model to represent the life of the application elements, the interactivity with the viewer, and the events that occur throughout the application. Users are not required to have knowledge of NCL.

SGAi [12] is a tool that automatically generates surveys for NCL-Lua applications, handling the return channel and preserving the result through a web application.

API TVD [13] is a wizart tool that consists of graphic templates. It handles the management of temporal synchronism between media and their lifespan. The purpose of this generator is to simplify the development process by allowing the user to engage with "what" the application should do rather than "how" it is done. To this end, the user does not require knowledge of the NCL language.

IT NEWs [14] is a tool that reuses previously created news templates to generate new applications. These templates consist of NCL code. By focusing on the elements of communicability and usability, this tool allows users to create journalistic applications without having to learn how to program.

Template Generator [15] is a tool that allows users to automatically create code for an interactive application by modifying the relevant fields of a pre-established template. The templates are based on usability parameters such as level, service, and type of interactivity.

SPL-iDTV [16] is a tool whose features allow the design of the interaction; this tool then automatically generates iDTV applications for Ginga. Its optional and mandatory features represent the interaction pattern design.

Table 1 compares some characteristics of these automatic code generators to the automatic code generator proposed in the present work. The table highlights the level of usability that is supported, because these tools are intended for end users. While several of the code generators have not taken usability into account, others offer elements or parameters that provide basic support. Dr Nau and SPL-iDTV support different aspects of usability because they support patterns.

Table 1. Comparison of automatic code generators

Tool	Artifacts	Function	Domain	Interactivity	Environment	Usability
ITV-Learning	Learning object	Code generator	T-learning	Simple	Desktop	Not present
Crea Digital TV	Code – diagrams	Code generator	General	Local	Desktop	Not present
SGAi	Customization of interactive applications	Code generator	T-voting	Simple	Desktop	Not present
API TVD	Graphic template	Code generator – Wizart	News documentary	Local	Desktop	Graphics template
IT NEWs	News template	Code generator	News	Local	Web	Usability elements
Template Generator	Code template	Code generator	General	Simple	Desktop	Usability parameters
SPL-iDTV	Media	Template and code generator	General	Local	Desktop	Usability patterns
Dr. Nau	Media	Code generator	General	Local	Web	Usability patterns

3 Ginga-NCL

Brazil, Argentina, Chile, and other Latin American countries have adopted the Integrated Service Data Broadcasting (ISDB-Tb) or Integrated Services Digital Transmission standard. This standard consists of a set of Japanese standards that define ways to transmit digital content over the air. The content can be application updates or file systems. This standard uses middleware called Ginga [17], which enables execution of NCL/LUA applications [18].

NCL [19] is a declarative language based on the conceptual model NCM (Nested Context Model), which is basically an XML application. NCL clearly defines how media objects (elements of multimedia content: videos, images, sounds, etc.) are structured and related in time and space.

An NCL program, like every XML document, begins with a header. After the header, the structure of the application begins with the tag <ncl>, its id and xmlns attributes, and its <head> and <body> children elements, following the terminology adopted by the W3C standard. The <head> element contains the basis of elements referenced by the core of the NCL application (in the <body> element) and identifies them as regions, descriptors, transitions, connectors, and rules. The <body> element contains the elements that define the content of the application itself, such as medias, objects, links, contexts, and switch objects. The NCL structure is represented in Fig. 1.

```
<?xml version="1.0" encoding="ISO-8859-1"?>
  <ncl id="main"
       xmlns="http://www.ncl.org.br/NCL3.0/ EDTVProfile">
  <head>
     Region ---------------- where will the media be shown?
     Descriptor ------------ what properties do the media have?
     Connector --------------when will the media be shown?
  </head>
  <body>
     Port ---------------- which media runs first?
     Media --------------- which media will be shown?
     Link ------------------when will the media be shown?
  </body>
```

Fig. 1. General structure of an NCL document.

Medias or content objects are represented by the <media> element. The regions represented by the <region> element indicate the area of the screen where the mean component will be displayed; these can be indicated in pixels or as percentages. The descriptors represented by the <descriptor> element specify how the mean elements associated with the descriptors will be displayed. The gate, represented by the <port> element, indicates which medium will run at the beginning of the application. The <transition> element, defined as a child of the <head> element, specifies a group of transition effects.

The connectors and links allow specification of actions on media objects resulting from the occurrence of events. A connector defined through the <causalConnector> component represents a relationship that can be used to create link elements in the document. In a causal relationship, a condition must be satisfied to activate an action. A <link> element links an interface node with the connector roles, defining a space-time relationship between the NCL objects. The events that may occur are: onBegin, onEnd, onAbort, onPause, onResume, and onSelection. The corresponding actions that are triggered when an event occurs are: start, stop, abort, pause, resume, and set.

4 User-Centered Design Patterns for IDTV

Patterns play a very important role in software development. A pattern encapsulates a proven solution to a recurring software design problem, and a collection of interrelated patterns provides developers with a communication platform for disseminating elegant and reusable solutions to the challenges of commonly encountered specifications. Collections of patterns have become the major method for communicating design decisions and helping user interface designers cope with the growing number of applications for new devices in versatile domains.

A perfect example of such a collection of patterns is presented in [3]. The catalog describes each pattern from the perspective of the user rather than in terms of the technology that is used. It takes into account the context of use and the interests of the users with the objective of maximizing their experience, and each of the provided solutions has been evaluated and approved through a series of usability studies. The patterns that are presented are hierarchically structured and indexed according to design problems, which allows developers to conveniently navigate through the patterns or quickly jump to others in search of a particular design problem. The catalog consists of 41 patterns classified into ten groups that cover all aspects of interactive applications for DTV. Figure 2 shows the five groups of patterns that Dr. Nau implements in the generation of NCL applications and how these are linked to one another. These groups include a total of 15 patterns, almost 50% of the patterns appearing in the catalog. Use of these patterns enables the representation, selection, and design of the multimedia components that will participate in an iDTV application, since these patterns allow fundamental characteristics such as the screen distribution, basic functionalities, and navigation, among others, to be identified, specified, and configured in a standardized way. The patterns also predefine sets of values and/or ranges for other interaction parameters and thus guarantee usability and a certain validation level for the generated application.

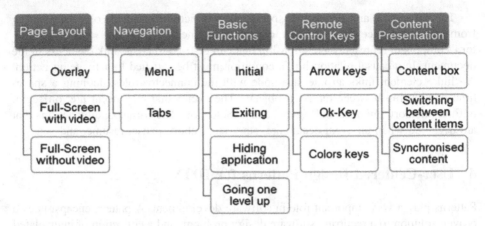

Fig. 2. Interaction Design Patterns supported by Dr. Nau

5 Vision of Dr. Nau

Dr. Nau, like any application generator, is oriented to a specific domain, which allows it to represent high-level abstractions. The coding or implementation of an NCL application using Dr. Nau is completely transparent to the user. At no time is it necessary for the user to enter source code, nor is any mention made of concepts related to the design of data structures (such as fields, DB tables, SQL statements, and NCL tags/attributes) or other technical issues surrounding traditional implementations.

The user can begin with an idea for a new or existing TV program. Dr. Nau offers the possibility of creating projects with which general information can be associated and then creating different prototypes. The prototypes combine different NCL elements and components, and each prototype can use different groups of media and apply different interaction design patterns. The user only needs to select these, and the code for the application is then generated automatically.

To generate a prototype, the user begins by selecting the screen distribution based on the volume of multimedia content to be presented. Options for the start of inter-activity are then presented, and the positions and timing can be chosen for displaying buttons on the screen. Next, based on the selected distribution, the system provides several designs for the presentation of the media objects and, if applicable, it will continue with the navigation section in order to finish loading the media, and finally the prototype is automatically generated. Figure 3 shows the set of screens just referred to as an example.

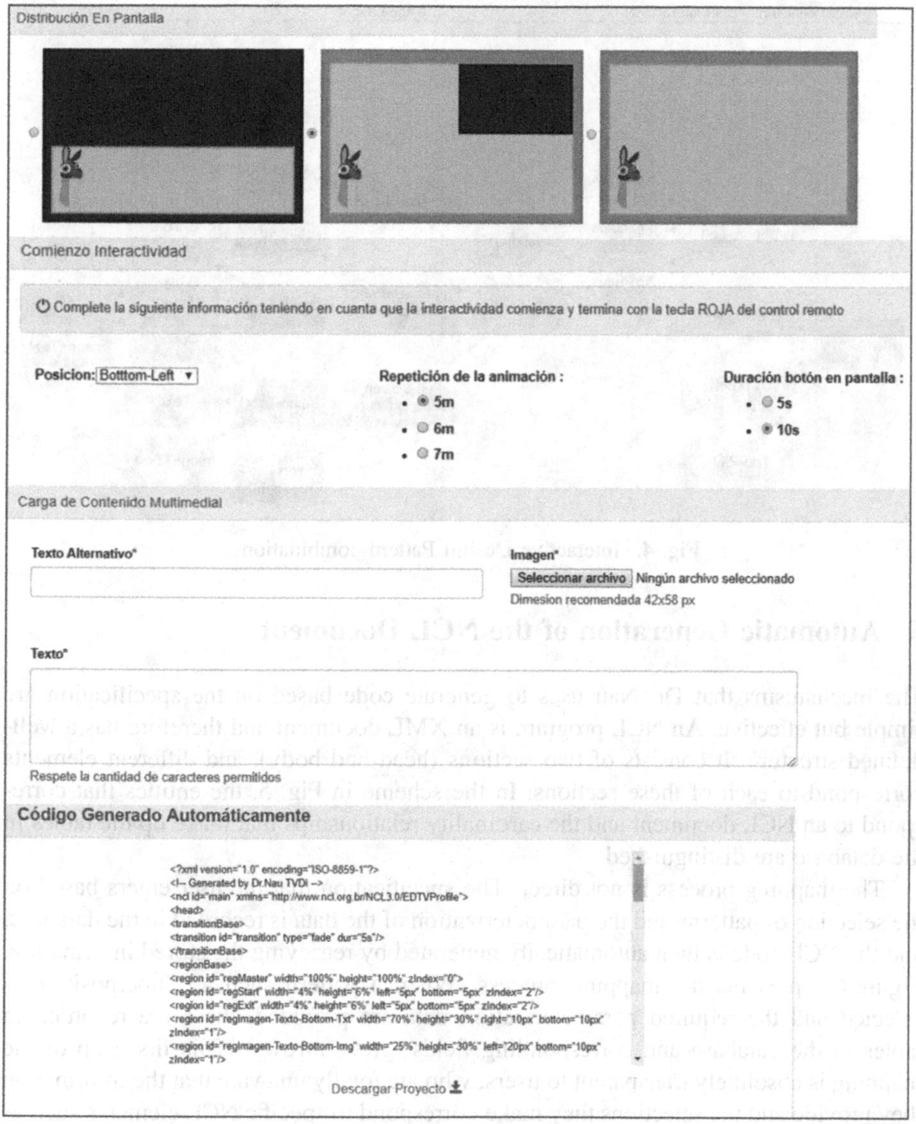

Fig. 3. Dr. Nau's web interface

The diagram in Fig. 4 depicts in summary form the possible combinations of patterns that Dr. Nau can generate as prototypes and the relationships between the patterns (basic functionality, layout and screen design, navigation, presentation of content). Based on the multiplicative principle [20], more than 6000 prototypes are possible, with no programming requirements.

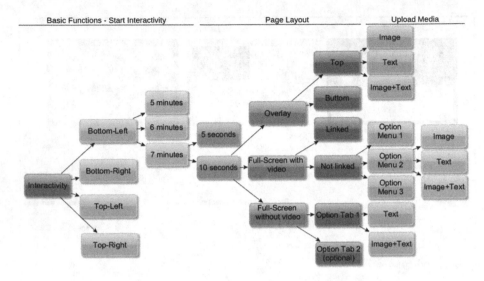

Fig. 4. Interactive Design Pattern combinations

6   Automatic Generation of the NCL Document

The mechanisms that Dr. Nau uses to generate code based on the specification are simple but effective. An NCL program is an XML document and therefore has a well-defined structure. It consists of two sections (head and body), and different elements correspond to each of these sections. In the scheme in Fig. 5, the entities that correspond to an NCL document and the cardinality relationships that make up the tables in the database are distinguished.

The mapping process is not direct. The specification that the user enters based on the selection of patterns and the parameterization of the data is recorded in the database, and the NCL code is then automatically generated by retrieving the stored information. Figure 6 represents the mapping process. When a pattern such as Superposition is selected and the required parameterization data are provided, these are recorded in tables in the database and corresponding fields (green arrows). This first step of the mapping is absolutely transparent to users, who are totally unaware that the information they provide and the selections they make correspond to specific NCL elements such as region, descriptor, media, bind, and so forth, nor do they know where these are stored in the database.

The second step of the mapping process executes the algorithm that generates the code. The algorithm retrieves the information from the database (red arrows), following the order, sequence, and structure of an NCL document, and writes the code into a text file that the user can later download as part of a project. This second mapping process is also absolutely transparent to users.

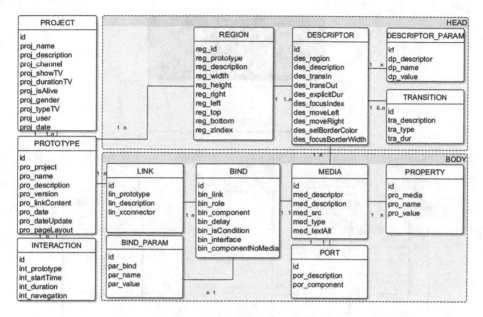

Fig. 5. Data entity scheme

Special consideration is given to the connecting elements and links. For the management of these properties, Dr. Nau employs a set of previously defined connectors. This connector base was specified to allow the connectors to be reused by the different link elements. In this way, the different multimedia components are linked through a link to the roles that are part of a connector, as either a condition or an action. When finalizing the creation of a prototype, Dr. Nau automatically inserts the NCL connector base into the project, which is necessary for being invoked from the main file.

7 Usability Evaluation of Dr. Nau

The questionnaires were utilized for the usability evaluation of Dr. Nau. The questionnaires can be electronic or in printed format. They are usually divided into two parts: in one part, questions are asked to analyze the quality of the interface and in the other, questions are asked to collect objective data from users as well as subjective impressions. To plan the points that will be covered by the questionnaire, the objectives of the evaluation should be determined, the users who test the system should be defined, and the final criteria used to qualify the interface should be identified. The users who are selected must be real users and must form a representative sample of real users. The evaluation should include a preparatory phase, development of the test, a post-test in which the users' answers are analyzed, and preparation of a report with the conclusions.

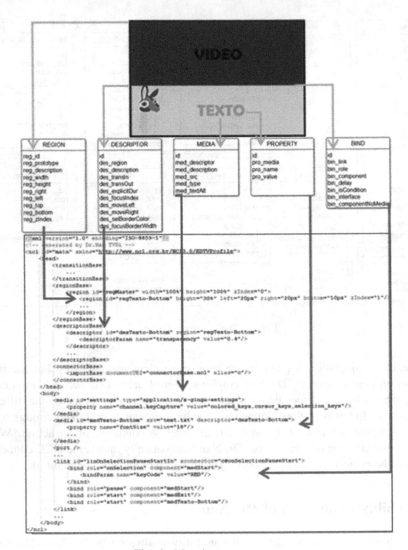

Fig. 6. Mapping process steps

The format selected for Dr. Nau's evaluation questionnaire is based on the scale for the usability of systems—SUS [21, 22]—developed by Digital Equipment Co. SUS is a widely accepted approach since it allows the usefulness of a system to be evaluated in a simple way. The questionnaire used to carry out the evaluations of Dr. Nau's user interface and the system is presented in the appendix.

Table 2 summarizes the user groups participating in the evaluation. Before answering the questionnaire, the groups were provided tutorial sessions about the tool, and then participants interacted with the application to develop different exercises and examples.

Table 2. Users' information

University	City	Users	Profile		Age	
			Professional	Student	20–30	31–40
Universidad Nacional de la Patagonia Austral (UNPA)	Río Gallegos, Santa Cruz	9	3	6	6	3
Universidad Nacional de Quilmes (UNQ)	Bernal, Buenos Aires	7	2	5	3	4
Universidad Nacional de la Plata (UNLP)	La Plata, Buenos Aires	5	3	2	2	3

SUS produces a unique number that represents a composite measure of the general usability of the system being studied. The scores for the individual items are not significant by themselves. The method used to obtain the score for an entire questionnaire applies simple calculations. First, the scores contributed by each of the items are added together. These scores fall between 0 and 4. For items 1, 3, 5, 7, and 9, the contributed score is the selected position on the scale minus 1. For items 2, 4, 6, 8, and 10, the contributed score is 5 minus the selected position on the scale. The sum of the contributed scores is then multiplied by 2.5 to obtain the general SU value. These final scores range between 0 and 100.

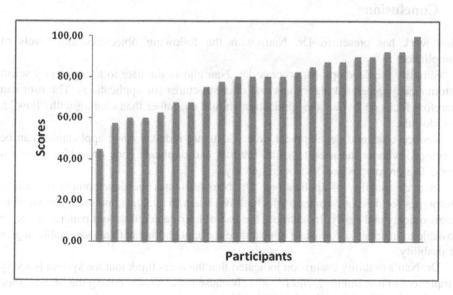

Fig. 8. Distribution of scores

Figure 8 graphically presents the distribution of the calculated scores, and the individual values per item of the questionnaires are shown in the appendix.

The general average is 77.27. The average values discriminating the data by city, profile, and age, balance with one another and with the general average, as shown in Table 3.

Table 3. Average scores by university, profile and age

Criterion	Average
University-City	
Universidad Nacional de la Patagonia Austral	75.83
Universidad Nacional de Quilmes	77.85
Universidad Nacional de La Plata	81.00
Profile	
Professional	75.38
Student	80.00
Age	
20–30	75.00
31–40	79.55

According to different authors and experts [23], group averages that are higher than 68–70 are considered acceptable. For the application in this study, all of the analyses by groups exceed these average values, although they do not reach the level of excellence, which requires an average higher than 84 points.

8 Conclusion

This work has presented Dr. Nau, with the following objectives and levels of compliance:

Simplify the development process: Dr. Nau allows the user to transparently select automatically generated algorithms and data structures for applications. The user can therefore focus on "what" the application should do, rather than dealing with "how" it will do this.

Reduce costs and development time: Costs are reduced since applications can be developed without the need to write, rewrite, and duplicate code or to hire programmers. The prototypes are developed quickly.

Increase usability of applications: Dr. Nau facilitates the development of various prototypes for the same content, which allows users to evaluate and compare usability levels quickly and easily. In addition, the use of user-centered design patterns makes it possible to maintain a consistent appearance for applications with an acceptable degree of usability.

Dr. Nau's usability evaluation indicated that the users think that the system is a very simple tool to use, intuitive, and friendly, because the evaluation using the SUS method exceeds the acceptability threshold by a high percentage.

Future work can explore adding various improvements to the tool. Dr. Nau is a scalable tool, since the remaining 50% of the pattern catalog has yet to be implemented to cover more content and/or provide more graphic options for interaction design, following the scheme proposed in the present work. Dr. Nau can generate code for other standards and Digital TV platforms; this can be done by modifying the module that automatically generates the code. Since Dr. Nau is a web application, it is possible to generate user communities that share resources and develop projects in a distributed and collaborative way.

Dr. Nau is a fully functional prototype that is available at http://170.210.92.36:8000/ and can be accessed with the username "taller" and password "taller.

Appendix

1. SUS questionnaire

	Strongly disagree				Strongly agree
1. I think that I would like to use this system frequently	1	2	3	4	5
2. I found the system unnecessarily complex	1	2	3	4	5
3. I thought the system was easy to use	1	2	3	4	5
4. I think that I would need the support of a technical person to be able to use this system	1	2	3	4	5
5. I found the various functions in this system were well integrated	1	2	3	4	5
6. I thought there was too much inconsistency in this system	1	2	3	4	5
7. I would imagine that most people would learn to use this system very quickly	1	2	3	4	5
8. I found the system very cumbersome to use	1	2	3	4	5
9. I felt very confident using the system	1	2	3	4	5
10. I needed to learn a lot of things before I could get going with this system	1	2	3	4	5

2. Individual values per item of the questionnaires

Q#1	Q#2	Q#3	Q#4	Q#5	Q#6	Q#7	Q#8	Q#9	Q#10
5	1	2	1	5	1	5	1	5	2
5	3	5	2	5	1	3	1	5	4
4	2	3	4	4	2	3	1	3	5
4	2	2	3	0	2	3	3	3	4
5	1	5	3	4	1	3	1	3	2
5	2	4	2	3	1	4	1	4	2
5	1	3	3	5	1	3	1	4	1
5	1	5	1	4	2	5	1	4	1
5	1	3	3	4	2	5	1	4	4
5	1	1	0	5	1	5	1	5	1
5	1	1	1	5	1	5	1	5	3
4	1	4	2	4	1	5	1	4	1
5	2	2	2	4	2	1	2	3	3
3	1	2	1	3	2	5	1	5	1
3	1	1	1	3	1	3	1	3	4
5	1	0	3	4	1	5	1	4	1
4	1	2	1	5	1	4	1	5	1
3	1	5	1	5	1	5	1	3	1
5	1	5	1	5	1	5	1	5	1
2	3	3	3	4	2	3	1	4	3
4	3	5	4	3	1	5	1	3	4

References

1. Rodrigues, R., Soares, R.: Produción de Contenido Declarativo para TV Digital. XXXIII SemiSH, Brasil (2006)
2. Kunert, T.: User-Centered Interaction Design Patterns for Interactive Digital Television Applications. Springer, London (2009)
3. Kunert, T.: Interaction design pattern in the context of interactive TV applications. In: Proceeding of the 9th IFIP TC13 - International Conference on Human-Computer Interaction (2003)
4. Laiola Guimarães, R., Monteiro de Resende Costa, R., Gomes Soares, L.F.: Composer: Authoring Tool for iTV Programs. In: Tscheligi, M., Obrist, M., Lugmayr, A. (eds.) EuroITV 2008. LNCS, vol. 5066, pp. 61–71. Springer, Heidelberg (2008). https://doi.org/10.1007/978-3-540-69478-6_7

5. Honorato, G., Barbosa, S.: NCL-inspector: towards improving NCL code. In: Proceedings of the ACM Symposium on Applied Computing, pp. 1946–1947. ACM, Sierre, Switzerland (2010) https://doi.org/10.1145/1774088.1774500
6. Pequeno, H., Gomes, G., Castro, M.: FrameIDTV: a framework for developing interactive applications on digital television environments. Int. J. Netw. Comput. Appl. **33**(9), 503–511 (2010). https://doi.org/10.1016/j.jnca.2010.01.002
7. Barboza, D., Clua, E.: Ginga Game: a framework for game development for the interactive digital television. In: Proceedings of the VIII Brazilian Symposium on Games and Digital Entertainment, pp. 162–167. IEEE Computer Society, Rio de Janeiro, Brazil (2009) https://doi.org/10.1109/SBGAMES.26
8. Segundo, R., da Silva, J., Tavares, T.: ATHUS: a generic framework for game development on Ginga middleware. In: Proceedings of Brazilian Symposium on Games and Digital Entertainment, pp. 89–96. IEEE, Florianopolis, Brazil (2010) https://doi.org/10.1109/SBGAMES.2010.28
9. Gutiérrez Duarte, S.: Guía para el desarrollo de aplicaciones interactivas en TDT para Colombia. Bdigital Repository. Universidad Nacional de Colombia, Bogota (2013)
10. Neto, S., Bezerra, P., Dias, D.: ITV-Learning: a prototype for construction of learning objects for interactive digital television. In: Proceedings of the International Conference on the Future of Education, pp. 486–490. Pixel, Florence, Italy (2012)
11. Arroyo, M., Schwartz, S., Cardozo, S., Tardivo, L.: Crea TV Digital: Composición Visual de Aplicaciones Interactivas para TV Digital. In: Proceedings of the 41st Jornadas Argentinas de Informática, pp. 305–321. SADIO, La Plata, Argentina (2012)
12. Bernal, I., Cabezas, G., Quezada, M.: Sistema de Generación de Aplicaciones Interactivas para TV Digital para la evaluación de servicios masivos. Revista Politécnica **32**(2), 11–22 (2013)
13. Oyarzo, F., Herrera, F., Casas, S.: API TVD: a wizart for interactive applications for digital TV. In: Proceedings of the XL Latin American Computer Conference, pp. 1–8. IEEE, Montevideo, Uruguay (2014)
14. De Souza, V., Galabo, A., Fernándes Pinto, R., Araujo, F., De Salles Sores, C.: Plataforma Online Orientada a Templates para a Criação de Aplicativos de Telejornalismo. In: Proceedings of JAUTI 2014, pp. 102–108. Palma de Mallorca, RedAUTI, Spain (2014)
15. Ochoa, S., Pillajo, A., Acosta, F., & Olmedo, G.: Template Generator: Software para la generación de aplicaciones interactivas para la televisión digital terrestre a partir de plantilla Ginga y LUA. In Proceedings of III Jornadas Iberoamericanas de Difusión y Capacitación obre Aplicaciones y Usabilidad de la TVDi, pp. 109–113. Palma de Mallorca, Spain (2014)
16. Miranda, M., Casas, S.: Línea de producto de software para aplicaciones interactivas de TV digital. Simposio Argentino de Ingeniería de Software (ASSE), JAIIO - Argentina, vol. 46, pp. 15–24 (2017)
17. Barbosa, S., Soares, L.: TV digital interativa no Brasil se faz com Ginga: Fundamentos, Padroes, Autoria Declarativa e Usabilidade. Em T. Kowaltowsky & K Breitman (orgs). Atualizacoes em Informátic. Rio de Janeriro, RJ. Editora PUC-Rio, pp 105–174 (2008)
18. Soares, L., Rodrigues, R., Moreno, M.: Ginga-NCL: the declarative environment of the Brazilian digital TV system. J. Braz. Comput. Soc. **12**, 37–46 (2007)
19. NCL: http://www.ncl.org.br/
20. Lutfiyya, L.: Finite and Discrete Math Problem Solver. Research & Education Association Editors (2012)

21. Sauro, J., Lewis, J.: Standardized Usability Questionnaires in Quantifying the User Experience, 2nd edn., pp. 185–248. Morgan Kaufman, San Francisco (2016)
22. Sauro, J.: Measuring Usability with the System Usability Scale (SUS). https://measuringu. com/sus/
23. Brooke, J.: SUS - A quick and dirty usability scale. In: Jordan, P.W., Thomas, B., Weerdmeester, B.A., McClelland, A.L. (eds.) Usability Evaluation in Industry, pp. 189–194. Taylor and Francis, London (1996)

Interaction Techniques, Technologies and Accessibility of IDTV Services

Interaction Models for iTV Services
for Elderly People

Daniel Carvalho[1,2(✉)] [ID], Telmo Silva[1,2] [ID], and Jorge Abreu[1,2] [ID]

[1] Communication and Arts Department, University of Aveiro, Aveiro, Portugal
{daniel.carvalh, tsilva, jfa}@ua.pt
[2] CIC.DIGITAL/Digimedia, University of Aveiro, Aveiro, Portugal

Abstract. The increase of longevity is one of the most important advances in modern societies. However, as people get older there are multiple changes that occur at physiological, social and psychological levels. On the one hand, aging can generate more opportunities to have free time to consume products or services that are informative or playful. On the other hand, it is also more likely that social and digital exclusion situations would appear. In this framework, the use of television as a device to support dedicated services has been a viable solution to overcome the referred problems because it is a close technology to the elderly population. However, in the process of developing a product or service (in this case, for television), it is necessary to consider the users' needs and expectations, being this a continuous challenge in the connection between different modes of interaction with different services. The present study will begin to explain what an interaction model is, adapting this definition later to interactive television services. Subsequently, literature on existing iTV projects and the interactions they offer (last five years) will be reviewed, providing a clear knowledge about the modalities that were used. Following the analysis, the current situation of iTV services for the elderly and their interaction paradigms will be addressed, in order to identify the most common practices on the design of interaction models for future projects in the field.

Keywords: iTV services · Elderly · Interaction models · Inclusive design

1 Introduction

With the evolution of the ICT's (information and communication technologies) the television started to offer more forms of interaction than just 'push' media and one-way mass communication [1]. Users have started to interact directly with television content, being able to control notifications that appear on the screen [2], access social networks, contact other users, or even insert text on the television screen [3]. Another example is the possibility of extending the interactive capabilities of iTV (interactive television) services by using an second screen (a tablet or smartphone) [3, 4]. Yet, user experience is not only enriched by an interactive television content, but also, pertinent to include, the interaction models provided by different iTV services. An interaction model can be defined as *"a conceptual model that represents the communication between the user and the Information System by means of a user interface"* [5], being iTV the

© Springer Nature Switzerland AG 2019
M. J. Abásolo et al. (Eds.): jAUTI 2018, CCIS 1004, pp. 89–98, 2019.
https://doi.org/10.1007/978-3-030-23862-9_7

Information System provider in this study. Regarding the communication, this is carried out by different channels of input and output, being the medium through which the information travels. The interaction is then performed when the user output is the input of the computer (in this case, of the iTV service) and vice versa [6]. However, the interaction performed in iTV systems can not only be performed in graphical interfaces, being also possible for the user to resort to other modalities such as voice, touch or even gestures. It is important to emphasize that in the human being, his input channels are vision, hearing and touch, and output is the movement of fingers or hands, voice, eyes, head, among others. Almeida [6] emphasizes the touch as the most used modality, being used normally in smartphones or tablets. Other modalities such as body gestures and eye gaze are equally important. Although, voice outputs and inputs are gaining popularity in current technologies, being the most natural interaction for the human being [6]. Taking into account these arguments and the objectives of this study, "*a conceptual model that represents the communication between the user and the iTV service by means of a set of interactive modalities*" is suggested as a definition for interaction models to interactive television services. However, although this definition emphasizes that an interaction can resort to different modalities, it does not explain what modalities to use in an iTV service. In order to meet a better design [7], the product or service should be adapted to the needs of the widest range of users as possible, i.e., to be inclusive in order to provide a good experience and a sense of belonging [8]. For the validation of this argument, the present study focuses on elderly users, being people who normally have difficulties in interacting with smart televisions, electronic program guides (EPG) or due to lack of accessibility television interfaces [9]. This is mainly due to the natural process of aging, leading to physiological, social and psychological changes [10, 11]. However, it is noteworthy that these users use television as the main means of information and entertainment [2], making viable the iTV services as a means of improving the user's quality of life. Although there is an increasing research on interactive television field, it is essential to provide a clear picture about which are the recent approaches in iTV interaction and which are their strengths and limitations, namely on elderly people. Thus, recent literature about the general existent iTV projects and the interactions they offer will be reviewed, providing a clear knowledge about the modalities that were used. Then, the iTV projects suitable for elderly people and how they fulfil users' needs will be analysed separately. In the end of the study, the actual challenges and opportunities provided by these iTV projects will be identified.

2   Method

A systematic review was carried out to analyse the different modalities existing in different iTV projects and later analysed those that are directed to elderly users. This review was based on the PRISMA Statement [12]. It was reviewed articles written in English and Portuguese that were published between 2013 and 2018 (last 5 years), which covered interactive television projects. Subsequently the results were manually filtered to find projects targeting elderly users. From the obtained data, the conditions to analyse the interaction models that were used by each iTV project were given, in order to understand the existence of possible similarities or differences in their interaction models. The research was conducted in SCOPUS and Web of Science databases using the following keywords in the search: ("interactive television" OR "itv" OR "interactive tv") AND ("app*" OR "application*" OR "project*"). In order to restrict the results according to the content of this study, specific filters of each database were also used.

Regarding the inclusion criteria, the age of the user was used as reference to the manual filtering, in order to understand which projects were developed for elderly people (ages above 60 years were selected according to the information obtained in the analysed projects). However, it is important to consider in later analysis the iTV projects in general, due to World Health Organization [13] definition of *Healthy Aging*, highlighting the diversity among people where "*Some 80-year-olds have levels of physical and mental capacity that compare favourably with 30-year-olds. Others of the same age may require extensive care and support for basic activities like dressing and eating.*". Thus, the obtained results should be analysed and take into account those that "*improve the functional ability of all older people*" [13] and that are accessible to the widest range of users. All articles that did not address iTV projects, or did not present enough data that characterize the interaction model that they have, were excluded, being pertinent to this study to identify and understand the modalities adopted.

Regarding the study selection and data extraction, the obtained results were explored through a detailed review of the articles' and conferences' titles and abstracts, enabling to exclude all documents that did not met the required criteria. It was also excluded all documents that were not available to review or were duplicated.

2.1 Results

Throughout the research, 802 potentially eligible articles were identified, of which 562 were from SCOPUS and 240 from the Web of Science (Core Collection) databases. Following a refinement by date range and subject area, it was possible to obtain 365 results from SCOPUS and 89 from Web of Science, resulting in a total of 454 potentially eligible articles. After the removal of duplicates (n = 77), of results that do not address iTV projects and that are not for review (n = 144), 233 articles were obtained. At the end of the refinement process, projects that did not have a functional iTV system (n = 174) were excluded, ending with 59 articles that identifies 49 iTV projects. The whole process of refinement of the research is illustrated in Fig. 1.

3 General Findings

The main findings and details of the 59 selected studies, which characterize 49 iTV projects, were organized by the name of each project, articles' author and year, the user's age, hardware available for interaction and the respective interactions[1].

---

[1] To consult the tables with all the obtained iTV projects, access the URL: https://zenodo.org/record/2583119.

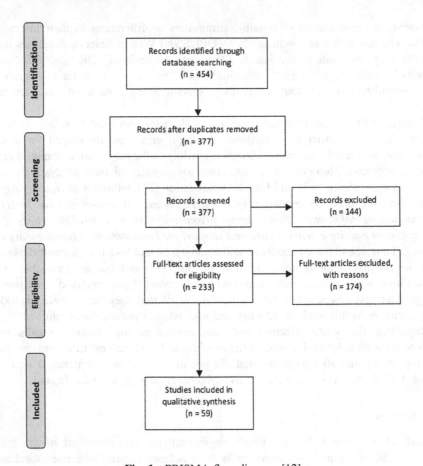

Fig. 1. PRISMA flow diagram [12].

Afterwards, all the studies that were more oriented to elderly users were selected manually, obtaining 10 iTV projects.

3.1 User's Age

From the analysed projects in general, 26 articles showed the age of the users. Regarding the different stages of age, there was a great diversity, from projects like "UltraTV"[2] [14] that was tested with users from 12 to 54 years old (and that the age contributed to the respective project to obtain different results), or the "TV DISCOVERY AND ENJOY"[3] [15] that was tested by young adults between 22 and 26 years of age. Nevertheless, from the obtained data, it was possible to observe that the average age of the users is 44.04

---

[2] More information about the "UltraTV" project: http://www.alticelabs.com/site/ultratv/.

[3] More information about the "TV DISCOVERY AND ENJOY" project:http://socialitv.web.ua.pt/index.php/projects/sponsored-projects/tv-discovery-enjoy/.

years (projects that do not address users age were excluded), being considered as middle-aged adults. Of the more oriented studies for elderly users, the first reference to this age phase was found in the "IDTV-HEALTH"[4] [16] project, identifying the users as elderly from the age of 55; And in the project "+TV4E"[5] [2] from the 60 years. However, the most referenced age among iTV projects for elderly users was 65 years (n = 5). Regarding the highest age found in user tests, it was 99 years in the "SIX" [17] project, as well as 93 years in the "IDTV-HEALTH" [16] project, and 80 years in the "Nutrition Tracker & Photo Browser" [18] and "Vital Mind"[6] [19]. Therefore, it was possible to observe that the average age of the elderly users is 66.05 years (considering only the projects where the user was considered elderly).

3.2 Hardware

It is important to consider that television was not counted as hardware to be analysed, for which it is already associated its use in the projects under study. Thus, it was analysed the hardware or devices used by the users to interact with iTV services. In most projects, the use of the smartphone or tablet (n = 35) is preferred, followed by remote control (n = 12). An example of a project that used the smartphone or tablet is the "Senior Cloud"[7] [4], a social iTV system, where the elderly users can communicate with other users who are watching the same TV content, tapping the application to navigate between content and write to other users. Regarding remote control, the "+TV4E" [2] is given as an example, being a service that provides informative content through the injection of videos in the linear transmission of television. The user, while watching certain television content, receives a notification, which can interact by clicking on the remote control buttons, having access to the additional content. However, there are some projects that have resorted to unconventional hardware for television interaction. In the project "Don't open that door"[8] [20], the user interacts with gestures with the contents of the TV show "Supernatural", using a camera setup (Kinect; n = 8). Another example is the "Bubble UI" [21] that uses a remote control (Arduino Uno microcontroller board and sensors) that controls the television contents when doing tilt, press or even puff the device. In "immersiaTV"[9] [22], the user interacts with the TV content through a Head Mounted Display (HMD; n = 2), which enables new ways of producing television content, such as immersive multi-screen tv experience or omnidirectional content viewing. In the "SIX" [17] project, a remote control with the shape of a cube and with an Inertial Motion Unit (IMU; n = 1) was created, that when turning to respective side of the cube upwards, it plays a certain function in the television.

---

[4] More information about the "IDTV-HEALTH" project: https://cicant.ulusofona.pt/noticias/idtv-health/.

[5] More information about the "+TV4E" project: http://tv4e.web.ua.pt/.

[6] More information about the "Vital Mind" project: http://dcgi.fel.cvut.cz/en/research/vital-mind-vm.

[7] More information about the "Senior Cloud" project: http://sc.cyber.t.u-tokyo.ac.jp/en/index.html.

[8] More information about the "Don't open that door" project: https://gvu.gatech.edu/research/projects/dont-open-door.

[9] More information about the "ImmersiaTV" project: http://www.immersiatv.eu/.

As a final example of the analysed projects, "Windy Sight Surfers" [23] allows to create immersive experiences by simulating the wind (n = 1) of a particular video using a "wearable" camera (GoPro Hero 2), a 360° camera for cylindrical projection (Sony Bloggie Handy Cam1) and a wind accessory (Arduino Mega ADK that controls two fans). Regarding the more oriented hardware for elderly users, the remote control (n = 7) is highlighted. In 40% of the projects, the smartphone/tablet (n = 4) was addressed. However, the use of unconventional hardware such as cameras setups (n = 2) was relatively low.

3.3   Interactions

From the analysis of the hardware, it was possible to observe some of the interactions coming from the iTV projects/services. However, it is intended in this section to present all interactions found in the analysed projects, as well as the modalities necessary to carry out the respective interactions. In Table 1 it is possible to observe the number "n" of projects that present a certain modality and the interactions that come from it, as for example, in the modality touch gesture, it is possible to identify tapping as one of the possible interactions.

Table 1. Modalities and the resulting interactions of the iTV projects from the last 5 years.

Modalities	Interactions
Visual Output (n = 49)	Graphical/Textual (n = 48) Lightning (n = 1)
Tangible (n = 3)	Vibration patterns (haptic) (n = 3)
Audio (n = 37)	Text-to-speech conversion (hearing) (n = 1) Verbal or any audio output (hearing) (n = 28) Sound/voice recognition (speech-to-text conversion) (n = 7) Non-verbal vocal interaction (NVVI) (n = 1)
Touch Gesture (n = 34)	Tapping (n = 27) Dragging (n = 4) Screen-pressing (n = 1)
Breathing (n = 1)	Puffing (n = 1)
Proprioception (n = 1)	Body perception or context awareness (n = 1)
Thermoception (n = 1)	Feeling on the skin or experience sensing (n = 1)
Gesture (n = 37)	Body movement (n = 3) Object movement/manipulation (with tilt, press, turn a specific cubes' face, etc.) (n = 5) Reactive (n = 2) Mimetic (n = 2) Head movement (n = 2) Hand movement (n = 4) Grabbing and dropping (n = 1) Sling (n = 1) Sit (n = 1) Swipe (n = 1) Pinch to zoom (n = 1) Key pressing/click (n = 14)

Concerning the obtained modalities from the studied interactions, the most used was visual output (n = 49), followed by audio (n = 37) and gesture (n = 37) and touch gesture (n = 34). The least used were tangible (n = 3), breathing (n = 1), proprioception (n = 1) and thermoception (n = 1). From the interactions inside these modalities, it stands out the use of graphics and texts for visual output interaction (n = 48), audio outputs and text-to-speech conversions for hearing (n = 29), key pressing (n = 14) and movement of objects as gesture (n = 5), and the tapping as touch gesture (n = 27). Concerning the less used interactions, there is vibration patterns from tangible interaction (n = 3), puffing modality from breathing (n = 1), body perception or context awareness from proprioception (n = 1) and experience sensing from thermoception (n = 1).

Subsequently, a second table (Table 2) was also created, where the analysed projects were manually filtered, being included only those that were oriented for elderly users.

Table 2. Modalities and the resulting interactions of the iTV projects that are more oriented for elderly users (Filtered from Table 1).

Modalities	Interactions
Visual Output (n = 9)	Graphical/Textual (n = 9)
Audio (n = 9)	Text-to-speech conversion (hearing) (n = 1)
	Verbal or any audio output (hearing) (n = 5)
	Sound/voice recognition (speech-to-text conversion) (n = 2)
	Non-verbal vocal interaction (NVVI) (n = 1)
Touch Gesture (n = 4)	Tapping (n = 4)
Gesture (n = 10)	Object movement/manipulation (with tilt, press, turn a specific cubes' face, etc.) (n = 1)
	Hand movement (n = 2)
	Key pressing/click (n = 7)

Concerning the obtained modalities from the studied interactions, the most used was gesture (n = 10), highlighting the use of physical key-pressing or button-pressing gesture (n = 7). However, the hand movement (n = 2) and manipulation or movement of objects (n = 1) were among the less commonly used interactions by the elderly users. The second most used modality was visual output (n = 9), using graphics and texts; As well as the modality associated to audio (n = 9), more specifically to its output, such as text-to-speech conversions for hearing (n = 6). However, the sound or voice recognition (n = 2) and non-verbal vocal interaction (n = 1) were the least used interactions. Regarding the least used modality, it was touch gesture (n = 4), finding the tapping interaction in 40% of the projects.

4 Discussion

This review intended to understand the different iTV projects that have been developed in the last 5 years concerning the interaction models that have been adopted, as well as which hardware used to provide the means of interaction between the user and the iTV service. It was also possible to analyse and filter data to understand the current situation of iTV services targeting elderly people. The way to differentiate projects oriented for elderly people from projects to a wider audience depended on user's age, which varied. I.e., in projects such as the "+TV4E" [2], a 60-year-old user was considered an elderly user, while in "IDTV-HEALTH" [16] was considered elderly user at 55-year-old, and in some other projects, users were considered as elders only from the age of 65. However, it was concluded that iTV projects in general are usually targeted at middle-aged adults, with a mean age of 44.04 years. Although age is a questionable variable to define when a person is elderly [13], it should be considered as an indicator in the findings of this study. This is corroborated through the differences found in the results between projects for elderly people and middle-aged adults. In general, the hardware most used for iTV projects has been television and the smartphone or tablet (second screen). Yet, in projects that are more oriented for elderly users, the remote control was more used than second screen. Derived from this change of devices in the projects for the elderly, more physical gestures, such as the push of a button, were evident, while in the projects oriented for middle-aged adults the tapping was the most used, being an interaction carried out on the touch screen of a smartphone or tablet. From the studies of Bobeth et al. [18], the use of the remote control works well for linear tasks (e.g. zapping). However, elderly users have difficulties in performing non-linear tasks when compared to younger users, being the touch screen a solution to provide a more dynamic interface according to user needs [18], as well as providing a greater variety of modalities, being able to interact with different graphics, texts, audio or touch gestures like tap, drag, press, draw or pan. Other hardware that was little used on projects for elderly users were camera setups that can track gestures. According to Bobeth et al. [18], if the system can assure accurate real-time tracking, then it may apply short point-and-click gestures (hand gestures), being also possible to add sound or visual feedback on the system. Other opportunities for interaction are the implementation of voice recognition for audio assistance; Or even apply new technologies such as HMD devices, which provide more immersive television experiences that may require gestures like body movement, making possible to *improve the functional ability of all older people*" [13]. The creation of projects together with elderly users ,also provided new opportunities to create new objects that facilitate interaction with television. For example, in the "SIX" project [17] it was developed a cube designed to work like a remote control, being customized by the user to play certain function in the television whenever it turns the respective side of the cube upwards. As it was highlighted the opportunity to implement more technological solutions found in iTV projects for middle-aged adults, the elderly user-oriented projects, present interaction solutions themselves that take into account the physical, psychological and social changes of these users, developing more inclusive iTV systems.

5   Conclusion

Despite the differences between iTV projects for elderly and middle-aged users, this inequality is what prompts to the creation of more forms of interaction to satisfy the needs of a wider spectrum of users. However, it has been shown that the projects oriented to elderly users have the potential to improve their interaction models, for example using the gestural dynamism present in the touch screen from second screens, or even use devices that can track freehand or body gestures. Other solutions covered go through the virtual reality provided by immersion in HMD devices, the use of voice recognition or the creation of new physical interactive objects. Nevertheless, it should also be highlighted that this study is limited to the interpretation of the obtained data from the selected databases, serving as a recommendation for future work the addition of more sources. It should also be considered that this review was limited between the years of 2013 and 2018, being this document useful to apply on future research on this field.

References

1. Jensen, J.F.: Interactive television - a brief media history. In: Tscheligi, M., Obrist, M., Lugmayr, A. (eds.) EuroITV 2008. LNCS, vol. 5066, pp. 1–10. Springer, Heidelberg (2008). https://doi.org/10.1007/978-3-540-69478-6_1
2. Silva, T., Abreu, J., Antunes, M., Almeida, P., Silva, V., Santinha, G.: +TV4E: interactive television as a support to push information about social services to the elderly. In: Martinho, R., et al. (ed.) Procedia Computer Science. pp. 580–585. Elsevier B.V. (2016). https://doi.org/10.1016/j.procs.2016.09.198
3. Abreu, J.F., Almeida, P., Silva, T.: iNeighbour TV: a social TV application to promote wellness of senior citizens. Inf. Syst. Technol. Enhancing Health Soc. Care **221**, 19 (2013). https://doi.org/10.4018/978-1-4666-3667-5.ch001
4. Miyazaki, M., Sano, M., Naemura, M., Sumiyoshi, H., Mitsuya, S., Fujii, A.: A social TV system for the senior community: stimulating elderly communication using information and communications technology. In: 16th International Conference on Network-Based Information Systems, pp. 422–427. IEEE (2013). https://doi.org/10.1109/nbis.2013.68
5. Valverde, F., Pastor, O., Valderas, P., Pelechano, V.: A model-driven engineering approach for defining rich internet applications: a Web 2.0 case study. IGI Global (2010). https://www.igi-global.com/chapter/model-driven-engineering-approach-defining/39163
6. de Almeida, N.F.C.: Multimodal interaction: contributions to simplify application development (2017). http://hdl.handle.net/10773/21768
7. Clarkson, J., Coleman, R., Hosking, I., Waller, S.: Inclusive Design Toolkit. Engineering Design Centre Department of Engineering, Cambridge (2007). http://www.inclusivedesigntoolkit.com/
8. Microsoft Design: Inclusive Microsoft Design (2016). https://www.microsoft.com/en-us/design/inclusive
9. Coelho, J., Rito, F., Duarte, C.: "You, me & TV" — Fighting social isolation of older adults with Facebook, TV and multimodality. Int. J. Hum. Comput. Stud. **98**, 38–50 (2017). https://doi.org/10.1016/j.ijhcs.2016.09.015
10. Paúl, C.: Envelhecimento ativo e redes de suporte social. Sociologia **15**, 275–287 (2005). http://ler.letras.up.pt/uploads/ficheiros/3732.pdf

11. Ferreira, S.: Tecnologias de informação e comunicação e o cidadão sénior: estudo sobre o impacto em variáveis psicossociais e a conceptualização de serviços com e para o cidadão sénior (Tese de doutoramento) (2013). http://ria.ua.pt/handle/10773/12336

12. Liberati, A., et al.: The PRISMA statement for reporting systematic reviews and meta-analyses of studies that evaluate health care interventions: explanation and elaboration (2009). https://doi.org/10.1371/journal.pmed.1000100

13. WHO: What is Healthy Ageing? http://www.who.int/ageing/healthy-ageing/en/

14. Almeida, P., De Abreu, J.F., Fernandes, S., Oliveira, E.: Content unification in TV to enhance user experience: the ultra TV project. In: TVX 2018 - Proceedings of the 2018 ACM International Conference on Interactive Experiences for TV and Online Video, pp. 167–172. Association for Computing Machinery, Inc. (2018). https://doi.org/10.1145/3210825.3213558

15. Abreu, J., Almeida, P., Teles, B.: TV discovery & enjoy: a new approach to help users finding the right TV program to watch. In: Proceedings of the 2014 ACM International Conference on Interactive Experiences for TV and Online Video - TVX 2014, pp. 63–70. ACM Press, New York (2014). https://doi.org/10.1145/2602299.2602313

16. Baptista, A., Sequeira, Á.D., Veríssimo, I., Quico, C., Cardoso, M., Damásio, M.J.: Using digital interactive television to promote healthcare and wellness inclusive services. In: Duffy, Vincent G. (ed.) DHM 2013. LNCS, vol. 8025, pp. 150–156. Springer, Heidelberg (2013). https://doi.org/10.1007/978-3-642-39173-6_18

17. Oliveira, A.P., Vairinhos, M., Mealha, Ó.: Proposal of a tangible interface to enhance seniors' TV experience: UX evaluation of SIX. Commun. Comput. Inf. Sci. 813, 135–149 (2018). https://doi.org/10.1007/978-3-319-90170-1_10

18. Bobeth, J., et al.: Tablet, gestures, remote control? Influence of age on performance and user experience with iTV applocations. In: TVX 2014 - Proceedings of the 2014 ACM International Conference on Interactive Experiences for TV and Online Video, pp. 139–146. Association for Computing Machinery, Newcastle Upon Tyne (2014). https://doi.org/10.1145/2602299.2602315

19. Miotto, A., Lessiter, J., Freeman, J., Carmichael, R., Ferrari, E.: Cognitive training via interactive television: drivers, barriers and potential users. Univers. Access Inf. Soc. 12, 37–54 (2013). https://doi.org/10.1007/s10209-011-0264-6

20. Clifton, P., et al.: Don't open that door: designing gestural interactions for interactive narratives. In: TEI 2013 - Proceedings of the 7th International Conference on Tangible, Embedded and Embodied Interaction, Barcelona, pp. 259–266 (2013). https://doi.org/10.1145/2460625.2460668

21. Bernhaupt, R., Desnos, A., Pirker, M., Schwaiger, D.: TV interaction beyond the button press. In: Abascal, J., Barbosa, S., Fetter, M., Gross, T., Palanque, P., Winckler, M. (eds.) INTERACT 2015. LNCS, vol. 9297, pp. 412–419. Springer, Cham (2015). https://doi.org/10.1007/978-3-319-22668-2_31

22. Gómez, D., Núñez, J.A., Montagud, M., Fernández, S.: ImmersiaTV: enabling customizable and immersive multi-screen TV experiences. In: Proceedings of the 9th ACM Multimedia Systems Conference, MMSys 2018. pp. 506–508. Association for Computing Machinery, Inc. (2018). https://doi.org/10.1145/3204949.3209620

23. Ramalho, J., Chambel, T.: Windy sight surfers: sensing and awareness of 360° immersive videos on the move. In: Proceedings of the 11th European Conference on Interactive TV and Video, EuroITV 2013, pp. 107–115. Como (2013). https://doi.org/10.1145/2465958.2465969

IOM4TV: An AT-Based Solution for People with Motor Disabilities Supported in iTV

Rafael Cardoso[1,2(✉)] , Andréia Rodrigues[1,2] , Matheus Coelho[2] ,
Tatiana Tavares[1] , Rita Oliveira[3] , and Telmo Silva[3]

[1] Technological Development Center (CDTec), Federal University of Pelotas (UFPel),
Pelotas, RS, Brazil
{rc.cardoso,andreia.sias,tatiana}@inf.ufpel.edu.br
[2] WeTech, Federal Institute Sul-Rio-grandense (IFSul), Pelotas, RS, Brazil
{rafaelcardoso,andreiasias}@pelotas.ifsul.edu.br,
matheusbarcelos.c@gmail.com
[3] Digimedia, Department of Communication and Arts (DECA),
University of Aveiro, Aveiro, Portugal
{ritaoliveira,tsilva}@ua.pt
http://wp.ufpel.edu.br/nulab/cdtec/ciencia-da-computacao/
http://www.ifsul.edu.br
http://digimedia.web.ua.pt

Abstract. One of the most common electronic devices available in homes around the world is the TV. Its high utilization rate in domestic environments opens a series of possibilities to meet the most varied needs of its viewers. In this context, projects developed for specific audiences can take advantage of the opportunities offered by TV. +TV4E is a solution designed for the elderly, which aims to provide their inclusion by displaying informative contents on topics of their interest. Applications such as this are very relevant because they directly affect a considerable portion of the world's population. However, many of the features available in applications such as the +TV4E are inaccessible to people with physical disabilities since the main features available must be accessed through conventional remotes. New forms of interaction, based on the principles of Assistive Technology (AT), aim to enable people with physical disabilities to perform daily tasks in a more autonomous way. An example of an AT-based initiative is the IOM (Mouse-Eye Interface) project, which focuses on developing a device that functions as an alternative form of computer interaction, designed for people with motor disabilities in the upper limbs. In this context, this paper introduces IOM4TV, a software prototype that allows its users to control the +TV4E application through the IOM device. The article presents the proposed architecture, highlighting the main steps involved during the development of the solution. The paper also highlights the results obtained with the first round of prototype testing using two evaluation tools: SAM and AttrakDiff.

Keywords: Assistive technology · Interactive television systems ·
People with disabilities · Alternative forms of interaction · Prototype

© Springer Nature Switzerland AG 2019
M. J. Abásolo et al. (Eds.): jAUTI 2018, CCIS 1004, pp. 99–114, 2019.
https://doi.org/10.1007/978-3-030-23862-9_8

1   Introduction

The TV set is one of the most commonly found home appliances in the homes around the world. This high availability facilitates its use for several purposes, in addition to its original application [1]. Combined to this, the quality of audio and video provided by digital TV and the new types of experience that interactive TV (iTV) can provide, considerably expand the universe of applications that can be created for TVs. An example of this kind of application is the +TV4E project, which aims to use TV as a channel for the diffusion of content related to public and social services customized for the elderly, intercalating these contents with ordinary TV programming [2].

However, despite the fact that these iTV applications reach a considerable part of the population, the use of conventional remote controls as the only form of user interaction makes it difficult, or even impossible, to use such applications by specific audiences, such as people with motor disabilities. In the world, it is estimated that about one billion people suffer from some form of physical disability. Particularly in Brazil, according to the 2010 census, 23.9% of the population declared some kind of physical limitation. Of this total, 7% of people reported specifically some kind of motor disability [3].

Assistive Technology (AT) is the research area dedicated to proposing and developing devices, tools or services that improve the quality of life and increase the autonomy of people with physical limitations due to birth problems, degenerative diseases or even accidents during their lives [4]. An example of a solution that uses AT concepts is the IOM project (acronym for Interface Óculos-Mouse, in Portuguese). The work developed in the project is specifically focused on people with motor limitations, consisting of the design of a wearable device, which allows simulating the movements and clicks of the mouse, from the movement of the head [5].

This paper describes the development of IOM4TV, a solution that uses the IOM device as an alternate form of interaction to control an iTV application. The IOM4TV is designed in such a way that it is possible for a user with motor disabilities to use the IOM to control the +TV4E application, by sending commands through head movements. The article is organized as follows: Section 2 presents the theoretical background necessary to understand the concepts used in the work. Section 3 details the design and development process of the proposed solution. Section 4 presents the tests performed to evaluate the developed prototype. In Sect. 5, the results achieved are discussed. Finally, Sect. 6 highlights the main conclusions, as well as indicating the next steps of the research project in which this work is inserted.

2   Theoretical Background

This section describes the essential concepts of the areas of research involved in the work, highlighting the projects that will be integrated and the main components involved in the proposed solution.

2.1   Assistive Technology (AT)

According to the World Health Organization report, today, more than one billion people have some physical disability worldwide. This large contingent of people produces a growing need for products and services to reduce, or even eliminate, the difficulties encountered by these people to perform basic tasks in their daily lives [6]. The area of research that is concerned with the design and development of solutions that allow this target audience to perform from basic daily tasks such as eating, communicating or moving, for example, to perform more complex activities in a way more autonomous and independent is called Assistive Technology (AT).

The term AT is relatively new, a definition that is still in the process of building and maturing. However, the use of AT resources is not recent, since it refers back to the beginnings of human history. At that time, the adoption of mechanisms to aid the daily life of people could already be observed in the use of primitive artifacts, such as a stick, used to function as a walking stick, for example. However, the emerging concern with AT issues in part must be credited to the more contemporary thoughts, which focus on the inclusion of all individuals in a society where everyone has the right to participate actively in it.

As stated by [7], AT is a generic expression that covers products, technologies and services used to increase the independence and participation of this public in society. There are several classifications that can be used to categorize AT [8]. One of these categories considers the cost and functioning of the resources adopted, dividing them into three levels:

1. Low-level AT: simple, non-electric and low-cost devices;
2. Medium-level AT: electrical devices, but without computational resources;
3. High-level AT: solutions that use specific software and/or hardware.

Figure 1 shows examples of some types of AT, grouped according to the three highlighted levels. The use of High-Level AT, specifically, may gather several fields of study, depending on the application requirements. Progress in research lines such as Universal Accessibility (UA), Decision Support Systems (DSS), Ambient Assisted Living (ALL) and Human Computer Interaction (IHC) enable a new generation of AT to emerge to improve the lives of people with disabilities [9].

In this sense, a systematic mapping of literature (SML) performed previously, allowed to find several works related to high level TA. These projects have been developed to soften or even solve specific problems faced by groups of people (or individuals) with physical and/or cognitive limitations. Different strategies and methods are used to design assistive solutions under different contexts. Projects such as [10–12], for example, invest in the development of AT games for entertainment or inclusion of their users. Other solutions allow the control of smart homes for people with disabilities [13,14]. There are also projects that define frameworks, services or software libraries aimed at simplifying the design of AT solutions [15–17]. Finally, there is a range of works focusing on providing access

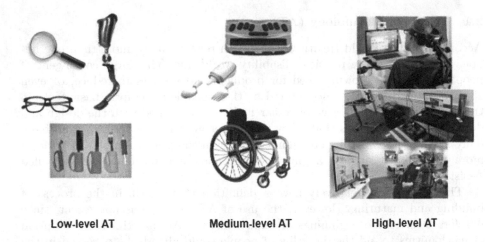

Low-level AT   **Medium-level AT**   **High-level AT**

Fig. 1. Examples of AT, grouped according to their level.

to resources primarily inaccessible to this considerable portion of the population, such as computer access [18–21].

In this last context of AT solutions related to computer access, the IOM device was created as a form of alternative interaction to allow control of computers through head movements of its users. Its primary goal is to be a low-cost option to enable people with motor disabilities in the upper limbs to interact with applications on computers in a simplified and independent way. The current version of the IOM consists of a spectacle frame with built-in sensors. The IOM uses the accelerometer sensor to capture the movement performed by its user. Figure 2 highlights the major elements of IOM version 1.0.

Fig. 2. IOM device and its main components.

The captured data is used as input, then sent through a serial connection, and finally translated into cursor movements on the computer screen. The interpretation and translation of the data is based on an internal communication protocol. This is necessary for the data exchanged to be properly understood and addressed on both sides of the communication.

To trigger click events, version 1.0 of the IOM adopts the Dwell Time technique, that is, clicks are simulated when the IOM device remains stationary for a preconfigured period of time. The gadget is accompanied by a setup application, which allows the customization of some parameters for use of the device.

2.2   Interactive TV

According to [22], interactive TV (iTV) is composed of two fundamental concepts: TV and interactivity. In this sense, conventional TV has spectators of what is being presented and not users, since there is no interaction happening between these two actors in fact. The non-participatory format is dependent on the content model, where there is advertising, cinema or pivots that serve as an intermediary of the interaction with the audience [22,23].

In turn, the concept of interactivity has two elements involved: the form of communication and the media environment adopted. The conjunction of interaction with TV, allows the content to be distributed according to the specific habits of the users, providing a more appropriate experience of use.

The +TV4E platform was conceived from the perspective just addressed, i.e making its target audience (seniors) users, not just passive viewers [24]. The idea is to provide the elderly with a simplified way to access information about public and social services, intending to make them more independent. The main focus is to provide and present informative content that facilitates access to relevant information in the context of users while watching TV. The main components involved in the operation of +TV4E are highlighted in Fig. 3.

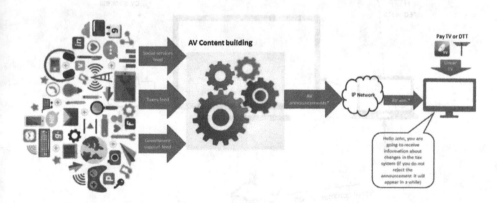

Fig. 3. General architecture of the +TV4E project. Source [24]

In order for the user to not miss any TV shows in progress, the +TV4E application pauses the broadcasting program, allowing users to watch the suggested video and then return to the TV program from the point where it was stopped. The platform also features a library that gathers the videos sent to users so they can be viewed later, as well as having an own recommendation system that selects the content that will be suggested according to users' specific profiles.

3   IOM4TV

This article details the design of IOM4TV, a software solution designed to integrate the +TV4E and IOM projects. The main goal is to use the IOM device as an alternate form of interaction to control the +TV4E system. To begin this development, the components involved in the solution were enumerated:

1. **TV set:** main interaction device for the user, responsible for displaying the contents presented by the iTV application;
2. **Set-top box (STB):** Equipment that connects to the TV with an external signal source and transforms it into content in a format that can be displayed on the TV screen. On +TV4E, the application runs on Android STB;
3. **IOM:** Alternative interaction device based on head movements;
4. **Execution Container:** Computer used to connect to the IOM and translate the head movements in cursor movement.

From the specification of these components, a high-level architecture was elaborated, which is highlighted in Fig. 4.

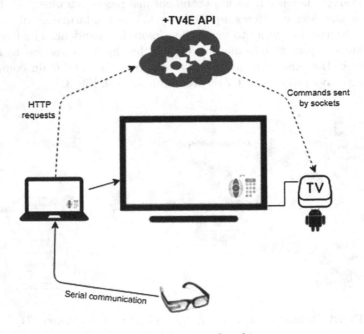

Fig. 4. IOM4TV's general architecture.

In addition to the previously listed elements, two software components have been created and are present in the architecture. They are responsible for allowing communication between all the devices involved in the interaction process:

1. +TV4E Integration Web Service (WS);
2. Interfaces for interaction via IOM device.

The general functionality of both software components are detailed in the following sections.

3.1   +TV4E Integration Web Service

To allow communication between the +TV4E's iTV system and the IOM device control interface, it was designed an intermediate layer of software. It functions as a facade that receives data from the interface, and translates it to commands on the iTV system. This software consists of a WS that receives HTTP (HyperText Transfer Protocol) POST calls and triggers instructions that are executed in the STB. To work correctly, two information must be passed in the HTTP request:

1. The STB unique identifier;
2. A numerical key that indicates which function should be triggered in the STB.

In the prototype interfaces developed in this work, the STB identifier is passed as part of the URL. The numeric key, which identifies the action to be performed, is passed as a parameter in the POST request. The values that can be assumed by this numerical parameter are summarized in Table 1.

Table 1. Actions and their corresponding numeric keys in the communication protocol.

Action	Numeric key
Go to next channel	40
Go to previous channel	38
Keys 1, 2, 3, 4, 5, 6, 7, 8, 9	49, 50, 51, 52, 53, 54, 55, 56, 57
Open or close library	48
OK command	13
Browse library to the left	37
Browse library to the right	39
Upload video	8

Through this protocol, as soon as it receives an HTTP request, WS identifies the requested command and establishes a connection, via Sockets, with the required STB. This command is then sent and then executed in the iTV application. Figure 5 highlights an example of an HTTP POST call that is mounted by the interface and sent for processing by the WS.

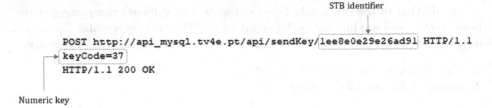

STB identifier

```
POST http://api_mysql.tv4e.pt/api/sendKey/1ee8e0e29e26ad91 HTTP/1.1
keyCode=37
HTTP/1.1 200 OK
```

Numeric key

Fig. 5. Example of HTTP request sent to the WS.

3.2   Interfaces for Interaction via IOM

To enable the IOM device to send commands to the WS two specific interfaces to perform the user interaction were designed. Different usage approaches were adopted at each of these interfaces. The particular features of both applications are highlighted in the following sections.

Prototype Based on IOM's Standard Operation. The interaction method used in the first developed interface was based on the IOM's standard operating approach. According to this method, the device simulates a mouse capturing the movement performed by the head to move the cursor on the screen and performing clicks using the Dwell time technique.

Considering such characteristics, a specific Graphical User Interface (GUI) was developed to promote the interaction between IOM users and the iTV application. This interface is highlighted in Fig. 6.

Fig. 6. Interface of the first prototype IOM4TV.

In this version, the user traverses the interface using the cursor (similar to the operation of the mouse) performing continuous movements of the head. When the user stops moving the cursor in a position for a time (preconfigured in the application) somewhere in the interface, the click action is triggered at the specific area where the cursor is.

When the click occurs on an interface button, the function responsible for assembling the HTTP request is triggered. This function sets up the HTTP request with the appropriate data (STB identifier and numeric key) to be executed, and then the HTTP request is sent to the +TV4E WS to perform its function. As soon as it receives this call, the WS communicates with the STB, executing the operation requested by the user. This interface has been developed as a Web tool, using HTML/CSS languages for its development, and AJAX for triggering HTTP requests to the WS.

Prototype Based on Interaction Through Events. The development of the first interface motivated the development an alternative form of interaction. The idea is to detect specific motion events with the IOM, to simplify application usage and reduce and discomfort that some users might feel due to an excessive amount of movement to navigate through the interface.

To achieve this goal, the IOM firmware has been adapted to allow its use through motion events. Initially, four motion possibilities were added to the IOM firmware: up, down, left, or right. From this firmware change, a second interface was developed using classes of listeners waiting for the occurrence of the predefined events to trigger the desired responses. This application is still in the early stages of design, having been developed in the Java programming language. Figure 7 highlights its primary interface.

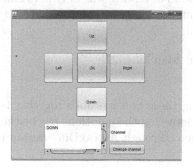

Fig. 7. Interface of the prototype based on events.

The limited number of monitored events, motivated the specification of a protocol to define the functions of each of the movements and, therefore, the interaction with this interface. The actions related to each event have been defined and are summarized in Table 2.

In this interface, the movement process that allows the user to cross the interface was simplified to use the commands presented in Table 2. For example, assuming that the "OK" button in the interface is what is initially selected, the user moves the head to the right, the focus will move to the next available button in this direction. The same happens when the user moves the head to the left,

Table 2. Relationship between events and actions performed on the application.

Events	Action
Move head to the left	Go to the left in the interface
Move head to the right	Go to the left in the interface
Move head down	Performs selected button action

causing the selection focus to move to the left side. This way of moving allows the user to move around the proposed interface in a relatively simple way.

Once the user has focused the desired button, the upside-down movement triggers the action related to the button. It is worth mentioning that the event-driven feature has been integrated into the interface, to work in conjunction with the modified firmware. However, nothing prevents future events from being programmed to call another function directly, such as channel switching.

4   IOM4TV Evaluation

To evaluate the IOM4TV properly, a controlled environment was organized. This environment was composed of all elements described in the proposed high level architecture, as highlighted in Fig. 4. Because the event interface is still in development, this first round of testing was only performed on the web interface. In order to evaluate the interaction process of IOM4TV in a qualitative approach, two techniques were used:

1. SAM (Self-Assessment Manikin) [27];
2. AttrakDiff [28].

The objective of using these two methods together is to achieve a complete evaluation of IOM4TV, detecting the emotions felt by the users (via SAM), evaluating the user experience (through AttrakDiff) during the use of the solution.

4.1   Materials

To perform the tests, an environment similar to that highlighted in Fig. 4 has been reproduced. The following components were used to create the test scenario:

1. a 32-in. smart TV device, $1920 \times 1080\,$p resolution, $60\,$Hz frequency, with 2 HDMI inputs;
2. a STB, Android version 6.0.1;
3. an IOM device, version 1.0;
4. computer with Intel Core i7 $1.8\,$GHz processor, and $8\,$GB DDR4 memory

These elements were interconnected and configured according to the layout highlighted in Sect. 3.

4.2   Participants

The test involved five end users over 60, (3) women and (2) men. This number of users, selected to test the application, is supported by the theory that states the best results come from testing no more than 5 users, running as many small tests as possible [29]. All testers reported using the computer daily, interacting with it through conventional interaction devices such as mouse and keyboard. None of the users had physical motor disabilities in the upper limbs. Another relevant fact is that none of them had used IOM4TV or even IOM previously. Before starting the test itself, the research project was explained, and the elements involved in the interaction were detailed. Before testing IOM4TV, each user performed a quick training with the IOM device. The goal was to familiarize users with the way the device works. Thus, for about 5 min each user was asked to execute the Fitts Law protocol using the IOM [30].

After this warm-up, the participants followed a roadmap of activities that should be carried out at the interface. This script was composed of simple tasks, such as channel changes and access to videos in the +TV4E library. All inter-actions were performed through the IOM device. After executing the activities, each user filled out the SAM and AttrakDiff questionnaires.

4.3   Emotional Evaluation Using SAM

In the context of this research, SAM was chosen because this self-assessment tool can evaluate areas that directly correspond to the domains of the Semantic Emotional Space Structure defined by [31]. This type of evaluation scale is composed of three sets of pictographs representing the domains of Valencia (satisfied - unsatisfied), Excitation (motivated - relaxed) and Control Feeling control (completely in control - out of control) [32]. Each domain is represented by a range of values, ranging from 1–9. The user is instructed to choose one of the five pictographs or intermediary between the two - which best represents their emotional state, concerning the domain evaluated. The values of the selected circles are checked to get the result - the domain is evaluated as positive for values between 1 and 4; the domain is evaluated as negative for values between 6 and 9; and value 5 evaluates the domain as neutral.

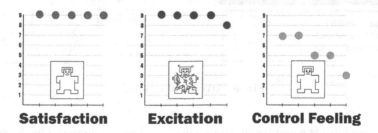

Fig. 8. SAM results.

When performing the self-assessment tool, the participants reported that they were completely Satisfied (all selected maximum level of satisfaction), Fully Motivated (4 participants answered maximum level) and concerning the differentiated interaction, reported that they were not in control of the situation as shown in Fig. 8. The elderly mentioned that since they had never used another device for computer interaction other than keyboard and mouse, and remote control for the TV, they would need more time to use the IOM so they could be more autonomous when interacting with it.

4.4   AttrakDiff Evaluation

AttrakDiff is an instrument to measure the attractiveness of interactive products and their relationship to the user experience. It uses pairs of opposing adjectives so that potential users can identify their perception of the solution that has been analyzed. The AttrakDiff questionnaire filled out by users generated a set of data, highlighted in Fig. 9.

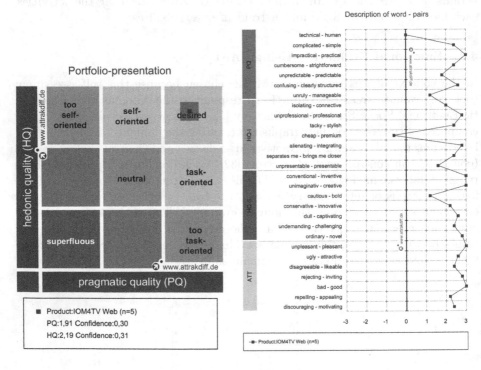

Fig. 9. AttrakDiff results.

Two axes form the first result graph (in the left side) generated by AttrakDiff. The vertical axis represents the Hedonic Quality (HQ), while the horizontal axis represents the Pragmatic Quality (PQ). Depending on the values, the solution is framed in one or more defined quadrants: too self-oriented, self-oriented, desired, neutral, task-oriented, superfluous and too task-oriented. On the other hand, the confidence rectangle represents the accuracy of the results. Thus, the smaller its size, the higher the reliability of the results obtained.

The PQ and HQ obtained in this evaluation were 1.91 and 2.19, respectively. Observing the relationship between the dimensions of HQ and QP, it is possible to note that the confidence rectangle is located in the "desired" quadrant. These data indicate that IOM4TV was entirely satisfactory for users who tested it. It was considered a product with desirable characteristics, not limited by its functional properties. IOM4TV also presented very satisfying HQ values.

Regarding the chart that describes the opposite keywords (right side), the exception with the cheap-premium pair, all other words were evaluated positively. This pair probably obtained this result due to the difficulty of users in monetizing the final value of the proposed solution, since it involves a series of technologies that may present an unknown cost. These data allow us to realize that the solution was well evaluated end-user perspective, emphasizing desirable characteristics like practical, inventive, creative pleasant and good, in the criteria related to the attractiveness of the application.

5 Discussion

The project follows the steps proposed by [25], trying to identify characteristics and recurring needs in different applications. Thus, in addition to IOM4TV, other initiatives have already been developed using IOM as the primary interaction object [10, 26].

Currently, the event-driven IOM4TV prototype is in development phase. The operation by events, although still at this stage of development, has been presented as a very relevant contribution, since once it is implemented, it will open up a range of possibilities for the development of applications that use this behavior. This functionality still lacks testing and evaluation with end users, which could not be achieved in this article. The web interface is more mature, having already been subjected to a round of functional tests with end users, as described in the previous section. These evaluations made it possible to verify that the solution had a very positive acceptance by the users.

Another relevant point was the development of interaction interfaces using different technologies: one based on Web technologies; and the second use object-oriented programming. This reinforces the understanding that a possible software framework should be developed regardless of the technology used in the final implementation.

The adoption of intermediate interfaces between the end user and the iTV application has proved to be an appropriate strategy in terms of interaction as it provides visual feedback to IOM4TV users. The use of a WS to integrate interfaces with the iTV application was quite effective. However, it should be taken into account that the tests were performed in controlled environments. Factors such as possible unavailability or poor quality of Internet connection can directly affect the functionality of the solution.

And although the tests revealed that the elderly evaluated as satisfactory and felt motivated to interact with the IOM4TV, they still expressed that they would need a longer time of interaction with this new device. And considering that the goal is also to be an AT, a relevant topic will be to carry out a new round of evaluation with the same participants so that we can analyze the learning curve.

6   Conclusion and Future Work

This work presented IOM4TV, a software solution to control +TV4E's interactive TV application, through the IOM interaction device. To achieve this goal, two main software components were developed: an integration WS; and two interaction interfaces to allow users to control the iTV system through the IOM.

The first interface was based on the IOM's default behavior. It was developed using web technologies and was tested with the target audience of the +TV4E project, the elderly. The evaluations of this application were very positive, both in the SAM method and in the AttrakDiff tool. During the tests, however, points were noticed that deserve attention and improvements, specifically in the behavior of the IOM device as a means of interaction with the system.

The second interface uses an approach based on response to events. Although it has not been tested with end users (because it is an unfinished application), development tests have shown that the interaction approach through events is quite promising, since it seems to simplify the interaction process. Thus, this new form of interaction can be considered a very interesting result of this work, and it will undoubtedly be incorporated as new functionality in the IOM software. It is worth noting that IOM4TV is another solution that is part of the set of applications developed in the context of the design project of a framework for AT solutions aimed at users with motor restrictions.

For the sequence of this work, it is expected to run another series of functional testing of the application with its target audience. Also, if possible, we will try to apply these tests to people with physical disabilities in the upper limbs, in addition to the elderly, to obtain feedback from these users as well. Also, in this second round, we expect to apply the tests to both interfaces, so that the two modes of operation can be evaluated and compared. The main idea is to combine the results of both approaches to obtain a more accurate assessment of both the IOM4TV and the IOM device in terms of attractiveness and usability.

References

1. Silva, T., Hernández, L., Caravau, C.: Building informative audio-visual content automatically: a process to define the key aspects. In: Ferraz de Abreu, J., Guerrero, M.J.A., Almeida, P., Silva, T. (eds.) Proceedings of the 6th Iberoamerican Conference on Applications and Usability of Interactive TV - jAUTI, pp. 132–143. University of Aveiro, Aveiro, Portugal (2017)
2. Silva, C.J.H.: Automatic generation of audiovisual informational content for seniors. Geração automática de conteúdo audiovisual informativo para seniores (Masters dissertation), Universidade de Aveiro, Aveiro, Portugal (2017)

3. IBGE, Instituto Brasileiro de Geografia e Estatística: Demographic Census. Censo Demográfico (2010). http://www.ibge.gov.br/home/estatistica/populacao/censo2010. Accessed 02 Feb 2017
4. Disability Rights Network of Pennsylvania Page: Assistive Technology for Persons With Disabilities, An Overview. http://www.disabilityrightspa.org/File/publications/assistive-technology-for-persons-with-disabilities---an-overview.pdf. Accessed 13 Mar 2017
5. Machado, M., Colares, A., Quadros, C., Carvalho, F., Sampaio, A.: Óculos Mouse: Mouse Controlled by movements of the user's head. Óculos Mouse: Mouse Controlado pelos movimentos da cabeça do usuário. Brazilian Patent INPI number PI10038213 (2010)
6. World Health Organization: World Report on Disability. https://www.who.int/disabilities/world_report/2011/report.pdf. Accessed 06 Feb 2019
7. Hersh, M.A.: The design and evaluation of assistive technology products and devices Part 1: Design. In: Blouin, M., Stone, J. (eds.) International Encyclopedia of Rehabilitation [online]. CIRRIE (2010)
8. Lauand, G.: Sources of information on assistive technology to promote inclusion of students with physical and multiple disabilities. Fontes de informação sobre tecnologia assistiva para favorecer a inclusão escolar de alunos com deficiências físicas e múltiplas. (Doctoral Thesis on Special Education), Universidade Federal de São Carlos, São Carlos-SP, Brasil (2005)
9. Alonso, E.C.: Some Contributions to Smart Assistive Technologies. (Doctoral Thesis), Universidade do Pais Basco (2015)
10. Cardoso, R., et al.: Sweet labyrinth: Game experience using interaction based on head-movements and tangible resources. Doce labirinto: Experiência de jogo utilizando interação baseada em movimentos da cabeça e recursos tangíveis (2016). XV Simpósio Brasileiro de Jogos e Entretenimento Digital (SBGames)
11. Ossmann, R., Thaller, D., Nussbaum, G., Veigl, C., Weiß, C.: Making the PlayStation 3 accessible with AsTeRICS. In: Miesenberger, K., Karshmer, A., Penaz, P., Zagler, W. (eds.) ICCHP 2012. LNCS, vol. 7382, pp. 443–450. Springer, Heidelberg (2012). https://doi.org/10.1007/978-3-642-31522-0_67
12. Lin, Y., Breugelmans, J., Iversen, M., Schmidt, D.: An Adaptive Interface Design (AID) for enhanced computer accessibility and rehabilitation. Int. J. Hum. Comput. Stud. 98, 14–23 (2017)
13. Paul, B., Marcombes, S., David, A., Struijk, L., Le Moullec, Y.: A context-aware user interface for wireless personal-area network assistive environments. Wirel. Pers. Commun. 69, 427–447 (2013)
14. Tripathy, D., Raheja, J.: Design and implementation of brain computer interface based robot motion control. FICTA 2, 289–296 (2014)
15. Ossmann, R., et al.: AsTeRICS, a flexible AT construction set. Int. J. Adapt. Control Signal Process. 28, 1475–1503 (2014)
16. Miesenberger, K., et al.: ATLab: an app-framework for physical disabilities. J. Technol. Persons Disabil. 1, 46–56 (2014)
17. Aced Lopez, S., Corno, F., De Russis, L.: Gnomon: Enabling dynamic one-switch games for children with severe motor disabilities. In: Proceedings of the 33rd Annual ACM Conference Extended Abstracts on Human Factors in Computing Systems, 995–1000. ACM (2015)

18. Antunes, R., Palma, L., Coito, F., Duarteramos, H., Gil, P.: Intelligent human-computer interface for improving pointing device usability and performance. In: 12th IEEE International Conference on Control and Automation (ICCA), pp. 714–719. IEEE (2016)

19. Mulfari, D., Celesti, A., Fazio, M., Villari, M.: Human-computer interface based on IoT embedded systems for users with disabilities. In: Giaffreda, R., et al. (eds.) IoT360 2014. LNICST, vol. 150, pp. 376–383. Springer, Cham (2015). https://doi.org/10.1007/978-3-319-19656-5_50

20. Karpov, A., Ronzhin, A.: A universal assistive technology with multimodal input and multimedia output interfaces. In: Stephanidis, C., Antona, M. (eds.) UAHCI 2014. LNCS, vol. 8513, pp. 369–378. Springer, Cham (2014). https://doi.org/10.1007/978-3-319-07437-5_35

21. Cruz, A.J.O., et al.: New solutions for old problems: use of interfaces human/computer to assist people with visual and/or motor impairment in the use of DOSVOX and microFênix. In: Rocha, A., Correia, A.M., Costanzo, S., Reis, L.P. (eds.) New Contributions in Information Systems and Technologies. AISC, vol. 353, pp. 1073–1079. Springer, Cham (2015). https://doi.org/10.1007/978-3-319-16486-1_106

22. Silva, T.: Identification of senior users on interactive television. Identificação de utilizadores seniores em televisão interativa. (Doctoral Thesis), Universidade de Aveiro (2014)

23. Soto, N., Ali-Hasan, B.: 8 Things to consider when designing interactive TV experiences. In: TVX 2015 - ACM International Conference on Interactive Experiences for Television and Online Video, pp. 1–2. ACM, New York, Brussells (2015)

24. Silva, T., Abreu, J., Antunes, M., Almeida, P., Silva, V., Santinha, G.: +TV4E: Interactive Television as a support to push information about social services to the elderly. Procedia Comput. Sci. **100**, 580–585 (2016)

25. Roberts, D., Johnson, R.: Evolving frameworks: a pattern language for developing object-oriented frameworks. Pattern Lang. Program Design **3**, 471–486 (1996)

26. Peroba, J., et al.: An IoT application for Home Control focused on Assistive Technology. In: Anais Estendidos do XXIII Simpósio Brasileiro de Sistemas Multimídia e Web, Webmedia 2017 pp. 119–122. SBC, Gramado (2017)

27. Bradley, M., Lang, P.: Measuring emotion: the self-assessment manikin and the semantic differential. J. Behav. Ther. Exp. Psychiatry **25**(1), 49–59 (1994)

28. Hassenzahl, M., Burmester, M., Koller, F.: AttrakDiff: A questionnaire to measure perceived hedonic and pragmatic quality. AttrakDiff: Ein Fragebogen zur Messung wahrgenommener hedonischer und pragmatischer Qualität. In: Mensch computer, pp. 187–196 (2003)

29. Nielsen, J., Landauer, T.: A mathematical model of the finding of usability problems. In: Proceedings of the INTERACT 1993 and CHI 1993 Conference on Human Factors in Computing Systems, pp. 206–213. ACM (1993)

30. MacKenzie, I.S.: Fitts' law as a research and design tool in human-computer interaction. Hum. Comput. Interact. **7**(1), 91–139 (1992)

31. Scherer, K.R.: The nature and dynamics of relevance and valence appraisals: theoretical advances and recent evidence. Emotion Rev. **5**(2), 150–162 (2013)

32. Mahlke, S., Minge, M.: Consideration of multiple components of emotions in human-technology interaction. In: Peter, C., Beale, R. (eds.) Affect and Emotion in Human-Computer Interaction. LNCS, vol. 4868, pp. 51–62. Springer, Heidelberg (2008). https://doi.org/10.1007/978-3-540-85099-1_5

A Review of Voice User Interfaces
for Interactive TV

Sílvia Fernandes(✉) ⬤, Jorge Abreu ⬤, Pedro Almeida ⬤,
and Rita Santos ⬤

Department of Communication and Art, University of Aveiro,
3810-193 Aveiro, Portugal
{silvia.fernandes, jfa, almeida, rita.santos}@ua.pt

Abstract. The design of interaction models for Voice User Interfaces is changing. The increasing number of home assistants, mobile devices and televisions supporting natural language interaction that are transforming and introducing voice interaction in multiple home scenarios is leading to important changes in the design of its interaction models. In the TV context, voice interaction is being introduced with multimodal interaction, supported on graphical interfaces or voice-first devices.

By compiling voice interaction best practices and guidelines of a significant range of voice user interfaces for the television context and analyzing commercial solutions, this paper presents an analysis of leading-edge use cases and trends. It also examines the applicability of various user input approaches, the integration of visual signifiers and elements, and how the user experience changes due to those variations. Combined with interactive television trends, use cases are analyzed on how they take the user's context and habits as personalization tools in the television experience. The analysis reported in this paper can support the development of advanced interfaces for natural language interaction solutions based on set-top boxes of Pay-TV operators.

Keywords: Voice user interfaces · Natural language interaction · Television · Conversational interface

1 Introduction

As the main communication method used amongst humans, voice – and the dialogue it supports – is a mean capable of quickly and clearly expressing feelings and desires [1]. While the technology for voice interaction between user and machine is still being improved, progress and advances in this area are becoming faster than ever [2], with the human language itself becoming a new User Interface (UI) layer [3]. Voice interaction occurs on what can be defined as voice user interface (VUI). The VUI is characterized by the interface for communicating with a spoken language application [4], where the input is primarily or exclusively speech, whereas the output can be audio or also visually supported [1]. VUIs are comprised by prompts, grammars and dialog logic, making it possible to enclose possible inputs and queries, as well as responses, in a call flow database [4]. The user's spoken speech is collected via microphone and is decoded

© Springer Nature Switzerland AG 2019
M. J. Abásolo et al. (Eds.): jAUTI 2018, CCIS 1004, pp. 115–128, 2019.
https://doi.org/10.1007/978-3-030-23862-9_9

by Automatic Speech Recognition (ASR) systems to generate a response and feedback. Advanced systems usually include a natural language understanding (NLU) component which could recognize and perceive more complex user intents.

Voice in multimodal platforms can enrich the user experience while allowing users not to "focus all their attention on one channel for feedback" [1] and lessening the cognitive load on the "ephemeral nature of output" in auditory-only interfaces [4] when combined with screens and visual information. In addition, the voice in multimodal solutions is a naturally more intuitive input for humans than touchpads, keyboards, or remote controls [1]. With technological advances in voice and speech recognition and word error rates dropping to near 5 percent, voice is at the forefront of interactive systems for the near future [5].

The referred opportunities are also true when considering interactive television solutions, associated with more private and domestic contexts of use with less noise than a public space where the user feels safe and at home. These contexts help to surpass some of the most common voice interaction user issues, regarding privacy concerns, distress in speaking to a machine or the influence of external noise (e.g. the speech of other users) [6]. To reach a successful VUI is a particularly important task when thinking of television systems, most of which are constrained by remote controls, making the user experience dependent on the interactions with the respective set of keys. And although industry experts believe that users are not ready to completely dismiss the remote control in the near future, they claim that voice is "set to play a significant role in the future of TV UI" [7] in a multimodal interaction.

The research pertaining the compilation of past and present voice user interfaces and its visual analysis is still modest. The study of user voice interaction with the television is mostly limited to the efficiency and accuracy of such systems, while its graphical representations and overall user experience has not been the object of indepth study. This paper analyses the interaction and visual elements that are being implemented on voice user interfaces supported in interactive television platforms, set-top boxes (STB), smart TVs or home assistants connected to the television. Cases were selected in a previous survey concerning trends for UI in interactive television platforms [8] and analyzed to provide a general outlook of VUI for interactive television made available in 2016 and first half of 2018. From the considered set of products, four examples were later selected due to distinguishable elements and characteristics to be further examined.

2 An Overview of Voice User Interfaces

This section presents briefly how voice user interfaces have evolved to today's standards. It explores on how voice user interfaces are built today and how they are affecting the day-to-day life, with a particular focus on the television and living room scenario.

2.1 A Brief History of VUIs

Starting with single digit recognition systems in the 1950s, VUI systems evolved in the following decades through research, by expanding the understanding of vocabulary and including NLU. In the 2000s, these systems evolved from labs to the real world as interactive voice response (IVR) systems, providing a new way to carry out automatized tasks using a landline telephone [6]. Business from banking to surveying resorted to IVR systems, allowing users to perform small tasks like checking the traffic or tracking a mail package.

In the subsequent years, voice user interfaces underwent little change, until the 2010s, with the emergence of new systems that started replacing IVR. These new systems are becoming mainstream, either with the growing use of voice-interacted mobile apps that combine visual and auditory information, or voice-only devices like smart-speakers or smart-displays. This "second era of VUIs" [6] is entering daily living much more significantly than earlier IVR systems. In 2016, Google reported that 20% of searches were done by voice when using the Google app and in 2017 almost 70% of smartphone requests done through the Google Assistant were expressed in natural language, contrary to the regular keyword-based input [9]. As Cohen [4] predicted, as these new VUIs are becoming more intuitive through the implementation of standards, technological efficient and overall ubiquitous, they could deliver a more enjoyable experience for the user.

2.2 Voice User Interfaces Today

Overall, expectations for VUI are different than when dealing with a graphical only interface, as users tend to expect a more natural interaction after activating a command or talking to the machine because "they are used to talk to other people, not technology" [10]. This affects the way users formulate their requests, using more complex utterances [11], which can implicate the success of the user experience.

VUIs are now slowly but steadily progressing into conversational user interfaces, with search expanding to more demanding and complex tasks (action-oriented) in digital personal ecosystems. Contrary to simple voice commands, that rely on a set of utterances and replies, conversational user interfaces are built to create interactions where both agents – the user and the machine – are "working towards a mutual goal" [1], pushing for a cooperative conversation in "quality, quantity, relevance, and manner", to be truthful, concise, relevant and clear [6, 12]. In this way, a successful conversational user interface should unfold like a negotiation, not with one-off questions and answers, but a "graceful interaction" [13]. Conversational user interfaces should thus not rely solely on user input but act one step forward of what the user wants or needs [14]. Cooperative conversation is therefore of the utmost importance: the more capable the machine is to perform conversation like a human with all that entails – continuous speech, management of answers in response to what was said before, speaking in turns – the easier the interaction will become with a system that "allows them to participate actively rather than one that leads them through a series of navigational obstacles" [1]. It is expected that data science and machine learning can improve systems to make that happen by developing "real insights and accurate answers to valuable individual questions" [14].

Voice-activated assistants are playing a defining role in making conversational user interfaces popular. Assistants are created to support a new personal user experience, by combining advanced Artificial Intelligence (AI) training towards the improvement of Natural Language Processing (NLP) and the creation of future two-way dialogues between humans and machines. The complexity in building a satisfying and successful conversational product and user interface is connected to the intricacies of human speech and dialogue. Considering a diversified audience, today's systems should not only be able to understand defined intents but to do so across generations, speech patterns, and accents.

The easiness provided by voice-activated systems combined with hands-free approaches are proving to be widely used for day-to-day tasks such as setting appointments or controlling smart home environments [15]. With Google Assistant, user queries are "40 times more likely to be action-oriented than Search" [16]. There is also a tendency for users to employ verbs and full sentences in their intentions in a complex conversational type of dialogue with voice-activated assistants [11]. In conclusion, today's voice interaction systems are increasingly allowing commands for actions – "play music", "set alarm" – instead of search-based queries.

2.3   Voice User Interfaces in Interactive Television

Voice interaction can be considered an "efficient input modality" [17], especially in an interactive television scenario where its addition could bring speed and ease of use to a complex remote-control dependent situation.

Regarding the television domain, most significant VUIs were introduced in the early 2010s. Television makers offered voice interaction to make the device more accessible to those with disabilities, while media centers and smart TVs resorted to external interactive devices to provide voice control, such as Xbox's Kinect or Google TV's companion apps with Google Voice [18]. However, these systems were still comprised of a defined limited set of controls and commands, made up of just a few words and actions.

Nowadays, VUIs are increasing in their number of applications regarding television. In most cases, they are used to skip tedious and slow text inputs when searching for content, providing the opportunity to bypass intricate navigation and the on-screen keyboard interacted with a remote control [19]. But the challenge is also in offering the user what he/she is asking considering the specificities of the television ecosystem. This includes a peculiar lexicon and language model to address actions including access to live and recorded catalog, user preferences, logged accounts and available offers.

Furthermore, from a design perspective, these interfaces and the visual components that integrate them are an intrinsic part of the user experience contributing to a successful or failed outcome. In this way, the design of systems that support voice interaction, built on big data and intensive training, should be able to clearly and conveniently convey information and responses to the user's requests and intentions. And while in voiceonly user interfaces there are no visual affordances, multimodal voice user interfaces presented in television screens can and should be designed with appropriate visual feedback to improve the user experience [20]. A screen allows the

VUI to present the user with options and suggestions of commands, setting clear expectations and improving discoverability [21], and the remote can provide a different input mode and help the user reach a valid answer to his request when voice is ineffective.

Additionally, the opportunity for the television to become a visual translator for voice-activated assistants and smart speakers is still highly relevant – half of the American owners say they would be interested in having this technology on their television [15]. The direct and instant connection to personal devices and platforms makes the home assistants perfect messengers in a hands-free environment as more than 50% of smart speakers are placed in the living room where most TVs are located [15]. Accessible from any place in a room, regardless of position and direction, smart speakers can be both convenient or influenced by multiple sounds in that environment – interactive television VUI with smart speakers should consider the sound and dialogue provided by TV content to avoid mistakenly triggering the system [22].

While speech technology has become commonplace in some operator's player devices and smart TVs, "only 50% of consumers occasionally talk to their device" [7], revealing that talking to a machine still leaves some users uncomfortable [6]. However, the number of voice-activated commands is increasing. Xfinity's X1 Voice Remote reports more than 500 million monthly voice commands generated and more than 1.5 billion in the first quarter of 2018 [23].

3 Current Visual Approaches for Voice User Interfaces in Television

To identifying current approaches and trends (Sect. 4) in voice interaction for the television, a set of VUIs from different contexts was analyzed. VUIs from technologically advanced players, media centers and Smart TVs were selected from a previous survey of 48 disruptive commercial interactive television interfaces [8]. Of these, 24 products incorporate a VUI solution – 15 that include remote-based voice interaction, 2 that provide native hands-free interaction and 7 that only work with an external smart device assistant. Additionally, brand new products such as conversational assistants (Google Assistant, Amazon's Alexa, Microsoft's Cortana, Apple's Siri, Samsung's Bixby) as well as voice-controlled TVs (LG's ThinQ, Roku's Enhanced Voice), and voice-enabled STBs (DirecTV and Swisscom) were considered. This selection considers a significant range of commercial options, supporting a general view of VUIs in television.

The analysis of VUIs shows that the recent advances in voice solutions in interactive television platforms have resulted in coherent interactions models supported on similar visual elements, such as microphone icons, animated visual signifiers of the start and duration of the interaction, textual input feedback and visual results to the queries made by users.

In this way, most contemporary VUIs in television follow a similar layout and visual elements, with commercial products setting the standard through two popular graphical VUI models.

The most popular is the creation of a superimposed layer to the existing interface that is activated when using a voice command and shown in the lower section of the screen (Fig. 1). This new layer upholds the overall visual elements such as typography or color palette but adds new visual components essential for the VUI feedback and interaction such a microphone icon and call-to-action elements related to the interaction. The visual break created by this over imposed layer allows for the user to focus on the voice interaction being completed, creating the cognitive and visual space for more complex interactions, such as combined searching, multiple voice queries or possibly, in the future, a dialogue with the system. This interface design option keeps the user on the same interface and content he/she was watching, while clearly showing that a new interaction is occurring.

Fig. 1. Examples of superimposed bottom layer VUI models: LG with Google Assistant integration (top), Infinity X1 set-top box (bottom).

A second VUI model for screens can be identified when visual cues are included from the start. In this voice-first approach, products make the voice interaction a priority. Although the design of these products still relies, on some part, on the user's touch and not simply on voice commands, the preferred input was designed to be the user's voice. The designing of screens in this second model differs as the visual cues and components are designed as an integral part of the layout. The visual elements are tailored to the voice interaction, reflecting on this with minimal interfaces through the disuse of menus and emphasis on text, and with visual wording an essential part of the screen by either representing prompts or user queries. Even though this interaction model is in its early steps, commercial products such as the Amazon Echo Show or the Lenovo Smart Display are breaking through in terms of offering new multimodal screens that prioritize voice, establishing the voice-screen combo as products that effectively set expectations [24] (Fig. 2).

Fig. 2. Examples of voice-first VUI models: Amazon Echo Show (left), Lenovo Smart Display with Google Assistant (right).

4   Trends in Voice User Interfaces for Television

To better understand what the future in interactive television VUIs might be, four cases that presented singular VUI solutions in their interaction or visually approaches were selected. These examples display solutions that personify today's trends:

- introducing the context of use as an influence for VUI possibilities – Xfinity One;
- presenting a conversational layout and visual elements – LG's Voice Mate;
- their popularity and the increasing number of users, along with the extensive use of data for personalization – Google Assistant and its use on Android TV;
- the growing number of open-source and development tools and products for VUIs – Amazon's Alexa Skills.

Following, the four cases are detailed on how user interactions occur and on the graphical elements that support and augment the user's interaction with the system.

4.1   Xfinity

First introduced in 2014, Xfinity's Voice Control[1] (combined with Voice Guidance) was designed to help the users find content through voice-activated search and allow them to set definitions on the X1 set-top box (e.g. programming DVR) with simple voice commands. Xfinity's voice control has been significantly updated in the last

---

[1] www.xfinity.com/learn/digital-cable-tv/x1/equipment.

couple of years, by adding features such as commands for finding an item through Bluetooth tracker Tile – "Xfinity Home where are my keys?" – or locking a smart lock – "Lock the front door". The control of smart home devices is thus an important part of Xfinity's Voice Control experience, providing a unified domestic user experience through the set-top box, assigning new values to the television [23]. Xfinity provides voice control for an ever-increasing number of user intents and incorporates the user's context to do so. One example showcased by the company is the display of soccer game stats about the game being watched (using the command "Show me soccer stats") with a specially designed sidebar infographic (Fig. 3 - top). Other examples included new voice commands to enjoy events such as the Winter Olympics (Fig. 3 - bottom)– "What Olympic events are on today?" – or voting on America's Got Talent.

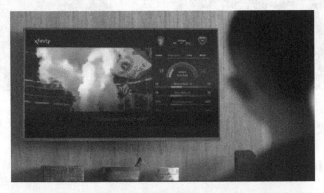

Fig. 3. Context-aware Xfinity VUI for soccer stats (top) and Olympic results (bottom).

4.2   LG Voice Mate (2016)

LG has released several VUIs across models of its smart TVs in the past three years. The 2016 Voice Mate VUI[2] version is visually disruptive, akin to the distinctive look & feel displayed by the graphical user interface [8]. VUI interaction occurs in the bottom

---

[2] www.lg.com/br/suporte/ajuda-produto/CT20096005-1436351544468-others.

right side, differentiating from other interfaces (Fig. 4). It was designed in a chat-like interface and, although it did not offer a conversational interaction, it clearly visually separates what is the user input and the platform's output. The interaction starts with a speech bubble on the left side with the instruction "Speak now" and an example of a possible command (e.g. "Voice guide"). Command suggestions are continuously changing although they are not related to the context of use. Visually feedback is given when the user speaks and results are shown in the same sidebar by extending it, covering the right half of the screen in a translucent dark layer. This allows the user to keep watching its content without completely replacing the interface while presenting results or further options.

Fig. 4. Voice Mate activated (left), Voice Mate search results (right)

Although this model was eventually disregarded for a more standardized lower-bottom layer as seen on the previous section with LG's integration of the Google Assistant, the evolution of voice user interfaces and NLU technologies and therefore, more complex conversations between the system and the user, could lead back to a more conversational graphical interface such as the LG's Voice Mate.

4.3   Google Assistant

The Google Assistant[3] was first introduced in 2016's I/O, Google's annual conference. It aims to create a new personal user experience, combining advanced AI with an everenhancing conversational persona and creating an ongoing two-way dialogue. The Google Assistant can be used to control an interactive television in different ways: using a Google Chromecast to receive commands via other devices (i.e. smart speakers like Google Home) or natively installed in smart TVs or media centers (e.g. Android TV). This allows for different interaction methods, as it can be accessed using the wakeup sentence "Hey/OK, Google" in hands-free devices, on remotes or the smartphone app. The importance of the Google Assistant usage is exponential, as the number of Android devices continues to grow, increasing the potential for its use with television-related commands [25].

Home assistants like Google Home allow for a hands-free interaction using a simplified interface with auditory signals and minimalist animations with 4 dots. The integration with the Google ecosystem also allows the user to search outside the TV platform or perform many commands with Google Actions (third-party "apps" for Google Assistant). Therefore, although it is not context-related, it provides widespread access to any information needed and displays it on the bottom of the TV screen (Fig. 5).

Fig. 5. Google Assistant VUI on Android TV - Weather results (top), search results (bottom)

---

[3] https://assistant.google.com.

4.4   Amazon Alexa

Amazon Alexa[4] was announced in 2014 alongside the smart speaker Amazon Echo. In recent years, Alexa has been adapted to provide results visually with smart displays like the Amazon Echo Show and on the TV with devices such as the Amazon Fire Cube. Therefore, interaction with Alexa can be initiated both by a wake-up word (e.g. "Alexa"), on a remote or on a smartphone. The number of different Alexa-enabled devices is increasing (surpassing 20.000 compatible devices) but there is still the need for the user to have an external device with Alexa support. Furthermore, Alexa skills (third-party "apps") are growing at an exponential rate, with more than 50.000 skills listed worldwide [25].

While using a smart speaker the interaction follows a minimalist approach with a blue gradient LED light as visual feedback. If integrated into the TV, that same visual signifier is adapted into a horizontal line on the top of the TV screen (Fig. 6). Additionally, Alexa commands not related to the control of the TV intents generate new interfaces occupying the entire screen as seen on Fig. 6 (e.g. weather, movies showing in cinemas). Visual affordances are regularly available and are adapted to the user's context (e.g. Try "Alexa, scroll right").

Fig. 6. Wake-up word activated Alexa VUI on Amazon Fire Cube (top), Alexa VUI results for movies showing in cinemas (bottom).

---

[4] https://amazon.com/Amazon-Echo-And-Alexa-Devices.

5   Conclusion

VUIs can become the interaction model that truly offers a new television experience, reinventing the regular use of the remote-control and bringing interaction to the flux and open space that is the living room. Screens like the television can "become the canvas for conversational AI" [26], providing visual output for voice-activated inputs. While voice by itself cannot single-handedly offer an optimal user experience, the combination of both voice and remote control is a solution adopted by many.

The introduction of voice activated commands into Smart TVs, STBs or through the control of smart assistants is increasing, allowing users to replace the remote control with their voice with an impact on their television-related behaviors. However, the addition of voice interaction to an already designed and tested system should be made intentionally and carefully. Because it will introduce a new interaction model into one already known by the user, the VUI designed for a commercial interactive television should become a part of the original's "look and feel" while asserting a new space without disrupting the existing design system.

The analysis showed that two main models are becoming the standard for the design of VUI for television. The first introduces a super imposed layer that does not disrupt the user experience and maintains the interface's look and feel, allowing the user to make a smooth transition between interaction methods. The second model responds to a voice-first approach, where voice is the main input method and the design of the interface validates that by focusing on providing the user with textual and auditory cues.

Visually coherent models have been developed and are deployed in most devices. However, the use case analysis reveals that the VUIs should not follow a one solution fits all approach. Context-aware VUI and conversational interfaces in interactive television can adopt different visual outputs, taking advantage of a bigger screen and the multimodal interaction with a remote-control.

In the future, a more personalized experience can be provided by taking the interaction further beyond the use of a couple of commands, to proactive solutions that should work continuously as a service to help the user with his individual needs and take advantage of the contextual and user data. UX designers face important challenges to work on VUIs in interactive television that integrate, in a balanced way, visual and auditory signifiers with privacy, context, and content.

The analysis reported on this paper attends the more common approaches in VUIs in interactive television and distinctive visual elements and interactions. However, further research has been developed towards identifying what is becoming standard, outlining guidelines based on industry applied interaction patterns and models. Subsequently, this research will support a preliminary stage of an industry and academic R&D project that aims to develop an interface for a natural language understanding (NLU) solution for a broadcaster's set-top box. Additional research concerning voice user interfaces for TV products and applications can also benefit from this study.

References

1. Harris, R.A.: Voice Interaction Design: Crafting the New Conversational Speech Systems. Morgan Kaufmann, San Francisco (2005)
2. Nordrum, A.: CES 2017: The Year of Voice Recognition, 04 January 2017. https://spectrum. ieee.org/tech-talk/consumer-electronics/gadgets/ces-2017-the-year-of-voice-recognition
3. Nadella, S.: Microsoft Build. Speech presented at Build 2018, Seattle, 7 May 2018
4. Cohen, M.H., Giangola, J.P., Balogh, J.: Voice User Interface Design. Addison-Wesley, Boston (2007)
5. Cuthbertson, A.: Microsoft speech recognition achieves 'human parity', 24 October 2016. www.newsweek.com/microsoft-speech-recognition-achieves-human-parity-511538. Accessed 12 Sept 2018
6. Pearl, C.: Designing voice user interfaces: principles of conversational experiences. O'Reilly, Beijing (2017)
7. Giles, K.: What will the TV of Tomorrow look like? – W12 Studios – Medium, 05 July 2017. https://medium.com/w12studios/what-will-the-tv-of-tomorrow-look-like-cd61029380e8
8. Abreu, J., Almeida, P., Varsori, E., Fernandes, S.: Interactive television UI: Industry trends and disruptive design approaches, in Abreu, J., Guerrero, M. Almeida, P. Silva, T. (eds.), Proceedings of the 6th Iberoamerican Conference on Applications and Usability of Interactive TV – jAUTI 2017, pp. 213–224. UA Edit. (2017). ISBN 978-972-789-521-2
9. Google: 5 ways voice assistance is reshaping consumer behavior (2017). www.think withgoogle.com/data-collections/voice-assistance-emerging-technologies. 12 Sept 2018
10. Mortesen, D.: How to Design Voice User Interfaces (2018). https://interaction-design.org/ literature/article/hot-to-design-voice-user-interfaces
11. Guy, I.: The characteristics of voice search. ACM Trans. Inf. Syst. **36**(3), 1–28 (2018). https://doi.org/10.1145/3182163
12. Grice, Paul: Logic and conversation. In: Cole, P., Morgan, J. (eds.) Syntax and Semantics 3: Speech Acts, pp. 41–58. Academic Press, New York (1975)
13. Hayes, P.J., Reddy, R.: Steps toward graceful interaction in spoken and written man-machine communication. Int. J. Man Mach. Stud. **19**(3), 231–284 (1983)
14. Krishna, G.: The Best Interface is no Interface. New Riders, San Francisco (2015)
15. National Public Radio: The Smart Audio Report (2018). www.nationalpublicmedia.com/ smart-audio-report/latest-report/#download. Accessed 12 Sept 2018
16. Huffman, S.: Five insights on voice technology, 21 August 2018. www.blog.google/ perspectives/scott-huffman/five-insights-voice-technology/. Accessed 12 Sept 2018
17. Whitenton, K.: Voice First: The Future of Interaction? 12 November 2017. www.nngroup. com/articles/voice-first/. Accessed 12 Sept 2018
18. Buskik, E.: Google TV Revealed: One Screen to Rule Them All (2010). www.wired.com/ 2010/09/google-reveals-google-tv
19. Tivo. Television Content Discovery: The Need for Improved Usability and User Experience (2016). http://business.tivo.com/content/dam/tivo/resources/tivo_tvcontentdiscovery_wp.pdf
20. What are Voice User Interfaces? (2019). www.interaction-design.org/literature/topics/voice-user-interface
21. Babich, N.: (2018, February 20). UI of the Future: The Basic Principles of Conversational User Interfaces – Shopify 20 February 2018. https://www.shopify.com/partners/blog/ conversational-user-interfaces. Accessed 12 Sept 2018
22. White, J.: TVs are getting smart assistants but they're not much use yet 03 January 2018. www.wired.co.uk/article/lg-adds-google-assistant-to-tvs. Accessed 12 Sept 2018

23. Comcast: Voice Control, 06 December 2017. www.corporate.comcast.com/company/xfinity/tv/voice-control
24. Pasztor, D.: Combining Graphical and Voice Interfaces for a better user experience – Smashing Magazine (2017). www.smashingmagazine.com/2017/10/combining-graphical-voice-interfaces
25. Kinsella, B.: Google assistant to have 60 percent virtual assistant smartphone share in 2022 (2017). http://voice-bot.ai/2017/11/12/google-assistant-60-percent-virtual-assistant-share-smartphone-share-2022-46-percent-today
26. Lafferty, M.: TV is dead, long live TV! — Crafting compelling living room experiences. Speech presented at Interaction 18 in La Sucrière, Lyon, 6 February 2018

Testing and User Experience of IDTV Services

Field Trial of a New iTV Approach: The Potential of Its UX Among Younger Audiences

Ana Velhinho(✉) ⓘ, Sílvia Fernandes ⓘ, Jorge Abreu ⓘ,
Pedro Almeida ⓘ, and Telmo Silva ⓘ

Digimedia, Department of Communication and Arts,
University of Aveiro, Aveiro, Portugal
{ana.velhinho, silvia.fernandes,
jfa, almeida, tsilva}@ua.pt

Abstract. The actual video consumption behaviors are blurring the traditional boundaries between linear and non-linear viewing, leveraged by On-demand and Over-the-Top (OTT) content offers. The Managed-Operated Networks (MON) adapted to this shift by providing flexibility to content access via Catch-up and Time-shift TV services. In addition, manufacturers of Smart TVs and high-end media centers (e.g. Apple TV) are offering their commercial solutions with a silo-based approach, lacking a fluid User eXperience (UX) when the user switches between proprietary applications (apps) displaying different settings and User Interfaces (UIs). In this framework, OTT providers have been taking the lead on setting the trends with partially unified cross-source UIs, enriched with personalization features to enhance the UX. These trends also contrast with Pay-TV solutions based in UIs mostly oriented to the traditional TV channel's line-up. Based on this opportunity, an operator-based iTV solution, delivered over a set-top box (STB), was developed within the UltraTV R&D project. This initiative brought together the academic and the industry fields to design, develop and validate a concept of a profile-based and cross-source recommendation UI (offering, at the same level, content from linear and non-linear TV, Netflix, YouTube and Facebook videos). After an iterative evaluation through expert reviews and laboratory tests, a field trial validation, with end users, of a fully functional prototype was set. Qualitative data collection methods along with a triangulation of UX scales were applied to gather opinions and measure usability, hedonic and emotional parameters. The results were arranged by age groups and viewing dynamics to reveal motivational indicators related to the achieved viewing experience. The unified access to different sources fostered content discovery and was particularly valued by younger audiences. The outcomes from this empirical study aim to provide valuable contributions to push the next generation of television platforms and bring younger audiences back to the TV screen.

Keywords: Content unification · Field trial · Interactive television ·
User experience · Viewing behaviors

© Springer Nature Switzerland AG 2019
M. J. Abásolo et al. (Eds.): jAUTI 2018, CCIS 1004, pp. 131–147, 2019.
https://doi.org/10.1007/978-3-030-23862-9_10

1 Introduction

The growing relevance of non-linear video over linear TV is highlighted as the main transformation within audiovisual consumption in recent studies [1], primarily due to the increase of OTT offers and the convenience of mobile viewing as a complement/alternative to the TV screen. This framework has promoted new behavioral phenomena like a) the "cord-cutters" (users that drop their Pay-TV services in favor of streamed OTT content making the regular TV service disposable) and b) the "binge-watching" (refereeing to a continuous marathon viewing of several episodes from the same show). Both phenomena are mainly associated to the users' groups "Mobility Centrics" (that essentially use mobile screens) and "Screen Shifters" (that consume all kind of TV and video content across multiple devices and anywhere) which are pushing new TV and video services [1]. To cope with this new context where OTT players are gaining space, Pay-TV suppliers react with commodity bundle TV and Internet services which include Video-on-Demand (VOD), time-shifted, and catch-up features also available on the move, anytime and anywhere [2–4].

Often this demanding new type of viewers is being studied from the perspective of generational groups [5], which are also associated with viewing behaviors classified by Ericsson Consumer Lab reports [1] TV groups. The "Silent Generation" (ages 65+), "Baby Boomers" (ages 50–64)" and "Generation X" (ages 35–49) are the ones that preferably watch video on the TV screen, mostly sports, news and movies [1]. Contrariwise, computer, tablet and mobile phone-based viewing is more popular among youngest consumers – "Millennials" (ages 21–34) and "Generation Z" (ages 15–20) – not because they totally dismiss the TV screen but because they adopt multitasking practices. This also has an impact on the number of hours dedicated to video consumption, being a total of 33 h per week attributed to groups of users between 16–19 years old, with 54% of this time dedicated to On-demand content. Users between 20–24 years old have similar behaviors. In contrast, the group of users between 45–49 dedicate only 31% of their time watching On-demand content (from a total of 29 h per week) whereas the 60–69 age group have a similar total amount of viewing time, however with only 21% of this period dedicated to VOD [1].

Within this framework, the personalization of the experience, along with a content-first approach delivered through a UI based on aggregation and unification of content and sources may represent leading features to meet current users' media behaviors. Such topics are targeted by an R&D project that brings together the academic and the industry fields to design, develop and validate a concept of a profile-based and cross-source recommendation UI that offers, through a STB based prototype, TV content at the same level with videos from Netflix, YouTube and Facebook [6, 7].

The main goal of this paper is to present insights provided by younger generations towards a unified iTV solution based on the results obtained through an empirical study with the UltraTV prototype. The prototype was developed according to an iterative User-Centered-Design (UCD) methodology [8] that included three evaluation phases: (i) an expert's review [9, 10], (ii) tests in laboratory [6] and (iii) a Field Trial (FT) [11].

After integrating the feedback from previous tests, the focus of the FT procedure was to validate the unification concept and assess the overall User eXperience (UX) of the system using a triangulation of validated instruments (described in section three): the System Usability Scale (SUS); the Self-Assessment Manikin (SAM), and; the AttrakDiff. Also, a characterization questionnaire was applied. Complementary to these instruments was the permanent monitoring of the interactions during the FT and phone interviews conducted afterwards.

The paper is structured into five sections. After this introductory part, the next section presents recent content unification solutions in the iTV domain, including the UltraTV R&D project. In the following section, the FT of the UltraTV prototype is described, detailing the UI of the tested version, the tests' procedures and the sample characterization. The final sections present and discuss the main results regarding the younger audience's behaviors, culminating with the conclusion that summarizes the contributions of the study.

2 Content Unification in the iTV Domain

Recently, online players have developed niche business models relying on OTT streaming technology. To face these OTT newcomers, cable Pay-TV subscriptions have started to offer additional On-Demand services. Despite the fast growth of such players, limitations on getting traditional TV channels and live content [12] kept them from taking over the TV market. Those restrictions prevent a seamless UX, perpetuating a behavior of using multiple apps displaying different settings and UIs. The lack of an integrated search feature and cross-source recommendations is also a limitation that leads to users having a scattered audiovisual consumption across devices. The interdependent dynamics between channels and Pay-TV operators and OTT providers is bringing both sides closer together in favor of more balanced solutions regarding a personalized and content-first viewing experience.

However, it was not before the turn to 2018 that new industry releases seemed to acknowledge the benefits from the synergies between OTT platforms and cable companies to more suitable services to meet the viewers' demands. The SkyQ[1] solution, from the UK Sky operator, led a paradigmatic change towards a cross-content approach by proposing a UI allowing the user to switch between live TV and Netflix content seamlessly (see Fig. 1). The other way around was the strategy adopted by the VOD platform Hulu[2], that integrated live content and channels alongside their original on-demand content, offering a "Lineup" section to display personalized content for different profiles (see Fig. 1).

---

[1] Sky Group: http://bit.ly/2LcigCg.

[2] Hulu Homepage: https://www.hulu.com/live-tv.

Fig. 1. Sky Q UI (left) and Hulu UI (right)

From beginning of 2017 until July 2018, an R&D project (UltraTV) unfolded from a partnership between the industry (a leading IPTV operator) and the academy. The goal was to target the new TV generation focused on the unification and personalization, by combining in the same UI, TV and OTT content (see Figs. 2, 3 and 4). With a MON-based framework [3] supported by the operator's offer, it provides unified access to a diversified bundle of content sorted by genres and sources. Content is displayed on a card-based grid with axis navigation and a fluid blob menu redirecting to the system's main features: "My Content" area (favorites and keep watching), filtering, profiles, unified search, and settings (see Fig. 3). Cross-content recommendations are also offered to foster the discovery of content (Fig. 4). Experts and end-users validated this solution during several UX assessment stages.

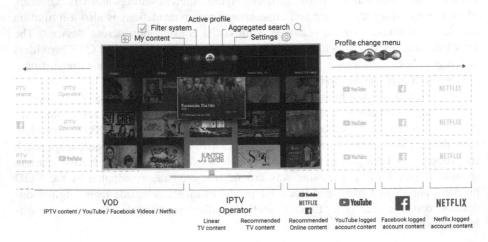

Fig. 2. UltraTV home screen interface architecture

For the assessment of the final version, as the culmination of all the previous developments, the goal of the team was to build a solution that allowed for the unification of TV content, aiming to enhance the entertainment experience offered to different consumer profiles, including younger generations. On the one hand by providing content beyond the traditional broadcast channels to the classic TV consumers

Fig. 3. UltraTV home screen interface with the active focus on the first card of the navigation grid (left).and with active focus on pea menu on top to change profile (right).

Fig. 4. UltraTV full screen interface with the active focus on the contextual menu (left) and with active focus on the cross-reference content on the side menu (right).

(promoting the diversification of their choices). And on the other hand, by aiming to regain the attention in TV content and improve the quality of OTT content viewing on the large TV screen for those who are used to watch videos on their computer and mobile devices. By targeting a different approach to zapping the prototype fosters the discovery of content from different players and sources, based on the user's profile and tracked behaviors.

3 FT Evaluation of the UltraTV Prototype

A FT plays a crucial role in validating a product, allowing it to be tested in conditions close to the real context of use, revealing potential problems that would not appear in controlled environments like the tests in laboratory. Therefore, a FT is an essential UX evaluation stage integrated in the iterative process for design and development of a product or service [13]. The tests with users (in laboratory and the field) followed the CUE (Components of User Experience) model [14] as a framework to evaluate the components of UX (based on four key dimensions, namely visual/aesthetic, emotion, stimulation, and identification [15–17]. As proposed by the team's previous work [13], a combination of qualitative data-gathering combined with a triangulation of specific validated UX instruments were applied, namely the SUS [18–20], SAM [21] and AttrakDiff [22] questionnaires. Qualitative data was also collected through interviews to gather complementary opinions [23].

3.1 FT Objectives and Procedures

A field evaluation spanning 20 days was carried out in the domestic context. The UltraTV FT took place in 2018 from 12 to 31 of January, using a total of 20 STBs installed at participants' households (see Fig. 5).

Fig. 5. Xiaomi MI Box 4 K HDR Android TV with Bluetooth remote control (left). A participant using the UltraTV STB in his house (right).

The home-installed test version (see Fig. 5) was an updated version of a previous prototype tested in the laboratory. In this sense, the FT evaluation had the following objectives: (a) Validate the technical solution for the concept of content unification; (b) Evaluate the UX of the prototype; (c) Validate the keys on the remote control used to interact with the system; (d) Evaluate the look & feel of the UI; (e) Validate specific system features (e.g. menus, cross-references, iconography, second level categories in the grid 'silos'); (f) Evaluate the personalization of experience (profiles with personalized grid and suggestions); (g) Evaluate the level of interest and appropriation of the system by the participants.

Some requirements were defined to be a participant in the FT, namely the need to have at least one TV set at home; willingness to use the prototype to access audiovisual content over the test period; have an internet connection at home; and be a regular viewer of online videos from sources like Netflix, YouTube or Facebook. Although only 20 STBs were available to be installed at different households, each STB supported up to 5 users, so participants were asked to invite their family members to join, which allowed the number of participants to rise to 48. This preparation phase (see Fig. 6) ended with the administration of a characterization questionnaire to know more about TV consumption habits.

The implementation phase (see Fig. 6) started with providing each evaluator with a trial package containing one STB, one remote control and an informative brochure. The participants just had to connect the STB to their TVs, set-up the Wi-Fi connection start using the system. The assessment phase also took place during this period (see Fig. 6): Google Analytics was set up to log all interactions on the prototype, by mapping the paths each participant performed in real time. Additionally, two different assessment moments using online questionnaires were applied, being one a halfway survey and the other the final one, including the UX scales SUS, SAM and AttrakDiff. A phone interview, for qualitative data collection, was conducted one week after the end of the FT.

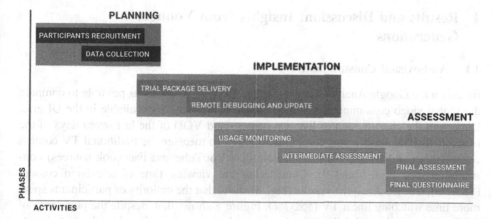

Fig. 6. Phases and activities of the FT dynamization

3.2 Sample Characterization

Prior to the FT, a characterization questionnaire was filled by all participants. The sample included students and power users, ensuring viewers from different age groups, especially target audiences of the UltraTV project – "Millennials" and "Generation Z". From the total of 20 STBs that started the FT, 12 STBs in 12 different houses were selected to be analyzed accounting for a total of 26 individual profiles and 9 family profiles. 8 STBs were not considered due to not complying with using the system for at least 6 h and registered more than 200 interactions. The 26 valid participants included 15 male (57.69%) and 11 female (42.31%) evaluators, aged between 12 and 54. Considering the completed level of education, high school education (38.46%) was most common, followed by a BA (26.92%) and MA (19.23%). According to an age stratification with 5-year intervals (see Fig. 7), the sample was most illustrative of four groups: 26.92% between 20–24 years old and 19.23% between 15–19 years old. These are followed by ages between 30–34, and between 35–39 years. For data analysis purposes participants were also grouped according to their family structure: (a) Families - 10 participants (38.46%); (b) Couples - 8 participants (30.77%); (c) Roommates - 5 participants (19.23%); (d) Alone - 3 participants (11.54%).

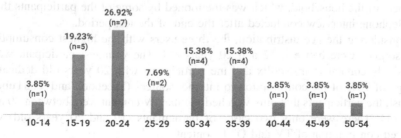

Fig. 7. FT sample by age groups

4 Results and Discussion: Insights from Younger Generations

4.1 Audiovisual Consumption

Based on the Google Analytics collected data from 26 users it was possible to compare the global video consumption stratified by the genres/sources available in the UI grid. Data from the consumption of live TV content and VOD of the last seven days of the associated IPTV service was combined to allow to measure the traditional TV content consumption and compare it to OTT (Netflix, YouTube and Facebook sources) consumption (see Figs. 8 and 9). Considering the viewing time of television content (88.17%), Google Analytics results (Fig. 8) show that the majority of participants spent more time watching linear TV (55.37%). Figure 8 shows that, despite the popularity of OTT sources consumed daily through various devices, as mentioned by the participants in the characterization questionnaire, only 11.83% of the time was spent watching these sources, being most of this consumption dedicated to Netflix videos (10.47%).

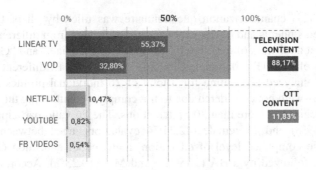

Fig. 8. Time spent watching TV per content source

However, considering that YouTube and Facebook videos are shorter, the number of videos viewed were also analyzed, showing a slight increase in both sources (see Fig. 9). Taking into account that access to Facebook videos and YouTube's subscriptions and recommendations implied the configuration of users' personal accounts, it is considered that this could have been an influential factor for the lower consumption. Besides the fact that the system is connected to a television shared by several members of the household, which was mentioned by some of the participants through the telephone interview conducted after the end of the test period.

Considering the age distribution, the three users with the highest consumption of OTT sources were between 12 and 20 years old. The youngest participant watched exclusively content from Netflix and the participants with 20 years old dedicated an average of 70% of the consumption to internet sources (Facebook and YouTube). By contrast, the participants that only watched regular TV content were between 20 and 34 years old. There were only two cases of participants (19 and 20 years old) with a balanced consumption of TV and OTT content.

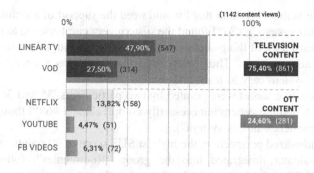

Fig. 9. Number of videos watched per content source

Considering the visualization groups, STBs associated with the "Family" and "Couple" groups achieved the highest total consumption means. Several participants preferred to use a generic family profile rather than their individual profile. These factors can be indicators that the UltraTV application promotes a collective consumption dynamic, a hypothesis acknowledged during the semi-structured interview conducted after the end of the test period. Another factor mentioned in the interviews that influenced the dismiss of individual profiles was the perceived lack of efficiency of the recommendation system (since it needed more time than the test period to make the content suggestions more accurate and more noticeable on the grid).

4.2   User Experience Metrics

The three quantitative UX scales adopted to evaluate the UltraTV prototype in the field were the SUS, SAM and AttrakDiff. Figure 10 provides an overview and highlights of the individual lowest and highest scores (SUS and SAM) according to age group:

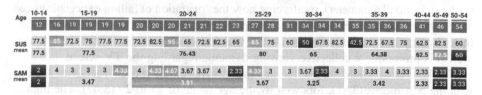

Fig. 10. SUS (0 to 100) and SAM (1 to 5) scores according to age groups

The System Usability Scale questionnaire (based on ten attitude items) addresses the global usability of the system using a Likert scale, regarding controllability, effectiveness, learnability. The global SUS score of 72.4 (from 0 to 100) points out the product as "Good" (Bangor et al., 2009). In addition to the overall SUS score, it was considered relevant to analyze the polarization of opinions for the different items (scores from 1 to 5) according to the participants' individual scores, to verify if their evaluation was related to age or viewing group patterns, associated with specific audiovisual consumption habits.

The positive item #4 ("I think that I would need the support of a technical person to be able to use this system"), #8 ("I found the system very cumbersome to use") and #10 ("I needed to learn a lot of things before I could get going with this system") obtained the more favorable opinions. Thus, suggesting that there was a strong conviction in considering the system easy to learn and use.

The only negative scores were pointed by two participants, 35 and 36 years old, in the item #2 ("I found the system unnecessarily complex") and #6 ("I thought there was too much inconsistency in this system").

In an individualized perspective, the highest SUS score of 90 points was given by a 20-year-old evaluator, integrated into the group "Roommates", followed by two evaluators aged 27 and 16 respectively, from the "Family" group, which scored 85 points (see Fig. 10). On the other hand, the worst scores (42.5 and 50 points) were attributed by two young adults, with 35 and 34 years old respectively (see Fig. 10). The first integrated into the group "Couples" and the second in the group "Alone".

In terms of hedonic and emotional aspects, the Self-Assessment Manikin, as a non-verbal pictorial questionnaire, measured the "satisfaction", "motivation", and "sense of control" associated with a person's affective reaction. Among the three parameters (from 1 to 5), the "sense of control" got the highest score (3.77), followed by "satisfaction" (3.23) and "motivation (3.12).

Regarding age groups, the lowest SAM score (1 point) on the "satisfaction" and the "motivation" parameters was given by the youngest evaluator of the sample (12-year-old) within the "Family" group. Another participant with 19-year-old, from the "Alone" group, also attributed 1 point to "motivation" and by contrast, gave 5 points to the "sense of control". When comparing with the qualitative data from the phone interview, this participant claimed to have no control over the recommendations, so it is possible that this score results from a confusion in the use of the SAM scale, which inverts the order of the figures in the parameter of the "sense of control". In this case, it means that this evaluator would have attributed the worst score (1 point) in two parameters related to emotional impact (having also assigned a low score of 2 points in the "satisfaction" parameter), reinforcing how the frustration of failing expectations can have a huge negative impact on the perception of a product. In contrast, the "Roommates" group got the best average (4.07), which may again suggest that the UltraTV system is promoting a collective viewing dynamic regarding the TV screen.

Looking at the SAM scores, the age group between 20 and 24 years was the one with the best means (3.81), followed by the age range of 25 to 29 (3.67). The highest individual mean score (4.67) was rated by a 20-year-old participant within a "Roommates" group. The second-best scores (4.33) were given by two evaluators with 19 and 20 years old, from the groups "Family" and "Roommates", all of them with an in-depth knowledge of OTT platforms and regular consumption of video content on multiple devices, specially the laptop. Therefore, there is also a willingness to use the system on behalf of these type of users because it provides access to OTT content, with personalized recommendations that can be watched on the television in the shared environment of the living room. As clarified in the phone interviews, this entertainment opportunity related to the TV is therefore clearly apart from the time spent working on the laptop, being perceived as a break time to leisure and relaxation.

As an extension of the SAM scale, the perception of the relational, emotional and aesthetic impact that a product causes on the user is becoming more relevant in the development of systems. For this reason, the AttrakDiff questionnaire, based on pairs of opposite adjectives that measure the pragmatic, hedonic (at the level of stimulation and identification) and aesthetic dimensions, constitutes a fundamental complementary tool to other UX metrics. Due to the limitation of the AttrakDiff platform[3] to 20 evaluators a downsampling process from the 26 participants was required. For this, the inclusion criterion was to be a regular user of the STB (at least 6 h and more than 200 clicks, in addition to filling all the data collection instruments). Aiming to a comparative analysis based on the age, two groups were defined: 10 participants with less than 25 years old and the remaining 10 over that age (see Fig. 11).

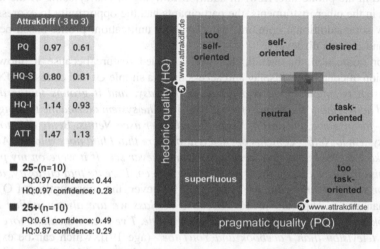

Fig. 11. AttrakDiff comparison of age groups: global scores (left) and confidence rectangles (right).

Similar scores between the two groups were achieved in the "stimulation" dimension (HQ-S), whereas the "aesthetic" dimension (ATT) was the best quality scored by both groups, although significantly higher in the under 25 group. The participants over 25 years old pointed the lowest scores to the "pragmatic" dimension (PQ 0.61) while the younger evaluators gave the lowest ratings to the "stimulation" dimension (HQ-S of 0.80). Considering the distribution by pragmatic and hedonic qualities (see Fig. 11) the UltraTV system was better received by the younger participants. The group under 24 pointed the product towards the "desired" quadrant, while the older group presented a more neutral and contained stance in terms of scores. Both groups display a similar confidence interval. Although younger participants have a best impression regarding the pragmatic qualities, since the system provides suitable answers to tasks integrated in their daily routines (e.g. OTT audiovisual consumption)

---

[3] AttrakDiff: http://attrakdiff.de/.

compared to the other group that did not consider the system as functional regarding their consumption habits ('scheduled viewing' in contrast to 'content discovery'), furthered clarified by the phone interviews.

4.3   Motivational Factors Towards a Content Unification System

The qualitative feedback provided by the participants was also valuable to understand the reasons for their scores and opinions.

Unification and Profile-Based Personalization Towards Content Discovery
The results obtained by all the instruments applied throughout the FT allowed drawing a profile of each user's consumption and identifying the most critical aspects that were addressed in the phone interview. In addition to trying to clarify some of the answers obtained in the other instruments, the participants had the opportunity to express in the interview some additional opinions, namely about unification, profile-based personalization and content discovery.

As for unification, in overall, this was a valued feature because it allowed the aggregation of content, its display and access using a simple UI and cohesive UX [*#118 "The design is simple, good and intuitive. It's easy, and it groups things that are scattered across other platforms"* (age 20)/*#131 "The system alerted me to things I had no clue – for instance, the part of Netflix. I had never used Netflix. Being able to access via this system to Netflix contents opened a door there that I had not explored. And then things like Facebook and stuff … things I would never see. If it were on my phone, I would miss it. And by being there on the home screen, I create that curiosity, and it is easier for you to see the contents"* (age 33)]. However, the consumption of OTT was lower than it was expected [#116 *"Because in class we are always online and on Facebook when we get home, we want to stop a little. I've been watching more movies and live television than Facebook and YouTube"* (age 19)], which can be explained with some limitations in the prototype regarding Facebook and YouTube pairing, that may have dissuaded some participants, and also some problems in the quality of the video streaming loaded from the IPTV provider application (paralyzed, blurred, pixelated image), which in some cases led to less regular use of the UltraTV STB [#173 *"I was never able to log in on Facebook. And on YouTube, the streaming was very bad"* (age 35)].

Also, the fact that not all users have paired their Facebook and YouTube accounts to their profile has also conditioned their UX for accessing OTT content [#128 *"I am not the type of user who feels the need to use social media on the TV set. That is, I do not see this profile need. And usually, here at home, we will all watch the same. I do not feel this need to change profiles depending on who is watching television. I would say this functionality will be most useful when our children grow up"* (age 37)/#117 *"I didn't notice which profile I was using. Usually, we were all together, or someone was already watching. As for me, I used the system together with everybody, and, it worked out well as it ended up improving a lot of suggestions that helped to find stuff, we all liked"* (age 22)]. Among participants who connected their accounts, some said they lacked native features of other platforms, such as commenting, liking, or sharing. Other users also mentioned privacy issues, highlighting the need for a PIN to access the profiles, which would also safeguard the personal social media accounts. Others indicated that the "family" profile fostered the discovery of content and collective viewing, in some cases with a preference for using this general profile rather than the individual profile [*#126 "I think it is because of our age group... Because we are students and we live together, we end up having all the same interests. So, we usually watch television together, or else the programs we see fit all within the same genre. But in our case, as a group of friends, we ended up opting to use a more general profile that ends up being shaped to our tastes"* (age 21)/*#126 "Just because this box has profiles and our operator doesn't have it, is already an advantage. And in your case, it helped us, for it has aggregated the content. And in the case of our operator's box, we have to actively search the contents to have references of things that we want to see, instead of having already some suggestions available"* (age 21)].

The validation of a content discovery proposal, fueled by the aggregation of TV and OTT content at the same level and using a profile-based recommendation system, suffered both from the regularity of the usage and the short duration of the test (20 days). If, on the one hand, the ease of access and automation of suggestions was recognized as an interesting premise [*#106 "This is great for me. I do not want to walk through looking at two hundred channels instead of what I am really interested, which is like... 10%."* (age 36)/*#114 "And also by showing related videos will also display shows that, for example, you would not discover if it were not so"* (age 36)], on the other hand, the lack of more accurate suggestions affected the expectations of the users [*#173 "I currently think the prototype has a skewed limitation of my preferences. But I think that's what a more advanced version would have improved and would encourage me to want the product. If you had the discovery of content with the search feature that would be great ... and perhaps fine-tune the related content on the right-side menu"* (age 35)]. Some users missed features to directly assign what you like to watch to help the recommendation system. This demonstrated that the context menu option of "I do not want to watch this content" went unnoticed to some participants, either because they did not find it or because they did not understand that by activating it would affect the recommendations on their profile-based grid.

Audiovisual Consumption in Other Devices

Although the UltraTV consisted of a television ecosystem, based on several consumer-oriented devices (television, mobile devices – smartphone and tablet – and computer), the prototypes tested focused exclusively on the STB version of the system. This option considered the TV consumption at home the most relevant use case scenario for the unification of content and UX proof of concept. Namely, regarding the acceptance of a disruptive approach to television consumption, and potential penetration in its context of excellence: the domestic leisure environment of the living room (simulated in previous laboratory tests and field tested in participants' homes). At the same time, the reconciliation with the television screen, to the detriment of the daily and ubiquitous consumption in the other devices, was considered another relevant issue to be validated. In particular, younger audiences tend to be further away from television in favor of the use of personal equipment such as the computer and mobile devices. Therefore, we tried to find in the initial, intermediate and final questionnaire and, in the last phase by phone interview (see Fig. 6), if the use of UltraTV would potentially have an impact on the consumption of audiovisual content in other devices. In particular, it was intended to verify if the participants anticipated a reduction of the consumption in these devices, privileging the visualization of videos on the television screen.

The participants highlighted the advantage of using the TV for collective viewing in a relaxed environment, compared to other devices such as the computer, more related to work and study tasks. The comfort and quick access to a range of recommended content on the home screen grid using only one-to-two-click (s) after connecting the TV/STB, without having to go to the browser or access to apps, were mentioned as advantages and motivations to reduce the consumption of audiovisual content at home through other devices.

In any case, a cross-platform solution was also considered to be relevant, especially for mobile use. Some participants also suggested the advantage of using mobile devices as a second screen to search for additional information about content without having to interrupt their viewing or even search before deciding to view it. Part of the prejudice of some participants, regarding the use of television, has to do with the limitation in the quantity, diversity and even up-to-date content available. Younger users continue to look at the television offer as old fashioned, assuming that the content programming provided by operators and channels will not match their tastes, compared to the ease of downloads made on the computer. The aggregation of OTT content, together with an integrated search and the personalized recommendation of contents that UltraTV offers, are precisely aimed at countering this view. This type of opinion confirms that there is a need for a product that unifies current and personalized content in a way that appeals to the most skeptical audiences about TV, especially the younger generations.

Willingness to Adopt UltraTV

The final questionnaire included a last closed question to perceive whether the participants were willing to change their current TV service for a commercial and fully functional version of the UltraTV system at the same price point, followed by an open-ended question to justify their choice. 76.92% of the participants replied they were willing to do so, which suggests a good indicator of the willingness for the unification concept and its validation.

Of the 26 respondents, only 6 participants – with 16, 34, 35 and 36 years – stated that they did not want to adopt the system. This result confirms the other UX scores that point to young adults (in their 30s) as the most skeptical audience to change their routines in favor of new products. The younger (16 years old) participant who stated that he did not want to adopt the system justified the answer by claiming that he was satisfied with his current service without further mentioning negative issues about the UltraTV prototype.

Regarding the negative issues, the need for more control over the system and the lack of advanced features and settings were considered the reasons to not adopt the UltraTV application if available on the market. The lack of control refers to some navigational difficulties that can be related to the disruptive interaction model of this system compared to regular services (namely the use of a grid with the use of directional keys without a channel alignment or numeric keys on the remote control). And also non-intuitive remote-keys for the activation of some specific areas (e.g. access to the side menu in full screen). The lack of other features and settings may also have been mentioned because some sections of the prototype were not fully functional during the test. This was the case of the lack of the "Search" feature, which did not allow quick access to channels and to browse specific content. Still, this qualitative set of data is in line with the quantitative results obtained in the SUS, SAM and AttrakDiff scales.

Finally, the feedback gathered in the phone interviews also allowed to clarify some of the results. The most negative issues referred by less than a third of the evaluators were: (a) the limited number of features as compared with the service they currently have and are satisfied with; (b) the lack of a chronologic channel surfing feature, usually called EPG (Electronic Program Guide); (c) some resistance to the organizational logic of the content on the grid. It should also be noted that users who are frequent consumers of TV, independently of the age, showed higher resistance to the regular use of this system.

5 Conclusions

The emergent iTV ecosystem leans towards on-demand content without dismissing the viewing of the shared linear experience on the TV screen, complemented by flexible access across mobile devices. Recent releases in the iTV industry confirm the growing expectations towards personalization and unification features, favoring the aggregation of sources, merging linear with non-linear videos. Despite some unification solutions released on the turn of 2018, the single UI horizontal unification embodies a different path from the prevailing offers that provide content in proprietary apps.

Acknowledging these challenges, the UltraTV project aims to enhance the entertainment experience by focusing on unification and personalization features. After several iterations assessed by experts and users in laboratory environment, the quantitative and qualitative UX results from the final prototype, tested in the field, reveal significant insights regarding younger generations, often detached from the TV screen and traditional TV content in favor for other devices and formats.

The outcomes from this empirical research sustained the motivation of users to have access to an iTV solution that includes content beyond the traditional broadcast channels, upgrading the offer with OTT content. Positive feedback was higher in young generations, across all instruments further corroborated and detailed by qualitative data from interviews and open-ended questions from a final questionnaire. This data provides interesting perceptions suggesting that unified iTV applications may be significant in retaining younger generations regarding the TV screen, including the cord-cutters. Nevertheless, there were limitations inherent to the trial procedure, namely the fact that not all designed features were fully functional, as well as API restrictions which prevented the inclusion of native features from Netflix, YouTube and Facebook. Despite these limitations, the validation of the unification and personalization concept, along with the recommendations provided by the participants, constitute an encouragement to further development and testing with more advanced functionalities. These may include content discovery and social networking tools embedded in the system, and also available on second screen devices to be used both as a remote control and a way to interact with complementary information.

In addition, the UCD methodological approach adopted by the UltraTV project, that recognizes industry trends and integrates the feedback of end-users in different stages of the UX evaluations using quantitative and qualitative instruments, may provide valuable contributions regarding frameworks for product development as well as user's insights agnostic to players' interests to push the next generation of television systems.

Acknowledgments. This paper is a result of the UltraTV - UltraHD TV Application Ecosystem project (grant agreement no.17738), funded by COMPETE 2020, Portugal 2020 and the European Union through the European Regional Development Fund (FEDER). Authors are grateful to the project partners.

References

1. Ericsson-Consumer lab. TV and Media 2017: A Consumer-Driven Future of Media. Ericsson, Stockholm (2017)
2. Abreu, J., Almeida, P., Teles, B.M.: TV discovery & enjoy: a new approach to help users finding the right TV Program to to Watch. In: Proceedings of the 2014 ACM International Conference on Interactive Experiences for TV and Online Video -TVX 2014, pp. 63–70. ACM, Newcastle (2014)
3. Abreu, J., Nogueira, J., Becker, V., Cardoso, B.: Survey of catch-up TV and other time-shift services: a comprehensive analysis and taxonomy of linear and nonlinear television. Telecommun. Syst. **64**(1), 57–74 (2017)
4. Vanattenhoven, J., Geerts, D.: Broadcast, video-on-demand, and other ways to watch television content. In: Proceedings of the ACM International Conference on Interactive Experiences for TV and Online Video - TVX 2015, pp. 73–82. ACM, Brussels (2015)
5. Nielsen-Company. Screen wars: The battle for eye space in a TV-everywhere world. Nielsen Insights, Nielsen, New York (2015)
6. Almeida, P., et al.: Iterative user experience evaluation of a user interface for the unification of TV contents. In: Abásolo, M.J., Abreu, J., Almeida, P., Silva, T. (eds.) jAUTI 2017. CCIS, vol. 813, pp. 44–57. Springer, Cham (2018). https://doi.org/10.1007/978-3-319-90170-1_4
7. Almeida, P., et al.: UltraTV: an iTV content unification prototype. In: Proceedings of the ACM International Conference on Interactive Experiences for TV and Online Video - TVX 2018. ACM, Seoul (2018)
8. Lowdermilk, T.: User-Centered Design: A Developer's Guide to Building User-Friendly Applications, vol. 1. O'Reilly Media, Inc., Sebastopol (2013). (M. Treseler, ed.)
9. Abreu, J., Almeida, P., Silva, T., Velhinho, A., Fernandes, S.: Using experts review to validate an iTV UI for the unification of contents. In: Proceedings of The 12th International Multi-Conference on Society, Cybernetics and Informatics (IMSCI 2018). Springer, Orlando (2018)
10. Almeida, P., Ferraz de Abreu, J., Oliveira, E., Velhinho, A.: Expert evaluation of a user interface for the unification of TV contents. In: Proceedings of the 6th Iberoamerican Conference on Applications and Usability of Interactive TV - jAUTI 2017, pp. 59–70. Universidade de Aveiro, Aveiro (2017)
11. Almeida, P., Jorge, A., Fernandes, S., Oliveira, E.: Content unification in iTV to enhance user experience: The UltraTV Project. In: Proceedings of the ACM International Conference on Interactive Experiences for TV and Online Video - TVX 2018. ACM, Seoul (2018)

12. Waterman, D., Sherman, R., Wook Ji, S.: The economics of online television: industry development, aggregation, and "TV Everywhere". Telecommun. Policy **37**(9), 725–736 (2013)
13. Abreu, J., Almeida, P., Silva, T.: A UX evaluation approach for second-screen applications. In: Abásolo, M.J., Perales, F.J., Bibiloni, A. (eds.) jAUTI/CTVDI -2015. CCIS, vol. 605, pp. 105–120. Springer, Cham (2016). https://doi.org/10.1007/978-3-319-38907-3_9
14. Mahlke, S., Thüring, M.: Studying antecedents of emotional experiences in interactive contexts. In: Proceedings of the SIGCHI Conference on Human Factors in Computing Systems - CHI 2007, pp. 915–918. ACM, San Jose (2007)
15. Bernhaupt, R., Pirker, M.: Evaluating user experience for interactive television: towards the development of a domain-specific user experience questionnaire. In: Kotzé, P., Marsden, G., Lindgaard, G., Wesson, J., Winckler, M. (eds.) INTERACT 2013. LNCS, vol. 8118, pp. 642–659. Springer, Heidelberg (2013). https://doi.org/10.1007/978-3-642-40480-1_45
16. Hassenzahl, M.: User experience (UX): towards an experiential perspective on product quality. In: Proceedings of the 20th International Conference of the Association Francophone d'Interaction Homme-Machine on - IHM 2008, pp. 11–15 (2008)
17. Hassenzahl, M., Tractinsky, N.: User experience - a research agenda. Behav. Inf. Technol. **25**(2), 91–97 (2006)
18. Bangor, A., Kortum, P., Miller, J.: Determining what individual SUS scores mean: adding an adjective rating scale. J. Usability Stud. **4**(3), 114–123 (2009)
19. Brooke, J.: SUS - a quick and dirty usability scale. Usability Eval. Ind. **189**(194), 4–7 (1996)
20. Martins, A.I., Rosa, A.F., Queirós, A., Silva, A., Rocha, N.P.: European Portuguese validation of the System Usability Scale (SUS). Procedia Comput. Sci. **67**, 293–300 (2015)
21. Bradley, M.M., Lang, P.J.: Measuring emotion: the self-assessment semantic differential manikin and the semantic differential. J. Behav. Therapy Exp. Psychiatry **25**, 49–59 (1994)
22. Hassenzahl, M., Burmester, M., Koller, F.: AttrakDiff: Ein Fragebogen zur Messung wahrgenommener hedonischer und pragmatischer Qualität, pp. 187–196. Vieweg+Teubner Verlag (2003)
23. Patton, M.Q.: Qualitative Research and Evaluation Methods Qualitative Inquiry, 3rd edn. Sage Publications, Thousand Oaks (2002)

Lessons Learned from Testing iTV Applications with Seniors

Telmo Silva(✉) , Hilma Caravau , and Liliana Reis

Digimedia, Department of Communication and Arts,
University of Aveiro, Aveiro, Portugal
{tsilva,hilmacaravau,lilianaareis}@ua.pt

Abstract. Despite the increasing number of solutions that come up every day with real usefulness to support the elderly, older people need to feel that the product is a real asset, often requiring more time to adopt solutions. The usage and satisfaction levels are highly influenced by the concern that development and design teams need to have by taking target audience's needs and expectations into account. Considering that the user is the key player, he/she should be the centrepiece in the development of a project. In the scope of the +TV4E project, that aims to develop an interactive television (iTV) platform to deliver informative contents about social and public services to Portuguese elders, several stages were carried out with potential end users based in a participatory design approach. These moments required that method and process' decisions were adopted, based on literature as well as on the experience lived during these moments. Likewise, dealing with older people requires extra care (physical, language, etc.) by the researchers, considering the anticipated and unexpected difficulties that can arise. Thus, the present paper aims to describe and discuss the challenges faced by the +TV4E project team members during all the project process, as well as the lessons learned concerning the used methodologies and tools and the implemented process. It is the intention of the authors that the presented findings can be used as guidelines in other studies involving the elderly.

Keywords: iTV platform · Elderly · Developing process · Lessons learned

1 Introduction

Faced by almost all countries, the ageing population, is a great human achievement that resulted from improvements made on living conditions. Facilitated access to better food and nutrients, water and enhancements in sanitation and health systems [1] were key aspects to perform this feat. Since 1970 the world average age of death has increased 35 years, with declines in death rates in all groups of the age pyramid [1]. Societies are increasingly aware and concerned with the needs that arise with the ageing process, both at individual and at collective level. One of the first public attitudes that reveal the societal aware concerning this phenomenon was the creation of the "active ageing" concept, by the World Health Organization (WHO) in 2002 [2].

Due to the population ageing, there are more and more politics, studies, interventions, products and solutions intending to provide answers to older people's needs.

© Springer Nature Switzerland AG 2019
M. J. Abásolo et al. (Eds.): jAUTI 2018, CCIS 1004, pp. 148–161, 2019.
https://doi.org/10.1007/978-3-030-23862-9_11

This greater attention for the elderly's needs has been actively contributing to the development of effective solutions for a healthier, autonomous ageing process. Traditionally several technologies focus on helping seniors with physical impairments but its potential is increasingly recognized as an important support for the promotion of social life [3]. Based in this phenomenon, the concept of *gerontechnologies* appears. This type of solutions aim to support older people to maintain their autonomy, increase the feeling of belonging to a community, enlarge the social networks, and improve the wellbeing and literacy [4, 5].

Recent studies have shown that the elderlies are increasingly demanding with the solutions they effectively use in their daily lives, which is also a result of the growing supply. In line with this, and in order to develop solutions with real impact in the individuals' lives, it is essential to construct products with and for seniors. However, development teams must balance the effort that the involvement of potential end-users requires on their part, to not saturate people which, often, generates some reluctance in collaborating in new initiatives.

Through time, one of the greatest media platforms with high importance in citizens' life, regardless the age group, was the television (TV). With the emergence of the internet and new ways to access information, television was losing prominence. However, regarding the Portuguese elderly population, this remains the preferred device for accessing information and entertainment contents [6]. The combination of television's functionalities with the potential of the internet led to the creation of interactive television (iTV) systems, which is the basis of the +TV4E project. This project, further explained in Sect. 2, aimed to develop an iTV platform to promote the info-inclusion of Portuguese seniors through the exhibition of informative contents about public and social services on TV.

As referred before, developing a product for a digital medium directed to a specific target group of users, implies worrying about their needs and optimizing the interface based on evaluation and tests, in order to create a good quality system as a whole. This framework, entitled co-creation process by Rosenberg and colleagues [7], is one of the most powerful design principles of new innovations as well as the user's experience. This was one of the key principles in the +TV4E project, which closely involved potential end-users in various phases of defining and testing functionalities. Developing tests with people implies that researchers can be able to adapt their behaviour to the situations, to the individuals and their specific needs, as well as having good levels of communication skills, empathy, etc. Although, it is recognized that the life stage of the participants in the tests may influence the session' dynamics and, consequently, the desired goals and required data.

In addition to the present introduction, this article is organized in the following sections: Sect. 2 offering a brief description of the +TV4E academic project; Sect. 3 presenting a quick analysis of the ageing process and some of its characteristics as well as a broader view on the importance of developing technologies with its final target audience; Sect. 4 which illustrates the methodological steps followed during the testing phases with seniors and the main lessons learned, disaggregated by type of technique applied, and finally, Sect. 5 that presents some of the conclusions drawn from this study and orientations for future work in this field.

2   +TV4E Project

The +TV4E project aims to promote the info-inclusion and improve the quality of life of Portuguese seniors by broadcasting video spots with informative content about social and public services. These videos include an audio track narrating the news content that is crawled from specific websites. This is an action-research project headed by the University of Aveiro, that comes up with an iTV platform, running in set-top boxes (STB), to enrich the TV viewing experience. Considering the user's preferences, needs and expectations, the system that supports the platform was created to only send relevant contents for the user. The information presented in the videos is aggregated into seven macro-areas of interest, titled *Assistance Services of General Interest for Elderly* (ASGIE), previously studied [8]. These areas are: (1) health care and welfare services; (2) social services; (3) financial services; (4) culture, informal education and entertainment; (5) security services; (6) local authority services and (7) transport services. Regularly, the system verifies if there are new contents on the information sources that feed the platform, and automatically generate new informative videos. This process is achieved through an algorithm that selects contents from different web sources and builds audio-visual pieces on its own.

The video spots are then injected into the linear television transmission. At this moment the regular TV broadcast is locally paused and resumed after the presentation of the informative video. It should also be noted that when the STB is turned on, a splash screen is shown with contextual elements: a welcome note based on the time of the day; information regarding the weather (temperature and an icon that visually represents the weather); the time and date; and the current season.

Regardless of the macro-area of interest, all videos have a similar structure and are composed by a set of elements, presented in a succession of cards' flow. The audio-visual elements included, specific to each macro-area of information, are: icon that identifies each specific ASGIE; specific colour background associated with each macro-area of information; background images defined to each ASGIE; opacity/transparency of images; background music; audio track that narrates the news article; font size shown as video caption [9]. Narration's speed; video length; reading's synchronization with transitions between screens and narration speed; transition effects between screens and news' interest, are the functional components integrated into the informative videos [9].

The research team defined two modes of presentation/visualization of the videos, analysed during the project execution with potential end users: (i) "injection", where the user receives an overlaid notification informing that a new video is available and it will start in 15 s; or (ii) "notification", where the user only receives a notification, localized at the top of the screen, requesting the user's express wish to start the video. In this last scenario, to accept the video, the user should press the "OK" button on the remote control. If the user does not execute any action, after 30 s, the notification retracts to the corner of the screen waiting for instruction. After 4 min it disappears irreversibly if no action is taken.

A video library was also implemented in the iTV system as an extra feature. This component allows the consultation of video spots, generated on the last five days, already seen, as well as accessing videos that were triggered to the user but that were not visualized.

Additionally, a mobile application for Android was designed, as an extension to the iTV platform, which aims to offer a higher freedom degree access to the users, not limiting the visualization of informative videos to the home context. This feature allows the user to access informative contents, on-demand, through the video library as well as recommended content.

3 Theoretical Background

Until a few years ago, getting older was a painful process deeply characterized by negative factors. However, parallelly, a new political and societal sensitivity had raised, marked by the implementation of new political frameworks and strategies that support and promote active and successful ageing.

Despite the heterogeneity that characterizes the group of people in advanced ages, there are restrictions that naturally appear, such as physical and mental health (changes at the organic and mental level), psychological (self-regulating changes of individuals relative to their age perspective), and social limitations [10, 11]. Although the responsible factors for ageing in their biological basis are not consensual, the gradual physiological and anatomical deteriorations that occur in the human body have real repercussions in individuals' lives.

Concerning sensory modifications, for example, seniors face visual changes related to alterations in the eye structure, such as declines in visual acuity, colour vision, contrast sensibility and adaptability [12]. Also, one of the most problematic modifications for seniors is hearing perception changes. Summarily, age-related changes in hearing are: loss of sensibility to pure tones, especially high frequency tones; difficulty in understanding speech; sound localization problems; problems in binaural audition; higher sensibility to loudness and more time needed to process audio information [13].

Obviously, neither these nor other modifications felt by the elderly should feed the stereotype that older people are "less capable", but it is undeniable that ageing makes some activities and tasks harder to execute.

The ageing phenomenon leads to societal changes that are increasingly focusing its attention to seniors' needs and desires, due to their growing importance in the demographic structure. The advances made to Information and Communication Technologies (ICT's) have been contributing to an efficient global distribution and diffusion of information, which improves well-being, satisfaction and comfort levels of developed countries' lifestyles. However, modern devices and new technologies are often difficult for older people to understand or to handle, hence one of the main concerns in developing ICT's for seniors is based on their ability of adapting to a new technological system. Physical and cognitive challenges, hesitation related to technology's benefits or even basic online services' complexity emerge as some of the factors for the dissuasion of ICT's usage by seniors [5, 14].

In this line of thinking, technological solutions for seniors should be designed and developed keeping their perspectives and necessities in mind, as well as considering their natural surrounding environment, for it to become a valuable instrument for them [14, 15].

4   +TV4E Phases and Techniques Applied

The +TV4E project involved various phases which consisted of several intermediate steps, in which different methodological techniques were applied. The results obtained in each one of the phases supported the development of the next phase, which mean the project is characterized by an evolutionary and sequential way. Although, several times there was the development of more than one task in parallel, which made some tasks benefit of the results of the following activities.

The choice for each one of the applied methodologies and techniques varied according to the defined objective, the guidelines of the international literature, but also of the previous experience of the researchers with the target public.

Through +TV4E project time, seven main phases were carried out (see Fig. 1).

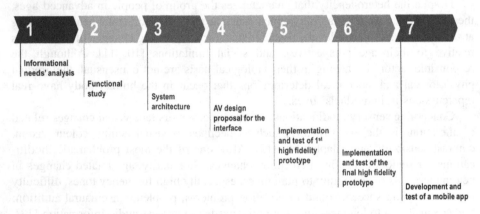

Fig. 1. Project execution phases of +TV4E project

Each project phase had specific aims as well as expected results, briefly explained next.

Phase 1: Informational needs' analysis encompassed the literature review, in international scientific databases, concerning the work developed in the area of iTV applications and their potential to support seniors; analysis of seniors' information needs namely the requirements related to social and public services, as well as their opinions and expectations regarding the development of iTV applications. Data was also collected about the information seniors' needs on social and public services in the Portuguese context regarding the lack of studies in the national framework in this field.

Phase 2: The definition of functional components of an iTV platform for seniors, able to deliver content about public services relied on a review of the STB primary specifications, exploring its functional potential and studying multiple solutions for each component. This task required on-field questioning to ensure the acknowledgment of the target audience, cultural probes (observation and informal conversation at seniors' natural environment) and focus groups (including gerontologists and researchers involved in the development of applications for elderly people).

Phase 3: The development of the system architecture and front-end interface were carried out concerning the inputs collected in phase 2 and was fully in charge of the +TV4E developers.

Phase 4: The main objectives were to design an initial graphical solution for the iTV platform; to develop an initial architecture for the iTV platform; to develop a low fidelity prototype of the overall platform that would allow: (i) testing interaction models, design decisions, architectural and communication decisions; (ii) perceiving if the content defined to be delivered to the users would be the most appropriate and if the algorithms used would be adequate. After defining the video's attributes and tuning the architecture system, it became essential to test the prototype with potential end users, which allowed the identification and closure of new problems in the platform under development as well as making sure that the data being used was trustworthy through improvements in the prototype.

Phase 5: This stage centered on the testing phase which included both lab-based studies and field trial studies. Thus, the aims were: using the prototype and perform tests with the target audience, considering their specificities; evaluate the design and functionalities with the target audience through tests; redefine, if needed, according to the test results, design, functionalities, delivered content, architecture and techniques to interrupt.

Phase 6: At this stage, the platform needed to be highly stable for the tests to provide accurate results for the project since software problems were very disruptive in the user experience (UX). Aside from fixing software and architectural problems, this task also comprised the optimization of already implemented layouts and interfaces, namely the video library. These were then presented to users in controlled testing scenarios, both in a senior university and in a senior home, where the research team was able to collect valuable feedback that helped to improve the overall usability of the platform. After that, the developed iTV platform were tested with the target audience at their homes (natural environment), as a final evaluation of the product.

Phase 7: Finally, a mobile application was created as an extension of the iTV platform. After the development of a first prototype of the mobile application, two test moments were performed with a limited number of potential users. Both test phases aimed to evaluate key aspects of the interface and the layout of the application.

According to the purposes of each step, several methods and technical approaches were applied. The selection of methodologies for data collection took their benefits for each moment into account.

Older people are an increasing user group of technologies and creating useful and easy-to-use solutions for them, regarding features and interaction, is of high importance, even for those with a poor technical background [16]. However, seniors are a special group of individuals with pronounced characteristics and different needs from younger age groups, which requires a special preparation and assembly of the researchers for the moments of interaction.

Several factors influence the choice of the technique applied, such as device used and previous experience with the technology [17]. Also, inherent factors to the individual must also be taken into account, namely age, education, academics and social background, specific diseases, etc. [18].

Concerning all these factors, during the +TV4E timeline, potential end-users of the iTV platform were involved in two major moments: (1) analysing their information needs about social and public Portuguese services and (2) developing the application's interface and components. In this second category of moments, the focus was on studying and analysing the quality of the interaction between the individual and the technology, which is based on the context of Human-Computer Interaction (HCI) [19]. During this study, the team was engaged with the co-creation principle, and whenever possible, potential end users were involved in the design and testing phases. The following topics explain in detail all methods and techniques that were applied to collect data with seniors, in which specific phases they were applied and the main lessons learned on how to run testing moments with older adults.

4.1   Questionnaires

The data collection methodology through surveys includes making questions to individuals, in order to collect information regarding attitudes, feelings, values, opinions or factual information. When questions are presented through an inquire in which the respondents answer by themselves, it is called a questionnaire or self-administered [20]. Overall, questionnaires are used to inquire a large number of people in order to characterize traits that identify large groups of subjects [21].

Phase 1 (Informational needs' analysis) and 4 (Audio-visual design proposal for the interface) included the application of questionnaires.

After assessing the information needs of the elderly from the research specialists' perspectives, in Phase 1, a focus group was carried out along with potential target users of the +TV4E platform to assess the feedback of senior population regarding the services in which they feel more necessity to access in a clear and concise way. The sample included 11 seniors, recruited in a Senior University. After presenting the project, a questionnaire was delivered to validate the 7 macro-areas of interest and their respective services. Participants were asked to score, in a Likert type scale (1 = unimportant to 3 = very important), a list of 23 services previously identified as key services important for them to receive information about [22].

Further, during Phase 4, all the audio-visual elements were created and tested, namely, sound elements, text elements (font type and font size), iconography, colours' video background, video library layout evaluation and final analysis of the +TV4E components [9, 12, 23, 24]. To achieve this, participatory design sessions were held in collaboration with a group of senior students from two Seniors Universities, who were invited to give their opinions about the proposed audio-visual elements and thus contributing to its design's improvement. To analyse the two desired variables regarding sound elements, specifically gender of the voice-over and the use of background music, the research team presented one video with a male voice and the second with a female voice as well as two videos with and without background music. During the analysis of all the other elements (text, iconography, colours' video background, video library layout and final analysis with all the elements gathered) the same approach was used. A set of proposals, concerning each element, was presented on a TV screen, and afterwards, participants were individually invited to select their favourite options in a paper supported survey.

The video library layout evaluation and final analysis of the +TV4E components also included a focus group moment.

One of the main lessons learned after applying questionnaires to senior population is that several participants need individual support to complete the surveys because they do not understand what is requested, even after explaining numerous times what is intended in the survey. Resorting to daily situations to explain what is intended is one of the easiest ways to solve such situations. Therefore, it is necessary to ensure that all participants answer with the same basic information, which means that it some extra information was always necessary and the same verbal examples were given. For example, during the survey applied on Phase 1, many seniors do not know which specific services information were included in social services ASGIE.

4.2   Focus Group

A focus group is defined as a method for data collection through interactions and group discussions, where topics suggested by a moderator with experience and leadership ability are discussed [25]. This technique may be considered as a mix of participant observation and in-depth interview to characterize participants' perceptions, spontaneous opinions, comments and attitudes [20]. Its usefulness is recognized for getting information about how people or a group of people think about a topic [25–27]. The focus group should be conducted with a limited number of participants and is advisable to have between 6 and 10 people.

During the +TV4E project, there were several focus group moments, such as in Phase 4 (Audio-visual design proposal for the interface) to the video colour background and colour for the corresponding icon, video library layout evaluation and the final analysis of the +TV4E components, and in Phase 7 (Development and test of a mobile app). In all these stages, the focus group was conducted after the team members presenting the components under analysis, individually or in group, with the aim of discussing participants' opinions.

Specifically, in Phase 4 was defined the video's colour background that identifies the ASGIE targeted to the informative content, which is the same for the corresponding icon. Colours intends to be an anchor element so that the user visually identifies the ASGIE under presentation. Considering the seven ASGIE, a set of 14 different colours was created, in order to minimize problems related to exclusion of hypotheses. To promote a free choice process, participants were presented with a greater number of colours than the number of ASGIE's, so that they did not feel limited in the choosing process. Additionally, other shades were available for each colour (darker or lighter), meaning participants could suggest adjustments for some specific colour. Afterwards, a focus group was held where, for each icon, the group discussed and decided, in consensus, the colour that would best represent the ASGIE in question.

During the focus group sessions, some special cares were taken concerning the target group. To ensure the evaluation of the same data, it was always necessary to give the same verbal examples and the research team needed to use the same test conditions. For example, the team always assured a distance of 3 meters between the television screen (a full HD TV set with 42") and the participants, to ensure that all the tests occurred under the same circumstances between individuals. The same principle was applied in the case of sound elements' evaluation, where the two samples included (from two different Senior Universities) adapted the sound volume to the natural hearing problems that arise with ageing and kept the same volume in both groups of participants.

Throughout some of these moments it was noticeable that the individuals' opinions were greatly influenced by the lack of awareness of how their choice would visually appear. This type of hesitancies made it difficult to decide on one of the presented options, for example, choosing one of three font types. Thus, considering that there was often a small number of participants and it is required a final decision on a specific element in these moments the research team asked participants to choose a unique option, agreed between all, through consensus. It is not overlooked that this type of decision may bias the obtained data, however, the moderator tried that the participants had the total idea of the options when making the final decision.

Finally, it should be mentioned that the research team would often like to have the opportunity to develop individual interviews with participants, however, this would entail further time, which led to the selection of the focus group technique.

4.3 Interviews

Interview is a data collection method that relies on pre-defined verbal questions to individuals [20]. It is guided by issues designed to collect data on the research topic and organized according to an Interview Guide. Based on direct interactions between the researcher and interviewee, this method makes possible to obtain information that would never be obtained through traditional questionnaires.

Often, the interviewer has a set of prepared questions to present to the interviewee in a structured and methodical way (structured interview). Alternatively, these questions can be used as a checklist to remind the researcher of key topics regarding the needed data (semi-structured or open interview). To interview can entail several challenges related to human interaction between the researcher and the study's participants [28]. It is essential that interviews take place in an open and flexible environment in order to foster reflections, ideas and presuppositions about the research theme [21].

Bryman distinguishes between structured interviews and qualitative interviews, referring that a qualitative interview typically includes semi structured/non-structured and open interview [29]. Structured interviews intend to maximize reliability and validity when defining key concepts, hence the predefined and well-planned questions. This type of interview is designed with the sole purpose of answer those questions [29]. On the other side, qualitative interviews tend to be less structured and it is not thought out to obtain highly specific results. At this type of interviews there is much more interest about the interviewee's point of view, while structured interviews reflect on the researcher's concerns. Bryman assumes that at qualitative interviews, "to ramble" or coming up with new conversation topics is frequently encouraged, as it offers a vision of what the participants think is relevant and important [29].

This method revealed to be advantaging for the course of this study, since it intended to obtain inputs from potential end-users to validate prototype versions of the platform. Due to the sample's characteristics, a more open approach of interviewing was considered a valuable technique to keep the participants involved in the data collections moments during the test phases of the prototype, as well as the testing phase of the mobile app development.

The interview technique was applied during Phases 5, 6 and 7, namely the test phases of the iTV platform and mobile app prototype versions. The researchers made use of a predefined structure of several questions exploring the participants' point of view regarding system overall functionalities, usability of the platform and their user experience. Nevertheless, the structured approach of an interview did not stop the users from giving additional inputs nor did make the researchers strictly focus on the pre-defined questions, encouraging a relaxed conversation environment for the participants to feel at ease and comfortable with the researchers. This led the users to be more open and express their opinions better, but also digressing sometimes from the subject in discussion.

A lesson taken from relying on interviews with older people is that these are moments that cannot afford to stretch for too long, especially when it comes to structured interviews, since this public tends to divagate from the topic on focus. The researcher needs to try to maintain the participants relaxed by not solely focusing on the needed data, but also keep an interest on the main conversation and try not to divagate too much. To test and prepare the interview beforehand may minimize potential difficulties that can arise while interviewing seniors.

4.4 Field Tests

Phases 5 and 6, both related to the development process of the high-fidelity prototypes for the platform, also included testing processes to evaluate the system's performance. In both phases, the prototypes were brought to seniors' homes for them to test it in a familiar setting, as close as possible to real usage of the product. The field trial approach was selected by the +TV4E team as the prototype would be tested in a "real life" setting as opposed to testing it under artificial laboratory conditions. The collected inputs from a "real life" background allows the gathering of valuable information for the development team that would not be identified in a laboratorial context, as well as detailed data that may not be immediately obvious to researchers and participants [30, 31].

End-users were prompted to test the 1st version of the prototype during a 5-week field trial at Phase 5 of the project, and then a 2-week field trial was conducted later after the prototype was improved. These tests aimed to identify potential issues on the system, to evaluate usefulness and functionalities of the platform and to understand usability levels and user experience the system offered, counting with the participation of senior end-users. Both field trials gave the participants the opportunity to explore the platform and understand how to use it alongside a researcher of the project on the first day. Afterwards, the prototype was installed in their homes and the users were free to use it for a certain period (5 weeks in the first field trial and 2 weeks in the final field trial), without compromising their daily lives. The team always made sure that the users were enlightened and without doubts about the system's usage but made them comfortable enough to contact by telephone anytime they needed during the field trial period. Nevertheless, during both field trials the team aimed to preserve a frequent contact with the participants, monitoring their experience by phone. This accompaniment was intended to register any incident or event that may have occurred and to promote a trust relationship with the end-users keeping them engaged with the project.

Despite phone monitoring keeping users in touch with the team, in some cases this was not enough to motivate the prototype's usage. Few users showed signs of a growing disinterest which led researchers to contact them more than one time in an attempt to keep them motivated. As it was not effective, the users were withdrawn of the tests due to the absence of useful data that could be included in the study. The researchers were conscious of these users' desires, respecting their decision of dropping out of the study.

The team learned that, while a field trial approach contributes to gather valuable data that would not be identified through another method, it is not easy to get full control of the participants' experience and potential incidents. Whenever there is a technical issue that an older user is not used to and is not able to overcome it without help, a phone call may not be a clear mean to orientate the user on how to fix the problem, due to the typical digital literacy levels this type of public presents, so choosing to work with end-users that are geographically closer can represent an added value for a field trial study.

Despite the challenges that field trials can present, developing tests of a technological solution in a real-life setting when it comes to older users, enables more profound and authentic insights from participants as it is easier for them to envision the idea of what a daily usage of the solution would be.

5   Overall Lessons Learned

Following the data presented above, there are some lessons learned that are transversal to all project phases, as well as to all methods and techniques applied.

One of the main difficulties, and perhaps the biggest obstacle, was to recruit participants. Concerning the inclusion criteria defined to the sample individuals (60 years old and over; being a literate person; watching television frequently and living close to the research team work place), with some variations depending on the test phase, it was learned that there were some available options regarding where potential participants could be found: seniors associations such as Senior Universities; day care centres and family and friends networks.

Once in the field context it is important to promote a relaxed environment, encouraging conversations not only about the project which will help to construct a trusting relationship and a connection feeling with the project. A clear and concise language is primordial, and the researchers need to adapt their communication according to each group of participants, for example, taking their education level and technological experience into account, as well as adjusting their voice tone to seniors' hearing acuity. The importance that each person represents for the work must be clearly stated, and each individual should be treated as a unique and irreplaceable participant.

Also, in all the interaction moments the aims and aspects of the data collection should be referred, allowing the participant to request additional information or quit at any time. The confidentiality of the collected data must always be explicitly guaranteed, verbally and written. Demonstrating that there is a constant monitoring and that the team is totally available to clarify any doubts without any repercussion for the person is also considered a good practice. Making it clear that participants are not under a test, withdrawing the concern that many of them feel when testing solutions, is also very significant.

As referred above, it is difficult to engage and bring together in a single space a reasonable number of people (around 30 individuals) to make decisions about a certain feature/aspect. In these cases, one reliable solution is to select a restricted number of participants in a focus group moment and require that in the end, the group makes a consensus decision among all.

This paper was created in line with the belief that sharing the knowledge and lessons learned over an academic or corporation project may represent an added value for other research teams that work in the same field or similar areas.

Acknowledgements. The research leading to this work has received funding from Project 3599 – Promover a Produção Científica e Desenvolvimento Tecnológico e a Constituição de Redes Temáticas (3599-PPCDT) and European Commission Funding FEDER (through FCT: Fundação para a Ciência e Tecnologia I.P. under grant agreement no. PTDC/IVC-COM/3206/2014).

References

1. He, W., Goodkind, D., Kowal, P.: An Aging World: 2015 International Population Reports., Washington DC (2016)
2. Kalache, A., Gatti, A.: Active Ageing: a policy framework. (2002)
3. Harrington, T.L., Harrington, M.K.: Gerontechnology: Why and How. Eindhoven, Netherlands (2000)
4. Rice, M., Carmichael, A.: Factors facilitating or impeding older adults' creative contributions in the collaborative design of a novel DTV-based application. Univ. Access Inf. Soc. **12**, 5–19 (2013). https://doi.org/10.1007/s10209-011-0262-8
5. Silva, T., Abreu, J., Antunes, M., Almeida, P., Silva, V., Santinha, G.: +TV4E: interactive television as a support to push information about social services to the elderly. Procedia Comput. Sci. **100**, 580–585 (2016). https://doi.org/10.1016/j.procs.2016.09.198
6. Marktest Group: Portugueses viram cerca de 3h30m de Tv em (2010). http://www.marktest. com/wap/a/n/id ~ 16e0.aspx
7. Rosenberg, P., Ross, A., Garçon, L.: WHO Global Forum on Innovations for Ageing Populations. Kobe, Japan (2013)
8. Silva, T., Caravau, H., Campelo, D.: Information Needs about Public and Social Services of Portuguese Elderly. In: Proceedings of the 3rd International Conference on Information and Communication Technologies for Ageing Well and e-Health (ICT4AWE), Porto, Portugal, pp. 46–57 (2017)

9. Silva, T., Reis, L., Hernández, C., Caravau, H.: Building informative audio-visual content automatically: a process to define the key aspects. In: Ferraz de Abreu, J., Guerrero, M.J.A., Almeida, P., and Silva, T. (eds.) Proceedings of the 6th Iberoamerican Conference on Applications and Usability of Interactive TV - jAUTI 2017, pp. 132–143. University of Aveiro, Aveiro, Portugal (2017)

10. Schneider, R.H., Irigaray, T.Q.: O envelhecimento na atualidade: aspectos cronológicos, biológicos, psicológicos e sociais The process of aging in today' s world: chronological, biological, psychological and social aspects. Estud. Psicol. **25**, 585–593 (2008)

11. Schroots, J., Birren, J.: A Psychological point of view toward human aging and adaptability. In: Adaptability and Aging, Proceeding of 9th International Conference of Social Gerontology, Quebeque, pp. 43–54 (1980)

12. Reis, L., Caravau, H., Silva, T., Almeida, P.: Automatic creation of TV content to integrate in seniors viewing activities. In: Abásolo, M.J., Almeida, P., Pina Amargós, J. (eds.) jAUTI 2016. CCIS, vol. 689, pp. 32–46. Springer, Cham (2017). https://doi.org/10.1007/978-3-319-63321-3_3

13. Czaja, S.J., Sharit, J.: Designing Training and Instructional Programs for Older Adults (Human Factors & Aging). Taylor & Francis Group, LLC, Boca Raton (2013)

14. Stojmenova, E., Debevc, M., Zebec, L., Imperl, B.: Assisted living solutions for the elderly through interactive TV. Multimed. Tools Appl. **66**, 115–129 (2013). https://doi.org/10.1007/s11042-011-0972-1

15. Nunes, F., Kerwin, M., Silva, P.A.: Design recommendations for TV user interfaces for older adults: findings from the eCAALYX project. In: Proceeding of 14th Int. ACM SIGACCESS Conference on Computers and Accessibility - ASSETS 2012, p. 41 (2012). https://doi.org/10.1145/2384916.2384924

16. Epelde, G., et al.: Providing universally accessible interactive services through TV sets: implementation and validation with elderly users. Multimed. Tools Appl. **67**, 497–528 (2013). https://doi.org/10.1007/s11042-011-0949-0

17. Silva, P.A., Nunes, F.: 3 x 7 usability testing guidelines for older adults. In: Calvillo Gámez, E.H., González, M., González, V. (eds.) Proceedings of the 3rd Mexican Workshop on Human Computer Interaction (MexIHC 2010), pp. 1–8. Universidad Politécnica de San Luis Potosí, San Nicolas de los Garza, Mexico (2010)

18. Pemberton, L., Griffiths, R.: Usability evaluation techniques for interactive television. Proc. HCI Int. **4**, 882–886 (2003)

19. Dix, A., Finlay, J., Abowd, G.D., Beale, R.: Human-Computer Interaction. Prentice Hall, New York (2005)

20. Coutinho, C.P.: Metodologia de Investigação em Ciências Sociais e Humanas, Almedina (2015)

21. Quivy, R., Van Campenhoudt, L.: Manual de investigação em ciências sociais. Gradiva, Liaboa (1998)

22. Silva, T., Caravau, H., Campelo, D.: Information needs about public and social services of portuguese elderly. In: Röcker, C., O'Donoghue, J., Ziefle, M., Maciaszek, L., Molloy, W. (eds.) Proceedings of the 3rd International Conference on Information and Communication Technologies for Ageing Well and e-Health. pp. 46–57. SCITEPRESS - Science and Technology Publications, Porto, Portugal (2017)

23. Silva, T., Caravau, H., Mota, M., Reis, L., Hernandez, C.: A process to design a video library for senior users of iTV. In: Abásolo, M.J., Abreu, J., Almeida, P., Silva, T. (eds.) jAUTI 2017. CCIS, vol. 813, pp. 105–116. Springer, Cham (2018). https://doi.org/10.1007/978-3-319-90170-1_8

24. Morgan, D.L.: Focus Groups as Qualitative Research. Sage, Thousand Oaks (1997)

25. Mack, N., Woodsong, C., MacQueen, K.M., Guest, G., Namey, E.: Module 4: focus groups. In: Qualitative Research Methods: A Data Collector's Field Guide, pp. 50–82 (2005)
26. Barrett, J., Kirk, S.: Running focus groups with elderly and disabled elderly participants. Appl. Ergon. **31**, 621–629 (2000)
27. Gray, D.: Doing Research in the Real World. SAGE Publications, London (2004)
28. Bryman, A.: Social Research Methods. Oxford University Press, Oxford (2012)
29. Nayebi, F., Desharnais, J.-M., Abran, A.: The state of the art of mobile application usability evaluation. In: 2012 25th IEEE Canadian Conference on Electrical and Computer Engineering, pp. 1–4 (2012). https://doi.org/10.1109/ccece.2012.6334930
30. Rauterberg, M.: USERfit Tools: Field Trial. http://www.idemployee.id.tue.nl/g.w.m. rauterberg/lecturenotes/UFTfieldtrial.pdf
31. Silva, T., Caravau, H., Ferraz de Abreu, J., Reis, L.: Seniors' info-inclusion through interactive television: results of a field trial. In: Proceedings of the 4th International Conference on Information and Communication Technologies for Ageing Well and e-Health, pp. 134–141. SCITEPRESS - Science and Technology Publications (2018)

Evaluating the Performance of ASR Systems for TV Interactions in Several Domestic Noise Scenarios

Pedro Beça$^{(\boxtimes)}$ ⓘ, Jorge Abreu ⓘ, Rita Santos ⓘ,
and Ana Rodrigues ⓘ

Digimedia, Department of Communication and Arts,
University of Aveiro, Aveiro, Portugal
{pedrobeca, jfa, rita. santos, ana. rodrigues}@ua. pt

Abstract. Voice interaction with the television is becoming a reality on domestic environments. However, one of the factors that influences the correct operation of these systems is the background noise that obstructs the performance of the automatic speech recognition (ASR) component. In order to further understand this issue, the paper presents an analysis of the performance of three ASR systems (Bing Speech API, Google API, and Nuance ASR) in several domestic noise scenarios resembling the interaction with the TV on a domestic context. A group of 36 users was asked to utter sentences based on TV requests, where the sentences' corpus comprised typical phrases used when interacting with the TV. To better know the behavior, performance and robustness of each ASR to noise, the tests were carried out with three recording devices placed at different distances from the user. Google ASR proved to be the most robust to noise with a higher recognition precision, followed by Bing Speech and Nuance. The results obtained showed that ASR systems performance is globally quite robust but tends to deteriorate with domestic background noise. Future replications of the evaluation setup will allow the evaluation of ASR solutions in other scenarios.

Keywords: Natural language interaction · ASR evaluation · TV interaction · Automatic speech recognition

1 Introduction

Noise robustness is one of the main concerns in automatic speech recognition (ASR) systems. While humans can naturally distinguish a specific audio (e.g. a human voice) from a mixture of multiple audio signals with little or no loss in intelligibility, ASR performance tends to be compromised in the presence of background noise. Although the recorded audio signal goes through a process of filtering and parameterization, the ambient noise can hinder the interpretation of the speech by the system [1, 2]. This is special relevant when ASRs are integrated in voice-interaction systems, which have been increasingly used on TV. Despite its enormous potential, voice interaction must tackle some social and technical barriers to be fully adopted as the future interaction modality with the television. TV-sets are usually located in common

© Springer Nature Switzerland AG 2019
M. J. Abásolo et al. (Eds.): jAUTI 2018, CCIS 1004, pp. 162–175, 2019.
https://doi.org/10.1007/978-3-030-23862-9_12

areas like the living room, where numerous sound emissions presenting a challenge for the performance of the ASR systems [3–5].

Previous studies on voice interaction and television such as those from [6–9] focused essentially on questions related with the interaction devices and the user interface. But not less important, is to better understand how ASR systems - a fundamental part in voice interaction - behave in different noisy scenarios resembling the living room environment.

The performance (in terms of noise robustness and efficiency) of the ASR component is particularly important as it is one of the main (and first) components of the voice interaction architecture.

The main goal of this paper is to perform an analysis of the performance of three commercial ASR systems (Microsoft API, Google API, and NUANCE ASR) on several noise scenarios resembling the interaction with the TV on a domestic environment and to present the results of the tests made for this purpose. The results here presented will be particularly relevant for the future development of a fully functional Natural Language Interaction (NLI) system in Portuguese (a language somehow unexploited in this domain). After this introductory section, this paper is structured as follows: Sect. 2 presents background information and state of the art regarding ARS systems; the Methodology is addressed in Sect. 3; Sect. 4 presents the Results and Discussion; and the Conclusions are presented in Sect. 5.

2 ASR Systems

ASR systems have become popular into different application areas as robotics and vehicles, telecommunications industry, assistive technologies or home automation and are being integrated in everyday devices such as mobile phones or TV-sets [10–12]. The two main usages of ASR are in voice command interactions, that is very strict, and interaction by natural language conversation, which attempts to approach a human-to-human dialogue [13, 14].

2.1 ASR Characterization

Each ASR system can be characterized through several aspects, from the type of speech recognized (continuous speech or composed by isolated words), style of speech supported (spontaneous or by codes), dependence of typical users on system training (speaker independent or dependent), linguistic variability and languages supported to the robustness to noise [5]. Nevertheless, the ASR systems provide the same process: the audio signal is captured by a microphone which converts sound waves into analog waves and then converted into digital data. Initially, the ASR system filter the audio to attenuate unwanted noise and adjusts the recording to constant sound levels and speed. The audio is then divided into phonemes, which can be understood as sound syllables that form the words, by the acoustic model (Fig. 1).

The number of phonemes recognized by the systems varies according to the language used in the conversation. To identify words (lexicon) with different intonations and pronunciations, the ASR systems use statistical models to simulate the most likely

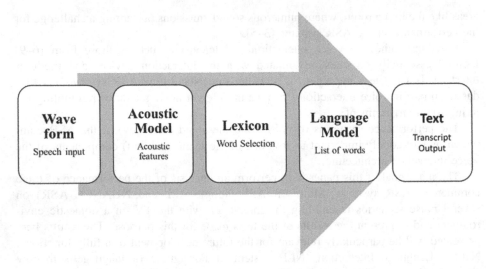

Fig. 1. Generic ASR component and respective functions.

combinations of phonemes (Fig. 1). Rather than individually processing each word, ASR systems are designed to process a much smaller list of keywords that works as contextual clues. Thus, the system can produce much more quickly an adequate response. This last step is a responsibility of the language model (Fig. 1). In the context of interaction with a TV device (either a Smart TV, an advanced Set-top-Box (STB) or a media player), for phrases like "I want to watch a movie" the keywords tagged by the system can be "movie" or "watch" and, from one of these, the ASR can find the context of the other words of the phrase [15, 16].

The improvement and training of ASR systems are fundamentally achieved in two ways: human synchronization and active learning. The first is relatively simple to perform and consists essentially of analyzing the conversation log of the ASR to identify words that are not part of the preprogrammed vocabulary and in the consequent addition of those words into the word list by human programmers. This allows the ASR system to expand its understanding of the speech system, which can range from the inclusion of words from the same base language, that were not previously included, to the inclusion of acronyms and foreignisms. In the second mode, active learning, the ASR is programmed to learn, retain and adopt new words autonomously, constantly expanding its vocabulary. This allows the system to evolve and to adapt to specific users so that it can better communicate with them [13, 14, 17].

For the optimal performance of the ASR, it is recommended to follow the manufacturer's instructions at the level of equipment setup, training, microphone selection, among others [5].

The assessment of the ASR performance can be done by several evaluation metrics, as the Levenshtein distance, the Word Error Rate (WER) or the Word Recognition Rate. Although WER is widely accepted as the standard metric for ASR evaluation, it only measures word errors at the surface level. It does not consider the contextual and syntactic roles of a word, which can be potentially critical on the next technical components of an NLI system [18, 19]. Works as [19] confirms the interest of using of the Levenshtein distance at the phonetic level instead of using it for words.

Among the several ASR solutions available, cloud-based systems have been gaining prominence. In addition to being reliable and secure, these systems also have unlimited storage capacity and ensure the required compatibility in terms of hardware and software. On a cloud-based system, for example, a system update is easily available to all users through a simple upgrade. Among the various solutions of existing ASR systems, it becomes very difficult to know which one to choose since there are several systems such as AT&T Watson, Microsoft API Speech, Google Speech API, Amazon Alexa API, Kaldi, CMU Sphinx, Nuance Recognizer HTK and Dragon [11]. While some are open source and available for free, others are paid but can be used in trial versions for a limited amount of transactions and/or minutes of processed audio. With respect to the full versions, the trial version of the APIs does not have any limitations on what concerns to the performance [18].

In what concerns the application domain of television, Nuance stands out for the development of Dragon TV, a voice recognition software specifically developed for this context that can be used on TV-sets, STBs, remote-controls and other products [20].

2.2   ASR Robustness to Background Noise

A voice system designed for a domestic environment, particularly for television, must be simple and robust to speakers' variations and environmental noises [21]. The common ambient noise level in a domestic environment varies between 30 and 40 dB and it has been experimentally determined that the comfortable regions for music or voice listening/conversation encompass dynamic ranges between 30 and 70 dB, above 75 dB is considered a noisy environment and the level of 120 dB corresponds to the threshold of discomfort [22].

In test-setups arranged to measure the performance (noise robustness and efficiency) of the ASR systems, the addition of noise to clean speech is often used to simulate a person talking in a noisy environment. Especially for certain types of noise and low signal-to-noise ratios, this assumption is not necessarily valid, as the Lombard effect, for example, influences the way the speaker is speaking dependent on the level and type of environmental noise. To deal with this problem, other studies suggested that audio should be collected with background noise. However, and despite the advantages these methods seem to present, it is important to consider its own limitations. Since different noise sources produce different types of noises, this method is not totally effective because it is not possible to consider all types of noise [23, 24]. Considering all these topics, on this paper, the audio will be collected in situ and with several background noises, to do an analysis of the ASR systems at stake in what can be considered distinct scenarios of voice interaction with the TV.

3 Methodology

This section presents the methodology that was followed to test the performance (noise robustness and efficiency) of the selected ASR systems on scenarios resembling the interaction with the TV in a domestic environment. Due to the main goal involved (the development of an NLI solution for a Portuguese context), the considered ASR were chosen based on the following criteria: their reliability, secureness, unlimited storage capacity, and Cloud-based approach, ensuring the required compatibility in terms of hardware and software, easiness and availability of system update; language support in Portuguese; and, output options – while a basic ASR output formulates the best hypothesis about the transcription of the speech input, some offer additional outputs options quite useful for the dialogue flow, by allowing the system to react while the user is still speaking. Based on these criteria, three commercial ASR solutions were chosen: Bing, Google, and Nuance.

3.1 Experimental Setup

The tests were carried out with several setup configurations, combining two distinct recording devices, three distances (from the participants' mouth to the microphones), and four different noise scenarios (Fig. 2).

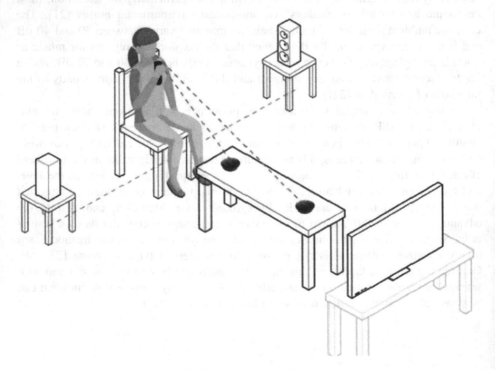

Fig. 2. Experimental Setup.

It was decided to carry out the evaluation in an audio studio since it allowed to have more control over the environmental noise and to create audio conditions as similar as possible for each participant. A pre-test was initially performed with six participants, not only to improve the audio recording procedure and to optimize the entire process but also to select the best setup configuration. In the pre-test phase, several configurations of the speakers, which spread the ambient noise, were considered. For example, it was tried to place the speakers from 1.0 m behind the user, separated by 1.20 m from each other, facing forward and making an angle of 45° with the participant, and laterally at 1 m and 2 m. After the pre-test, it was decided to place the columns laterally 2 meters from the participant, one on each side, since the other configurations caused some discomfort and participants get distracted even with a low noise level (Fig. 2). Instead of adding in post-production the background noise to the participants' audio, the chosen setup allows playing different types of noise while the participants were asked to say a set of phrases, allowing to better simulate what would happen in a real scenario of voice interaction with the TV in a domestic environment. In what concerns to the audio-noise, four scenarios were considered: (a)"Silence" – no extra sounds were added, only was considered the residual noise of the studio, around 30 dB; (b) "Domestic low noise" with a measured intensity around 40 dB; (c) "Domestic normal noise" corresponding to an intensity around 55 dB.; "normal conversation", corresponding to a sound between 50 and 65 dB. The chosen audio to simulate the (b) and (c) scenarios was a looped sound of a coffee machine, which was both continuous and constant, with few variations of amplitude. The audio was played twice at the two different levels. The audio for scenario (d) was a looping 10-second dialogue recorded in Portuguese by a male and female that did not include any of the words that were to be spoken by the participants.

Concerning the audio recording, two types of input devices with different technical characteristics were chosen: a remote control with an integrated microphone (from Ruwido©) and two far-field microphone (Jabra© Speak 510).The remote control was used at 20–30 cm from the participants' mouth, while the far-field devices were placed at 1,0 m and 2,0 m from the participants.

3.2   Experimental Procedure

The experimental procedure was based in the following steps: (1) participants' welcome; (2) fill-in of a consent form to record and use the participant's data; (3) explanation of the practical procedure; (4) performing the test with the 4 noise scenarios; (5) completion of the characterization questionnaire. During the test (Fig. 3), each participant was asked, for each noise scenario, to utter three phrases (corresponding to typical conversation scenarios with the TV), being the resultant audio signal recorded by each device (the remote control and the two far-field microphones).

The three utterances used in the tests were created considering commonly used verbs in the TV lexicon, with common intents such as "changing the channel", "searching for a movie", or "asking for a content by genre". The utterances also included an acronym (Portuguese TV broadcaster named "SIC") and an English-named character ("Mickey Mouse"). The utterances were conceived to be read without significant difficulty by participants of different ages. Extra care was taken to choose

Fig. 3. Test setup with participants.

foreign words of easy diction for Portuguese speakers and names of actors and programs commonly known in Portugal. The phrases used were: "Muda para a SIC" (Change to SIC), "Dá-me um filme do Mickey Mouse" (Give me a Mickey Mouse movie) and "Mostra-me desenhos animados" (Show me cartoons).

3.3   ASR Evaluation

To support the evaluation of selected ARS systems performance, a computer application was developed. Its inputs were a text file with the phrases to be pronounced by the participants (in .csv format) and the resulting audio files from the several recordings. As output, the application supplies a .csv file with the ASR output and the Levenshtein's distance for each phrase, enabling to calculate the similarity function (1).

The similarity score produced by these measures is a normalized real-number between 0 to 1. The ideal result is one (Sim = 1) which means that the original text coincides 100% with the ASR output 18.

$$Sim_{Levenshtein} = 1 - \frac{Levenshtein\ Distance}{Maximum\ Size\ (|S_1|, |S_2|)} \tag{1}$$

3.4 Sample

The evaluation tests were carried out in 2018, between July 16th and August 10th, with a convenience sample of 36 participants (none had participated in the pre-test phase). The average age of the sample was 27.25 years, the younger participant was 8 and the oldest was 51 years old. In what concerns to gender, there was as many women as men. Of the 36 participants, 32 showed a high level of digital literacy and all referred to use various technological devices in their daily lives. However, most of them were not regular users of any type of voice interaction systems.

4 Results and Discussion

From the 36 participants, 31 were receptive to use a voice interaction system for television in a domestic environment, 23 referred feeling uncomfortable while interacting with the television in the scenario with the conversational background noise, mainly because they had the feeling that the voice interaction might not work. The ASR systems were tested according to the setup previously explained, with four noise environment scenarios. However, due to the similarity of outcomes for both "domestic noise low" and "domestic noise normal", the research team decided to only consider the results for "domestic noise normal", in addition to the "silence" and "normal conversation" scenario. On the scenario with the 'normal conversation' background noise, it was noticed that participants get more distracted and tend to hesitate while speaking which can bring an extra challenge to the ASR systems. Those hesitations on the pronunciation of the words can lead to difficulties in the analysis of phonemes and consequently in the identification of the words uttered.

In overall, Google's ASR performs best for all devices and noise environments, followed by Bing's ASR and Nuance. Google's good performance corroborates the results presented by [11] in which a tool was designed to evaluate 3 ASR systems (Microsoft Speech API, Google Speech API, and Sphinx-4), however without the addition of background noise. When increasing the distance between the speaker and the audio input device the ASR performance reduces. This is more obvious on Bing's performance than on Nuance. It is also possible to notice that increasing background noise the performance of the ASR tends to deteriorate.

For a better analysis of ASR performance, on Figs. 4, 5 and 6 are presented the boxplots of the similarity by Levenshtein for the 3 considered distances/recording devices under the three mentioned noise scenarios. Looking for the similarity by Levenshtein for the remote control (Fig. 4), it is possible to notice that Google is the

ASR system that shows less dispersion of data followed by Bing and Nuance. This is also true for the far-field at 1 m (Fig. 5). It is in the far-field at 2 meters scenario (Fig. 6) that the decrease of the performance with the increase of the noise is more evident. This is the scenario that shows the greatest dispersion of results. Although Google's ASR performance reduced considerably from "domestic noise normal" to the "normal conversation" scenario, Google has less dispersion of data than Bing and Nuance. The remote control presents less dispersion of the results to all the ASR systems in analysis.

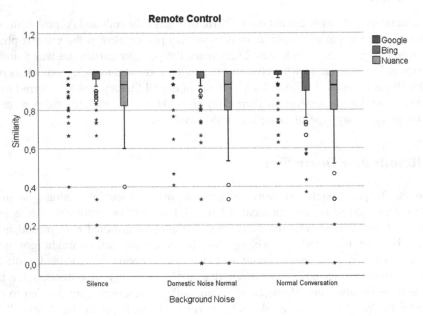

Fig. 4. Box-plot diagram showing the similarity by Levenshtein for the remote control with three background noise scenarios: 'Silence', 'Domestic Noise Normal' and 'Normal Conversation'.

Analyzing the performance and robustness of the ASR in the 'silence' scenario, the Google API performs best for all distances, followed by Bing and at last Nuance. Bing Speech API seems to be the most affected by the distance between the participant and the record device but performs best than Nuance ASR in all distance scenarios. Surprisingly, the Nuance ASR performs better with the far-field microphone at 1 m than with the remote control at 20/30 cm.

In the 'domestic noise normal' scenario, it is possible to observe that, by increasing the distance between the participant and the record device, was noticed a reduction on the performance, for all ASR systems. The Google API performs best for all distances, followed by Bing and at last Nuance. Google API performance for the remote control at 20/30 cm and for the far-field at 1 m show that the different ASR values have a high level of agreement with each other with a percentage of almost 100% of sentences with similarity values of 1. This value decreases in the far-field at 2 m, but it is up to 80%.

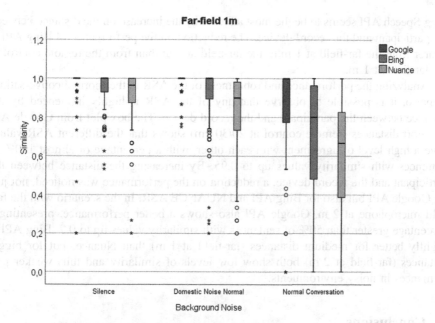

Fig. 5. Box-plot diagram showing the similarity by Levenshtein for the far-field at 1 m, with three background noise scenarios: 'Silence', 'Domestic Noise Normal' and 'Normal Conversation'.

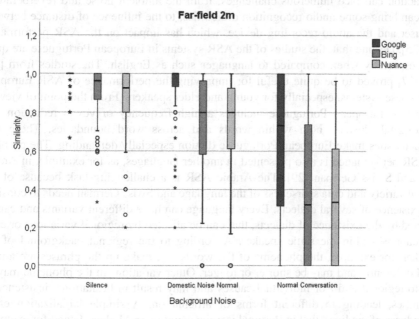

Fig. 6. Box-plot diagram showing the similarity by Levenshtein for the far-field at 2 m, with three background noise scenarios: 'Silence', 'Domestic Noise Normal' and 'Normal Conversation'.

Bing Speech API seems to be the most affected by the increase on the distance between the participant and the record device. The reduction on the performance of Bing API is clearer from the far-field at 1 m to the far-field at 2 m than from the remote control to the far-field at 1 m.

Analyzing the performance and robustness of the ASR in the 'normal conversation' scenario, it is possible to observe that any of the ASR is highly influenced by the distance between the participant and the record device. The box plot from Google API for short distances (remote control at 20/30 cm) shows that the different ASR values have a high level of agreement with each other, with a percentage of almost 100% of sentences with similarity values up to 0,95. By increasing the distance between the participant and the record device, a reduction on the performance was noticed, not just for Google API but also for Bing API and NUANCE ASR. In the scenario with the far-field microphone at 2 m, Google API also shows a better performance, presenting a percentage greater than 50% of sentences with similarity values up to 0.7. Bing API is slightly better for medium distances (far-field at 1 m) than Nuance, but for bigger distances (far-field at 2 m) both show low levels of similarity and thus weaker performances in noisy environments.

5   Conclusions

Several studies are still being developed for optimization and evaluation of the ASR systems in everyday environments. Particularly in domestic environments, voice interaction can face numerous challenges, from the ambient noise and reverberation, that can bring some audio recognition difficulties, to the influence of distance between the user and the audio recording device, which has impact on the ASR performance [23–25]. Despite that, the studies of the ASR systems in European Portuguese are quite few, especially when compared to languages such as English. The studies from [26] and [27] proved to be quite useful for improving the performance of ASR European Portuguese systems, especially for young and elder speakers. From the point of view of phonetics, European Portuguese includes a high frequency of vowel reduction and consonantal clusters, both within words and across word boundaries. These two characteristics make European Portuguese diction especially demanding. The problem of ASR performance is also presented in another languages, as for example, in Arabic [28] and Swiss German [29]. The Arabic ASR is a challenging task because of the lexical variety and data sparseness of the language and Swiss German needs to consider the existence of several dialects. Every language can have different variants and can be affected by the existence of dialects, that can be affected by regional variations or even fluctuations within the same speaker. According to the regional background of the speaker, for example, the phoneme of the words that make up the phrases are articulated differently and may be shorter or longer. Other variations in the phoneme may be due to regional and / or individual causes and may result in hesitations, insistence or emphases, leading to different forms of articulation. A simple labialization effect (roundness of the lips), that in Portugal is quite common in Madeira Island for example, can make the phoneme shorter or longer.

Considering the complexity of the language coupled with the constraints inherently associated with the domestic contexts of television usage, the results obtained in this study will contribute to the future development of a complete system of voice interaction for television. This paper in particularly, aimed to identify the most suitable ASR to be adopted in a Portuguese voice interaction solution for TV. Between the three ASR systems analyzed, it was observed that the Google API had a best performance, followed by Bing Speech API and at last Nuance ASR.

The methodology implemented to evaluate the ASR systems performance proved to be appropriate and the experimental setup configurations can be used fast and easily to test ASR systems for others domestic background noise scenarios.

In the near future, the ASR performance with other possible types of domestic background noise (e.g., air conditioning, blender, etc.) will also be performed and, other external aspects that might have a negative impact on the performance of ASR system should be considered and analyzed as well, as for example, the impact of the quality and type of microphone in the capture of the audio and the acoustic environment conditions and the furniture placement. [9] and [21] referred that the acoustic characteristics of the environment where the conversation takes place may, for example, influence the signal-to-noise ratio or the occurrence of echoes. The evaluation of the performance in real-context of a complete voice system solution for television on a domestic environment is already in preparation and will also be performed with a larger group of participants.

Another important issue for future consideration is the co-articulation that acts in the realization of the sounds that represent the phonemes of a signifier, in as much as a precedent phoneme influences the phoneme that follows and is also influenced by it [30]. All these concrete sounds that carry out the phoneme present sensitive diversities among themselves. To consider all these factors in subsequent researches will be a major contribution for the development of Natural Language Interaction.

Acknowledgments. This paper is a result of the project CHIC – Cooperative Holistic for Internet and Content (grant agreement number 24498), funded by COMPETE 2020 and Portugal 2020 through the European Regional Development Fund (FEDER).

References

1. Benesty, J.: Handbook of Speech Processing. Springer, Heidelberg (2008). https://doi.org/10.1007/978-3-540-49127-9
2. Bernhaupt, R., Boutonnnet, M., Gatellier, B., Gimenez, Y., Pouchepanadin, C., Souiba, L.: A set of recommendations for the control of IPTV-systems via smartphones based on the understanding of users practices and needs (2012)
3. Bernhaupt, R., Drouet, D., Manciet, F., Pirker, M., Pottier, G.: Using speech to search comparing built-in and ambient speech search in terms of privacy and user experience (2017)
4. Bohouta, G., Këpuska, V.: Performance of WUW and general ASR speech recognition systems in different acoustic environments. J. Acoust. Soc. Am. **143**(3), 1758 (2018)
5. Cordeiro, J.P.R.: Conversação Homem-máquina. Caracterização e Avaliação do Estado Actual das Soluções de Speech Recognition, Speech Synthesis e Sistemas de conversação Homem-máquina (2016)

6. Cultofmac. Nuance Beats Apple to Voice-Controlled Television with New Dragon TV Platform.   https://www.cultofmac.com/139335/nuance-beats-apple-to-voice-controlled-television-with-new-dragon-tv-platform/CultofMac. Accessed 20 Sept 2018
7. Gomes, R.: Teste de interfaces de Voz (2007)
8. Goto, J., Kim, Y.-B., Strl, N., Miyazaki, M., Komine, K., Uratani, N.: A spoken dialogue interface for TV operations based on data collected by using WOZ method (2004)
9. Hirayama, N., Yoshino, K., Itoyama, K., Mori, S., Okuno, H.G.: Automatic speech recognition for mixed dialect utterances by mixing dialect language models. IEEE/ACM Trans. Audio Speech Lang. Process. 23(2), 373–382 (2015)
10. Ibrahim, A., Johansson, P.: Multimodal dialogue systems: a case study for interactive TV. In: Carbonell, N., Stephanidis, C. (eds.) UI4ALL 2002. LNCS, vol. 2615, pp. 209–218. Springer, Heidelberg (2003). https://doi.org/10.1007/3-540-36572-9_17
11. Këpuska, V.: Comparing speech recognition systems (Microsoft API, Google API And CMU Sphinx). Int. J. Eng. Res. Appl. 07(03), 20–24 (2017)
12. Zajechowski, M.: Automatic Speech Recognition (ASR) Software - An Introduction - Usability Geek. https://usabilitygeek.com/automatic-speech-recognition-asr-software-an-introduction/. Accessed 30 Jan 2019
13. Morbini, F., Audhkhasi, K., Sagae, K., Artstein, R.: Which ASR should I choose for my dialogue system? In: Sigdial, pp. 394–403, August 2013
14. Nakatoh, Y., Kuwano, H., Kanamori, T., Hoshimi, M.: Speech recognition interface system for digital TV control. Acoust. Sci. Technol. 28(3), 165–171 (2007)
15. Shahamiri, S.R., Binti Salim, S.S.: Real-time frequency-based noise-robust automatic speech recognition using multi-nets artificial neural networks: a multi-views multi-learners' approach. Neurocomputing 129, 199–207 (2014)
16. Spiliotopoulos, D., Stavropoulou, P., Kouroupetroglou, G.: Spoken dialogue interfaces: integrating usability. In: Holzinger, A., Miesenberger, K. (eds.) HCI and Usability for e-Inclusion. USAB 2009. LNCS, vol 5889, pp. 484–499. Springer, Heidelberg (2009). https://doi.org/10.1007/978-3-642-10308-7_36
17. Stolfi, G.: Perceção auditiva e compressão de áudio. In Princípios de Televisão Digital, pp. 1–26 (2008)
18. He, L.D., Alex, A.: Why word error rate is not a good metric for speech recognizer training for the speech translation task? In: 2011 IEEE International Conference on Acoustics, Speech and Signal Processing (ICASSP), pp. 5632–5635 (2011)
19. Lecouteux, B., Vacher, M., Portet, F.: Distant speech processing for smart home: comparison of ASR approaches in scattered microphone network for voice command. Int. J. Speech Technol. 21, 601–618 (2018)
20. Turunen, M., et al.: User expectations and user experience with different modalities in a mobile phone-controlled home entertainment system. In: Proceedings of the 11th International Conference on Human-Computer Interaction with Mobile Devices, pp. 1–4. ACM, New York (2009)
21. Vipperla, R., Bozonnet, S., Wang, D., Evans, N.: Robust speech recognition in multi-source noise environments using convolutive non-negative matrix factorization. In: CHiME: Workshop on Machine Learning in Multisource Environments, pp. 74–79 (2011)
22. Ward, N., Rivera, A., Ward, K., Novick, D.: Some Usability issues and research priorities in spoken dialog applications. Departmental Technical Reports (2005)
23. Barker, J.P., Marxer, R., Vincent, E., Watanabe, S.: The CHiME challenges: robust speech recognition in everyday environments. In: Watanabe, S., Delcroix, M., Metze, F., Hershey, J. R. (eds.) New Era for Robust Speech Recognition, pp. 327–344. Springer, Cham (2017). https://doi.org/10.1007/978-3-319-64680-0_14

24. Lecouteux, B., Vacher, B., Portet, F.: Distant speech processing for smart home: comparison of ASR approaches in scattered microphone network for voice command. Int. J. Speech Technol. **21**(3), 601–618 (2018)
25. Nematollahi, M.A., Al-Haddad, S.A.R.: Distant speaker recognition: an overview. Int. J. Humanoid Robot. **13**(02), 1550032 (2016)
26. Pellegrini, T., et al.: A corpus-based study of elderly and young speakers of European Portuguese: acoustic correlates and their impact on speech recognition performance (2013)
27. Hämäläinen, A.: Automatically Recognising European Portuguese Children's Speech (2014). https://doi.org/10.1007/978-3-319-09761-9_1
28. Ali, A., Magdy, W., Renals, S.: Multi-Reference Evaluation for Dialectal Speech Recognition System: A Study for Egyptian ASR (2015)
29. Garner, P.N., Imseng, D., Meyer, T.: Automatic Speech Recognition and Translation of a Swiss German Dialect: Walliserdeutsch (2014). http://www.swissinfo.ch/. Accessed 12 Mar 2019
30. deMauro, T.: Linguística Elementar. Editorial Estampa, Lisboa (2000)

Broadcast Testing of Emergency Alert System for Digital Terrestrial Television EWBS in Ecuador

Gonzalo Olmedo[1](✉)(iD), Freddy Acosta[1](✉)(iD), Raúl Haro[1](✉)(iD),
Diego Villamarín[1](✉)(iD), and Nelson Benavides[2](✉)(iD)

[1] Departamento de Eléctrica, Electrónica y Telecomunicaciones,
Universidad de las Fuerzas Armadas ESPE, Av. General Rumiñahui s/n,
Sangolquí 170501, Ecuador
{gfolmedo,fracosta,rvharo,dfvillamarin}@espe.edu.ec
[2] PARCIF S.A., Quito, Ecuador
nbenavides@parcif.com.ec

Abstract. The results of transmission and reception broadcast tests of the Emergency Warning Broadcast System (EWBS) for Digital Terrestrial Television in the city of Quito-Ecuador with the ISBD-T standard are presented in this paper, in coordination with government agencies and private companies. The system consists of an EWBS server developed and implemented by the authors, which modifies the text overlay message and the PSI tables for some-emergency-codes transmission, as established in the EWBS international harmonization document, while re-configuring the multiplexing and transmission stage of the television station. The tests were carried out in two stages, on the one hand working directly with the multiplexers and modulators of digital terrestrial television from Pichincha hill, and on the other hand from television station with a microwave transport network to Pichincha hill. It was possible make the activation of the EWBS receivers in the coverage region, select codes, and reception of the overlay message, with an nearly imperceptible delay in the complete system, within real time requirements.

Keywords: DTT · EWBS · ISDB-T

1 Introduction

Ecuador's continental territory is crossed from north to south by a volcanic section of the Andes mountain range, and its coastline is part of the *Circumpacífico Belt*, which makes there is intense seismic and volcanic activity. The *Niño* phenomenon is another important event which is caused by the warming of the equatorial eastern Pacific, causing destruction of highways, roads and bridges, as well as damage to crops and fishing activity. There are certain institutions in Ecuador that focus on the study and prevention of this type of emergencies, which have been taken as a reference in the *"Escuela Politécnica Nacional"*

© Springer Nature Switzerland AG 2019
M. J. Abásolo et al. (Eds.): jAUTI 2018, CCIS 1004, pp. 176–187, 2019.
https://doi.org/10.1007/978-3-030-23862-9_13

(EPN) Geophysical Institute, which is the main research center for the diagnosis and monitoring of seismic hazards and volcanoes, the *"Centro Internacional para la Investigación del Fenómeno del Niño"* (CIIFEN), which is a research center that contributes to risk management and adaptation to climate change and the climatic variety.

Article 389 of the Constitution of the Republic of Ecuador mentions that *"The State will protect people, communities and nature against the negative effects of natural or man-made disasters through risk prevention, disaster mitigation, the recovery and improvement of social, economic and environmental conditions, with the aim of minimizing the condition of vulnerability ..."* [1]. The Public Safety and State Law establishes the Risk Management Secretariat as a technical body [2]. In accordance with the law of the matter: *"are functions of the technical governing body of the decentralized national risk management system, among others, articulate the institutions to coordinate actions to prevent and mitigate risks, as well as to stop them, recover and improve the conditions prior to the occurrence of a disaster emergency; and, carry out and coordinate the necessary actions to reduce vulnerabilities and prevent, mitigate, attend to and recover eventual negative effects derived from disasters or emergencies in the national territory ..."*.

Based on the foregoing, different means and communication technologies are sought to help generate early warnings of possible catastrophes or emergencies, which are massive, thus, it has been proposed to integrate the Emergency Warning Broadcast System (EWBS) in Digital Terrestrial Television (DTT), through the insertion of superimposition of emergency text, accompanied by a sound alarm, both controlled by the National Secretariat for Risk Management, which would allow early warning of the Ecuadorian population. The DTT system, Integrated Services Digital Broadcasting-Terrestrial (ISDB-T), was standardized by the Association of Industries and Radiocommunication Companies (ARIB) and implemented in Japan in 2003. Among the main features available, is the emergency warning generation called EWBS [3], which is received by fixed, portable and mobile terminals that have the system.

Most Latin American countries adopted the ISDB-T standard with Brazilian improvements, called ISDB-Tb, with Ecuador being defined in 2010. The EWBS system is coordinated by the ISDB-T International Forum in the harmonization document Part 3: *"EWBS Emergency Alert System"* [4], defined by the Japanese standard ARIB STD-B14 Version 2.0 Volume 1 [5], which specifies the details of the operation of area codes and superimposition of text. In Ecuador, there is currently a minimum number of models of DTT receivers with EWBS, since the transmitters of the country are in a process of testing coverage and transmission of audio and video programs, for this reason there was a requirement for field tests of the EWBS system to verify its applicability and response time.

With the cooperation of JICA (Japan International Cooperation Agency) expert, Peruvian states broadcaster IRTP conducted EWBS transmission trial on 6th December 2010. This was the first successful EWBS trial among those countries which adapted ISDB-T in South America [6].

The Philippine TV (PTV), Japan's NEC, and the Ministry of Internal Affairs and Communications evaluated the Emergency Warning Broadcast System (EWBS) and Data-casting System project on March 7, 2018. The Data-casting System the Japanese technology that will boost real-time reporting of updates on the weather, the movement of storms, floods, landslides, traffic, and grid-lock road conditions. Philippine is situated within the ring of fire with the tectonic movements crawling through fault lines throughout cities, towns and islands. The country's eastern seaboard faces the typhoon and storm surge highway. There are also the active volcanoes, heavy rainfall that causes flood and landslide. Davao City was chosen for the NEC's demo of the system because of its disaster preparedness and the availability of the all-modern Central 911 facility. Three areas received the signal, the coastal area of Barangay 76-A, Central 911, and the City Hall [7].

On March, 2018 Japanese experts in television digitalization trained officials from different public institutions to learn about the operation of the early warning signal EWBS using digital television in Nicaragua. Among the participants were public servants of the National System for the Prevention, Mitigation and Attention of Disasters (Sinapred) and members of the Army of Nicaragua [8].

In this article we present results of field tests in the city of Quito based on projects carried out by the members of the digital television laboratory of the University of the Armed Forces - ESPE, together with the opening and support of television channels, governmental organize and private companies.

2   Methodology

The transmission scheme of the Digital Terrestrial Television standard ISDB-T is show in Fig. 1, where the audio and video encoders of each of the programming or services are observed first, at its output packages are generated in a 188-byte Transport Stream (TS) format. It includes a PSI/SI and data generation server, defined as play out, that associates transmission of interactivity data, electronic program guide (EPG), Closed Caption, EWBS, parental control, among others, through packages TS. For the transmission of interactivity, the data packaging protocol DSM-CC is used [9], whose process is described by the authors in [10].

All audio, video and data TS packages are multiplexed via the MPEG2-TS transport communication protocol. At the output of the multiplexer to each TS packet, 16 bytes of configuration of the modulation stage are increased, which includes the hierarchical structure by layers, with their respective modulations and coding rates, as well as the configuration of the carriers that make up the signal OFDM with its respective segmentation, guard interval, mode of operation and synchronization signals, all this in a new type of package defined as Broadcast Transport Stream BTS of 204 bytes. The modulated signal is propagated through a radiofrequency system, which for the tests used the frequency of 635.143 MHz, within the UHF band, for channel 41. Additionally, the BTS output is monitored by a TS transport stream analyzer and BTS implemented by the authors in [11].

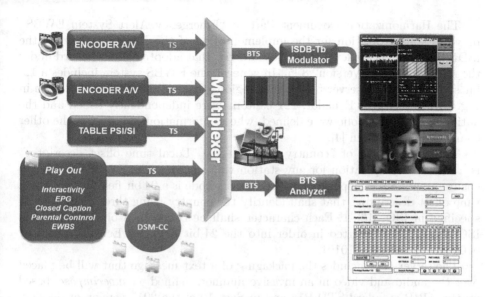

Fig. 1. Schematic of Standard Transmission of ISDB-T.

In the present project, the coverage of the propagating ISDB-T signal was validated through simulation and field tests, considering that the transmitter and its radiant systems are located in the Pichincha hill, covering the city of Quito and its surroundings, using the field monitoring procedures described by the authors in [12]. Figure 2 shows monitoring results from the Digital Television laboratory of the University of the Armed Forces - ESPE, located in a straight line at 19 km, without line of sight from the Pichincha hill, crossing small mountains at an average power of 500 W transmission.

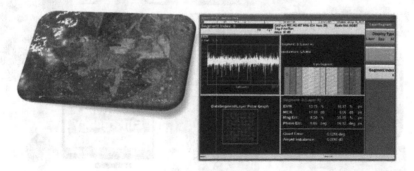

Fig. 2. Signal Range of the signal ISDB-T in Quito, transmission from Pichincha mountain.

The Harmonization Document Part 3: "Emergency Alert System EWBS" provides standardization for the implementation of the EWBS system for the ISDB-T system at the level of all the countries that adopted this standard under the ARIB STD-B14 Version2.8 [5]. In general, the EWBS system includes a 12-bit structure on the server to code the regions that will be alerted, as shown in Fig. 3. In the case of Ecuador, 221 cantons were independently coded and the national emergency code were defined, whose information and that of the other countries is detailed in [4].

The transmission of "country code" in the "Local time offset descriptor" is a mandatory operation for any station that operates the EWBS in order to ensure proper EWBS operations. The country code is a 24 bit field in the "Local time offset descriptor" that shall identify the country using three characters as specified in ISO 3166-1. Each character shall be coded in 8 bits according to ISO 8859-15 and inserted in order into the 24-bit field, for Ecuador given by 010001010100001101010101.

The server also includes the packaging of a text message that will be placed over the audio and video in an invasive manner, defined as *superimpose*, based on the ARIB standard STD-B14 and in Sect. 10 of the 2015 version of the document of Harmonization Part 3. The emergency bit is activated in the physical layer of the modulator, which corresponds to bit 26 of the configuration structure of the TMCC modulation stage (Transmission and Multiplexing Configuration Control), which is contained within the BTS packets generated by the multiplexer [4].

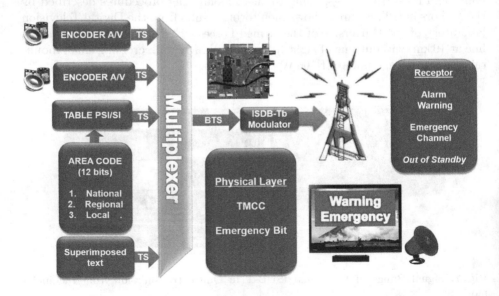

Fig. 3. Block diagram EWBS System.

In [13] the authors implemented the ARIB standard STD-B14 for tests of a single emergency code and tests with receivers that include sound alarm, performing laboratory tests with internal transmission control, in this work were presented reception results in relation to the activation of the alarm based on the discrimination of the emergency code. Because it is a controlled evaluation, the audio and video programming, as well as the inclusion of the emergency code restructuring the PSI tables, were constructed and multiplexed in a single system created in Java, whose interface is presented in Fig. 4(a). The activation of the TMCC bit was also configured independently.

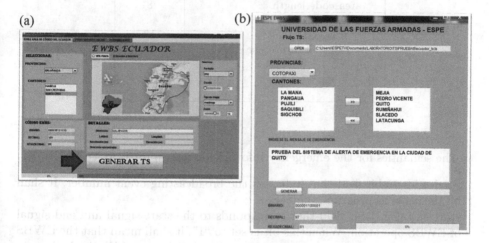

Fig. 4. (a) One Code Platform. (b) Several Codes and Warning Message configurable.

The EWBS receiving procedure comprises the following steps:

– The EWBS-ready receiver should continue monitoring the activation flag in the TMCC signal in stand-by mode.
– When the activation flag in the TMCC signal changes from "0" to "1", the receivers should start checking the emergency information descriptor in the PMT of the received transport stream.
– If the activation flag is "1" and the area code in the PMT matches the area code set in the receiver, the receivers should be activated. The receivers should then display the emergency information (Superimpose and program).
– If the activation flag is "0", it is a test transmission and no particular operation is required.

Receivers should continuously monitor the PMT while the activation flag in the TMCC signal remains "1". When the "Activation flag" in the TMCC switches to "0" and the emergency information descriptor is deleted, EWBS operation comes to an end.

The emergency information descriptor syntax shall be in accordance with Table 1, [4].

Table 1. Emergency information descriptor

Syntax	No. of bits
emergency_information_descriptor(){	
descriptor_tag	8
descriptor_length	8
for(i=0;i¡N;i++){	
service_id	16
start_end_flag	1
signal_level	1
reserved_future_use	6
area_code_length	8
for(j=0;j¡N;j++){	
area_code	12
reserved_future_use	4
}	
}	
}	

The semantics for the emergency information descriptor is given by:

– service_id: 16-bit field that indicates the broadcasting event number. It shall be the same as program_number.
– start_end_flag: 1-bit field that corresponds to the start signal and end signal of EWBS operation. When this bit is set to "1", it shall mean that the EWBS was started or is currently in operation. When it is set to "0", it shall mean that the EWBS has ended.
– signal_level: 1-bit field that corresponds to the emergency alarm signal specified by the responsible agencies. When set to "0", it shall mean that the emergency alarm signal is the first type of start signal. When set to "1", the alarm signal shall be the second type of start signal. This information should not be used to control EWBS-ready receivers.
– area_code_length: 8-bit field that indicates the size in bytes of an area code.
– area_code: 12-bit field that corresponds to the area code specified by the responsible agencies detailed in [4].

In [14] the authors included the selection of several emergency codes of cantons of Ecuador based on the document of Harmonization Part 3 and implemented the option to include the editable message of superimposition and multiplex it according to the norm ARIB STD-B14. The laboratory results were totally satisfactory, they responded to all the configuration tests on the services transmitted within a single laboratory system, whose interface is shown in Fig. 4(b).

3   Transmission and Reception Tests

The PSI implementations, specifically the PAT and PMT of an independent multiplexer [11], as well as the packaging of the text of superposition and preparation to perform the test with the transmission equipment of a channel private television in the frequency 635.143 MHz in the city of Quito, within its normal programming, making real field tests of the EWBS system. For the implementation, an ASI interface for communication with the multiplexer is shown, as shown in Fig. 5.

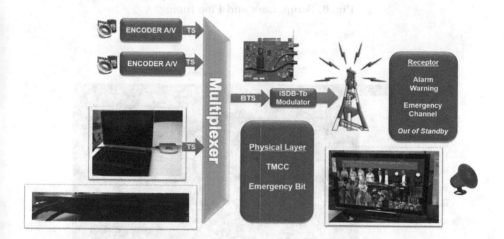

Fig. 5. Block Diagram EWBS Server.

The first tests were performed on December 19, 2016 directly from the Pichincha hill, the place where the multiplexer was located, as shown in Fig. 6. On that occasion, the monitoring places of the reception were placed in the city of Quito. Figure 7, in conjunction with government institutions and private companies in Digital Terrestrial Television, both in transmission and reception. The tests include the combination of the codes of all the cantons of the province of Pichincha and emergency text messages published in real time at the place of transmission. In addition, the design of the implemented EWBS server was used to include the configuration and packaging of interactivity contents created in Ginga-NCL [15]. Figure 8 shows the results of the reception of interactivity and EWBS in the laboratories of the University of the Armed Forces - ESPE.

With the validation of the system working, another test was performed on February 15, 2017, where the multiplexer was transferred to the television channel in the Quito studios, directly where the audio and video signal is produced, including a microwave signal transmission BTS to the modulator in the Pichincha hill, which allows the control of the emergency alert to be carried out in the place of better accessibility, as shown in Fig. 9.

Fig. 6. Setup, Link and Fine tuning.

Fig. 7. Transmission test from Pichincha mountain.

(a)   (b)

Fig. 8. Signal received (a) Interactive and (b) EWBS signal in ESPE labs.

Fig. 9. Server Setup, Link and Fine tunning, and Multiplexer setup at TV Channel with BTS Link to Pichincha mountain.

The results of the emergency signal, adding the times of reconfiguration of the BTS signal, the propagation of the microwave, the transmission to the whole city and the decoding is in the order of milliseconds, which is imperceptible by the human senses, which is shown as a real-time system from the generation of the signal. The test was replicated on December 1, 2017 for the authorities of the telecommunications sector and the National Secretariat of Risks of Ecuador. Figure 10 shows the places that the signal was monitored in the Quito city, and the results of the reception are shown in Fig. 11, which include tests on analog TV sets with digital terrestrial television decoders.

Fig. 10. Transmission and Reception Test from Pichincha mountain with management from Quito.

Twenty-five different codes of cantons from Ecuador were sent to the transmitter and the receivers were configured with Quito and Rumiñahui (location of the ESPE-University) codes. All codes were recognized in the reception process. It was also checked the standby output of the decoders and the superimposition of the edited text.

To better visualize the reception result of the emergency alert system, the link to a video has been included in the QR code of Fig. 12.

Fig. 11. EWBS Reception signal in Quito.

Fig. 12. QR code leading to EWBS reception demonstration video.

4   Future Works

The transport network is in design for the signal to be transmitted directly from the National Secretariat of Risks of Ecuador or through other governmental entities, for which it began with tests of control of the emergency alert system through the Internet, entering in the beginning by remote desktops that connect and control the EWBS or Interactivity server, the same ones that were evaluated and do not generate additional delays due to being permanently interconnected. The challenge is to design and implement a network of servers in different television stations with a single control, with the contribution of the server prototype that was evaluated in this article. Furthermore, the abilities of transmission and reception of data through terrestrial digital television allow us to create new proposals of encryption for security, as well as the possibility of implanting special receivers for EWBS that do not necessarily reproduce the audio and video signals, but that taking advantage of the transmission by broadcast to contribute to different geographical zones and specific populations, as it is the case of people with disabilities.

Acknowledgements. The possibility of bringing together several actors to contribute to the tests was thanks to the National Agency for Regulation and Control of Telecommunications (ARCOTEL) and the Ministry of Telecommunications (MINTEL). Special thanks to channel 41, TELESUCESOS and to the companies specialized in transmission, monitoring and reception equipment for DTT, EUACTRONIX and PARCIF S.A.

References

1. Constitución Política de la República del Ecuador. http://dpdba.georgetown.edu/Parties/Ecuador/Leyes/constitucion.pdf. Accessed 15 Feb 2019
2. Ministerio Coordinador de Seguridad. http://www.seguridad.gob.ec/wp-content/uploads/downloads/2012/07/01_LEY_DE_SEGURIDAD_PUBLICA_Y_DEL_ESTADO.pdf. Accessed 17 Feb 2019
3. ISDB-T Official Site. http://www.dibeg.org/index.html. Accessed 24 Feb 2019
4. International, I.-T.: Emergency Warning Broadcast System EWBS. ISDB-T HARMONIZATIOM DOCUMENT PART 3, Sao Paulo (2015)
5. ARIB STD-B14 Version 2.8 Volumen 3. http://www.arib.or.jp/english/html/overview/doc/8-TR-B14v2_8-1p3-E2.pdf. Accessed 24 Feb 2019
6. Digital Broadcasting Experts Group, Peru ISDB-T cooperation. https://www.dibeg.org/news/2010/1012. Accessed 24 Feb 2019
7. Philippine News Agency, PTV, NEC lauded for Emergency Warning Broadcast System. https://www.pna.gov.ph/articles/1027805. Accessed 24 Feb 2019
8. El 19 digital, Capacitan sobre señal de alerta temprana con el sistema de televisión digital. https://www.el19digital.com/articulos/ver/titulo:74941-capacitan-sobre-senal-de-alerta-temprana-con-el-sistema-de-television-digital. Accessed 24 Feb 2019
9. Olmedo, G., Mena, R., Paredes, N.: Transport stream generator and player for digital terrestrial television ISDB-Tb. In: CEUR Workshop Proceedings (2015)
10. Olmedo, G., Nuñez, A., Villamarín, D.: Design, implementation and evaluation of data carrousel extractor algorithm on MPEG-2 TS for digital terrestrial television. In: XLII Latin American Computing Conference (CLEI). IEEE (2016)
11. Olmedo, G., Benavides, N., Acosta, F., Paredes, N.: MPEG-2 transport stream analyzer for digital television. In: 35th International Conference of the Chilean Computer Science Society (SCCC). IEEE (2016)
12. Haro, R., Olmedo, G.: Evaluación del desempeño y optimización del sistema de televisión digital terrestre ISDB-Tb e IPTV de la ESPE. Escuela Politécnica del Ejército, Sangolquí, Ecuador (2012)
13. Segura, A., Olmedo, G., Acosta, F., Santillán, M.: Designing a system for monitoring and broadcasting early warning signs of natural disasters for digital terrestrial television. In: Latin-American Conference on Communications (LATICOM). IEEE (2015)
14. Recalde, C., Olmedo, G.: Análsis y generación del flujo de transporte con sobreimposición de texto para alerta temprana. Universidad de las Fuerzas Armadas ESPE, Sangolquí, Ecuador (2016)
15. Villamarín, D., Illescas, M., Olmedo, G., Lara, R.: Generating a transport stream for digital terrestrial television system in conformance with ISDB-Tb standard. In: Colombian Conference on Communications and Computing (COLCOM). IEEE (2013)

Author Index

Printed in the United States
By Bookmasters